WHAT IS POLITICAL THEOLOGY?

WHAT IS POLITICAL THEOLOGY?

LUKE BRETHERTON,
VINCENT W. LLOYD, AND
VALENTINA NAPOLITANO

Columbia University Press   *New York*

Columbia University Press
Publishers Since 1893
New York   Chichester, West Sussex

Copyright © 2026 Columbia University Press
All rights reserved

Library of Congress Cataloging-in-Publication Data
Names: Lloyd, Vincent W., 1982– | Napolitano, Valentina | Bretherton, Luke
Title: What is political theology? / Luke Bretherton, Vincent W. Lloyd, and Valentina Napolitano.
Description: New York : Columbia University Press, [2026] | Includes bibliographical references and index.
Identifiers: LCCN 2025021683 | ISBN 9780231222143 hardback | ISBN 9780231222150 trade paperback | ISBN 9780231564083 ebook
Subjects: LCSH: Political theology | Violence—Religious aspects—Christianity | Sovereignty—Religious aspects—Christianity | Justice—Religious aspects—Christianity
Classification: LCC BT83.59 .W46 2026 | DDC 261.7—dc23/eng/20250721

Cover art: Luke Bretherton

GPSR Authorized Representative: Easy Access System Europe, Mustamäe tee 50, 10621 Tallinn, Estonia, gpsr.requests@easproject.com

CONTENTS

Introduction: Trajectories in Political Theology   1

1 Political Theology as Testimony   37
   LUKE BRETHERTON

2 Political Theology from Below   101
   VINCENT W. LLOYD

3 An Anthropological Political Theology   155
   VALENTINA NAPOLITANO

4 Looking to the Future   207
   Emerging Pathways
   LUKE BRETHERTON

   Crossing and Deepening
   VINCENT W. LLOYD

   A Celebratory Roadmap
   VALENTINA NAPOLITANO

Notes   233
Bibliography   273
Index   299

INTRODUCTION
Trajectories in Political Theology

We each were drawn to political theology in the early 2000s as a conversation, a set of resources, and a critical orientation. We found political theology highly generative for our research. The topic has framed books we have written, and we have each, in different ways, drawn nourishment from and contributed to developing an intellectual community around political theology. We realized the term *political theology* is highly problematic given the first-order political commitments of key figures, most notably the Nazi jurist Carl Schmitt. But we waved off the skepticism of colleagues who took the term to be unredeemable. Surely concepts can take on new life. Surely political theology could be just as—if not more—useful as a critical tool, helping us notice what the wealthy and powerful would prefer to conceal rather than being a means of legitimizing or sanctifying the state.

By the middle of the 2010s, however, we became increasingly concerned about new bedfellows who, like us, were being drawn to conversations around political theology. These were not just liberals, a few of whom have long toyed with political theology, or conservatives with a nostalgia for "Judeo-Christian civilization." These new bedfellows had authoritarian, antidemocratic intentions, and many seemed well on their way to fascism. Under the banner of ethnoreligious nationalism (Christian, Jewish, Hindu, or Islamic), we saw political and religious leaders making claims about the connection between political and theological concepts that licensed militarism, autocracy, and authoritarian cultures, from the national level to the local, from the United States to India to Hungary to Israel.[1] We noticed some of the same scholarly resources that we had found inspirational, such as Alasdair MacIntyre's writings on tradition and Stanley Hauerwas's writings on communities of character, taken up by those clearly on an antidemocratic path.[2] Even our own earlier work was being well received in circles that we found surprising. The most frequent accessor of the journal *Political Theology*, where we have all published, is Liberty University, founded by the conservative Christian leader Jerry Falwell. We started to worry: Had the skeptics been right? Was political theology unredeemable?

No. As we talked with one another and with colleagues and students, we were convinced that the skeptics were wrong. We have seen too many instances, around the world and across history, of religious ideas, practices, and modes of imagining fueling struggles for liberation. We decided to write this book because we are convinced that the term *political theology* need not be ceded to demagogues, authoritarians, and fascists, religious or otherwise. Our task, then, is to separate the sort of political theology that lends itself to domination and exploitation from the sort of political theology that lends itself to democratic renewal and liberation.[3]

If one form of political theology is taking shape on the Right, is there another community and conversation available, one that attracted us to political theology in the first place?[4] The answer to this question can be elusive. We have seen colleagues and students from many corners of the academy drawn to political theology—as a slogan, method, set of theories, a multidisciplinary field, or a topic of study. But first and foremost they were drawn to it as an orientation, that is, as a commitment to bring out the political dimensions of conversations about religion, or to bring out the religious dimensions of conversations about politics.

There is much intellectual energy invested in the term *political theology*. However, strangely, it is not yet possible to say that there is *a* political theology conversation or even *several* political theology conversations. Tracking where the term *political theology* appears raises the question of whether there are any shared qualities in what it marks; the fragmentation of the discourse occurs along multiple axes, to the point that it is tempting to throw up one's hands in exasperation.

Even more perplexing, particularly to students and newcomers to the conversation, is that the term *political theology* is often used with a great deal of confidence, as if it really is pointing to something clear and its meaning is almost self-evident. When we focus on very local conversations (say, in Protestant social ethics, in the history of political thought, or in debates about secularism), scholars use *political theology* without hesitation, sometimes even claiming it as their method or identity ("a political-theological analysis," "as a political theologian"). But when we zoom out and look across disciplines, fields, and national academic contexts, even just by searching through books for the term, what we find is vitality amid chaos and confusion.

One of our purposes in writing this book is to demonstrate why political theology is so vital. Our hypothesis is when the multiple uses of the term *political theology* rub up against one another, sparks fly. Consider, for example, the way anthropologists like Talal Asad, Saba Mahmood, and Fenella Cannell have engaged with philosophers such as Alasdair MacIntyre and Charles Taylor as well as Christian theologians such as John Milbank. The resulting theorizing has been highly generative, not only in anthropology but also in religious, literary, and cultural studies, as well as in Christian theology. Or consider the way scholars of US literature, including Jared Hickman, Peter Coviello, and Emily Ogden, attend to religion in the texts they study by turning to political theology, revitalizing a conversation that brings together religious studies and literature. These are moments that demonstrate proof of concept: If an eclectic set of scholars talking about political theology could share a meal together, what results would be not only advances in political theology but also exciting developments across disciplines and fields.

A task of our book is to offer snapshots of such a feast. While each of us approaches political theology from a different disciplinary orientation—Christian theology, anthropology, and critical theory—we are all committed to a deep, careful engagement with an eclectic mix of interlocutors across disciplines, methods, and regions. We do not share a canon. Part of our purpose is to demonstrate that, against conventional wisdom, political theology need not take as its starting point any one theorist, concept, question, or location. We do not need to write about Carl Schmitt, Jürgen Moltmann, or Giorgio Agamben, or discuss sovereignty or the status of conceptual analogies, or begin the conversation in Europe. We each have been shaped by our encounters with these people, ideas, problems, and places, but they are small parts of a much wider array of conversation partners.

One way of naming what we mean by *political theology*, then, is deflationary: We are simply working in the space created by those using that term. We navigate that space differently, based on our academic formation and disciplinary orientation, but ultimately, we are trying to model new paths through that space.

Another way of naming what we mean by political theology is minimalist rather than deflationary, fixing the concept as the intersection of politics, critical theory, and various formations of religious belief and practice. Across the many uses of the term, in different corners of the global academy, something like this minimalist account seems to be at issue. Political theology asks more fundamental questions than who voted for whom: questions about the connections between religion and politics, about the nature of the nonsecular, about the entanglement of different ways of being alive (both human and nonhuman), about the meaning, purpose, and sacred values of different forms of life, or about who is sacrificed so that others live. And political theology digs deep by turning to the tools of critical theory (broadly understood, and shifting over time, from the German, French, and Italian philosophical tradition in generations past to, today, Marxist and anarchist currents, Black studies, feminist theory, queer theory, and decolonial theory). Political theology also attends to the critical and constructive role of religious beliefs and practices in constituting social, economic, and political life at different scales.

In a sense, then, all three of us answer the question "What is political theology?" in the same way, as a space of intellectual exchange, critique, and imagination. But we share more than that. Some themes surface again and again in our chapters, thus making an argument about what political theology ought to be, about the topics that should be at the heart of the field.

Four themes unify the chapters. First, we are oriented against a politics of domination in all its guises. Part of our project is rooting out the ways that domination manifests in colonial, racial, gendered, nationalist, and capitalist formations—and, particularly, the ways that religious ideas, affects, and practices conceal or naturalize modes of oppression. Second, although sovereignty as a political fact necessarily factors into our analysis, we attend to and explicate politics outside or at a threshold of the framework of sovereignty. This does not mean that we equate sovereignty and domination, but we worry about the tendency of sovereignty to license domination and about how the conceptual charisma of sovereignty can distort political analysis. Third, we are interested in the way that liberal political theory neglects or obscures questions of life and death as well as the affective and material remnants of violence. These questions are especially urgent today, as the problem space generated by the myopia of liberalism must not be conceded to reactionaries and fascists. Fourth and finally, we are oriented toward a just and generous future, even as we worry that articulated hopes for the future are usually captured by those invested in maintaining their own mastery. To imagine rightly, we must grapple with eschatological interruptions of the present, sometimes named explicitly and sometimes expressed as an apophatic shape of thought.

Why are we arguing for these themes to be central to political theology? We are writing to our political moment, one that is quite different from the Weimar republic of Carl Schmitt, from the tumultuous 1960s of Jürgen Moltmann, from the post-9/11 United States of Charles Taylor, and from the global social movements of the 2010s. As with these earlier moments, we are at a time when liberal assumptions about politics are under pressure: The largest war in Europe since the Second World War is raging; we witness the wholesale destruction of a people, land, and culture in Palestine; communities are being broken up and displaced in Pakistan, Sudan, Venezuela, and elsewhere; refugees receive a cold welcome at the borders of the United States and Western Europe; and the constant hum of environmental devastation that will precipitate planetary destruction grows louder by the day. In this context, we cannot afford to fiddle at the margins, and the project of reformist political theology rings hollow. Equally as important, these uncertain times fuel reactionary political theologies, and we must be prepared to combat them, pairing critical analysis with experimentation, imagination, and normative judgments about what enables life to flourish.

And yet this is not quite right, either, for the chapters that follow do not subordinate their thought to any secular, this-worldly political project. In the background of each chapter is the critique of secularism, an ideology entangled with forces of mastery. Political theology promises to give life to new ways of responding to a moment of crisis. It brings together rigor and creativity to conjure paths not yet imagined, not reducible to worldly terms, to the terms of the present. This effort requires intimacy with the claims of religious thought that make the committed secularist uncomfortable.

DIFFERENCES AND DISAGREEMENTS

While the three of us come to this project with similar or at least complementary motivations, we do not write with a unified voice. We do not answer the question "What is political theology?" in the same way. We hope that our disagreements, or at least the moments when our ideas grate against one another as they move in differing directions, illuminate fractures in the conversation about political theology more generally. That said, these fractures are not the obvious ones: They are not the battles of Christian theologians versus secular philosophers, or conservative partisans versus radical intellectuals. But they are also not fractures that can be written off as merely differences of temperament, of national or institutional context, or of scope or scale of analysis.

Napolitano writes as a sociocultural anthropologist, trained in the United Kingdom, teaching in Canada, and studying global Catholicism. She focuses on the negative represented by theology (irreducible to the species "negative theology"). For Napolitano, theologies undo political authority not only at the register of society but also in and through the body. Theologies that are materialized as thought, and especially as performed, create clearings, holding back the whirlwind of established power structures, allowing new things to emerge—new things that promise justice. While Napolitano's thinking grows out of an engagement with global Catholicism, the framework she puts forward is informed by and offered to scholars of various religious traditions, as well as to those who think about religion beyond the terms of religious tradition. While Bretherton and Lloyd are both sympathetic to the sort of negative moments that Napolitano embraces, they are wary of the uncertain futures that an emphasis on the negative and negating aspects of political life produce, wondering if those futures necessarily tend toward justice. Additionally, in Bretherton's case, there is an often implicit, sometimes explicit, concern about religious particularity, about the singularity of Christian commitments and contexts (and of the commitments and contexts of every religious tradition)—a concern that Napolitano's contribution may not fully satisfy. In Lloyd's case, there is a parallel concern about tradition, even as it figures differently: For Lloyd, the organizing of social movements is itself a tradition that brings obligations, capacities, and limitations, and grappling with the specificity of such contexts is, for him, the prerequisite for speaking rightly about politics.

Lloyd writes as a scholar located at the intersection of religious studies and critical theory. He is trained in both fields in the US academy, and he now teaches about race, religion, and critical theory at a Catholic university. His contribution is rooted in traditions of revolutionary socialism that take as authorities the insights and practices of justice movements, seeing these as opening vistas onto a world beyond domination. For him, political theology is a way of clarifying and orienting left political practice, in a sense girding it against the temptations of liberalism (and its avatar, secularism). While Napolitano and Bretherton are broadly aligned with Lloyd's political commitments to a more-left-than-liberal politics, both give more priority to the theological. From the perspective of Bretherton's contribution, the theological in Lloyd's work can appear nearly superfluous, at best a pragmatic tool to be discarded when it does not seem to do analytical work. From the perspective of Napolitano's contribution, what Lloyd classes as "theological" can flatten into the rhetorical, ignoring the multimodal nature of the theological at its most incisive: bodily, ritualized, disciplining, and imaginative.

Bretherton is the only contributor who writes as a Christian theologian, though he takes account of and speaks to critical conversations about political theology across the humanities and interpretive social sciences. Trained in the United Kingdom, he has taught in both the United States and the United Kingdom, mostly in institutions where he trains Christian ministers, and he is himself an ordained priest in the Church of England. Bretherton's scholarship puts foundational elements of the Christian tradition in dialogue with democratic thought and practice as exemplified in the practices of community organizing. In his contribution, Bretherton deepens his positioning as a confessional theologian in a way that is shaped by and contributes to the insights of theorists and practitioners reaching toward liberation. Not only do Napolitano and Lloyd locate themselves quite differently with respect to religious commitment, but their contributions also suggest a suspicion of the possibilities of expansive engagement with visions of liberation from a Christian perspective, not least because of the history of Christian triumphalism, whether crude or sanitized with the veneer of a search for justice. Napolitano's contribution, in contrast to Bretherton's, sees Christianity in need of a kind of self-abasement through apophasis lest its political impact be that of furthering the powers that be. From a different direction, Lloyd's contribution suggests starting with the spiritual-but-not-religious ethos of the contemporary North Atlantic context, and he worries that the critical potential of political theology is lost when it no longer involves an emphasis on unveiling—the theological behind the secular, the existential dimension of politics behind the settled comforts of liberal democracy. By way of contrast, Bretherton sees the lack of particularity and the absence of a defined eschatological horizon in Lloyd and Napolitano as collapsing political theology back into a wholly immanent frame. For Bretherton, what it means to be human is thereby reduced to materialistic and deterministic frames of reference that jeopardize human freedom and creativity and lack a moral frame of reference by which to judge questions of what is just and unjust.

ORIGIN STORIES

There is no single point of origin for political theology: Political theology is "creole," wrought in the commercial and violent entanglements of Europe, the Middle East, Africa, Asia, and the Americas.[5] One vital crucible of modern political theology is the "Black Atlantic" and the configurations and disruptions of the relationship between metropole and colony that circulated within it.[6] For example, Christian and post-Christian humanitarianism, Black liberation theology, and Anglican and Pentecostal political theologies cannot be understood unless situated within this context.⁷ From Bartolomé de las Casas bearing witness from Hispaniola through to the Black nationalism and pan-Africanism of Marcus Garvey and then the development of Rastafarianism in the 1930s, the Caribbean exemplifies this vibrant creolization. Likewise, Africa has birthed distinctive conversations on political theology that discuss the interplay between inculturation and liberation, as well as a drive to reimagine what democracy is and how it is lived in the current century. An African-centered story of political theology stretches from the interaction of African, Islamic, and Christian cosmologies and their respective political imaginaries in the fifteenth century onward, through the emergence of millenarian African independent churches in the nineteenth century, on to the formal Christian theologies of figures such as John Mbiti, Jean-Marc Ela, Mercy Amba Oduyoye, Desmond Tutu, and Kwame Bediako, and through to contemporary instantiations of political Islam. Another thread of this story in both the Americas and Africa is the interaction between Christianity and decolonial movements such as Negritude and the formation of contemporary Pentecostalism as a lived economic theology.⁸

The dialogue between these Black Atlantic political theologies and those from the Pacific basin is another vital context for the emergence of modern political theology. This interaction is represented institutionally by the Ecumenical Association of Third World Theologians, founded in 1976, and the Council for World Mission, founded in 1977. Kwok Pui-lan argues that the development of liberation and then postcolonial theology from the nineteenth century onward in places like Korea, India, the Philippines, and China develops in parallel, and is entwined with, similar developments in the Atlantic world.⁹ Mohandas Gandhi's influential thought, which we class as political theology, exemplifies these intersections, forged as it was from his own traversing of European, African, and Indian intellectual and religious life and the respective experiences of modernization and imperialism each refracted.

Understanding the Atlantic and Pacific basins as contexts from which political theology emerges also helps us see how the story of political theology might be told over a longer time horizon. When situated within a *longue durée*, the interactions of Judaism, Christianity, and Islam appear in relationships that are mutually constitutive yet often violent, producing a variety of political visions and settlements. Contemporary political theology, which involves a conversation across multiple religious and philosophical traditions, stands in continuity with this history of interaction and cross-pollination. Creolization is not just a feature of modern political theology; it has always been a feature of political theology.

Another approach to political theology's origins is to see it as a distinct response to the internal crises of modernity and, at the same time, as constituting modernity's self-understanding. From this perspective, we might plot the interaction and intersections between the revolutionary, reformist, and reactionary wings of political theology and their critiques of, and imagined alternatives to, the dominance of a liberal bourgeois, capitalist way of being modern. While revolutionary and reactionary political theologies share a desire to abolish liberal bourgeois capitalism, its more reformist strands contend that liberal capitalist modernity can be moderated and metabolized in fruitful ways.[10]

The revolutionary and reactionary strands supplement and feed into a standard origin story for contemporary political theology that envisages it emerging out of debates in Germany and Austria between the two world wars. These debates focused on whether or not there is a necessary identification between theological and political concepts and the implications of this question for understanding both the nature of political order and the form and meaning of modernity itself. Key figures in this story include the Nazi jurist and heterodox Catholic Carl Schmitt, the Catholic theologian Erik Peterson, the historian Ernst Kantorowicz, the jurist Hans Kelsen, and the Marxist-influenced Jewish philosophers Walter Benjamin and Ernst Bloch. But this German-language constellation should be extended to include parallel debates in Russia, Italy, Britain, and France during this time. For example, debates in France from the 1920s to the 1950s between existentialists, Marxists, and Catholics (particularly Jesuits and Dominicans) produced distinctive political theologies, both reactionary and democratic.[11] These debates also need situating in a "Black Atlantic" setting because their active participants were figures such as Léopold Senghor and Alioune Diop, who represent what Elizabeth Foster identifies as a distinctly Catholic strand of the Negritude movement with its critique of racism and European colonialism.[12]

A Germany-centered story continues after the Second World War with political theology developing in constructive, theological, and revolutionary directions at the hands of the Protestant theologians Dorothee Sölle and Jürgen Moltmann and the Catholic theologian Johann Baptist Metz. Sölle, Moltmann, and Metz envisaged political theology as a corrective to the privatization of Christianity and the ways in which theology overly spiritualized Christian beliefs and practices and legitimized oppressive regimes. They called on Christian churches to become "social-critical institutions," envisaging salvation as having as much to do with political, economic, and social transformation in the here and now as with the eternal destiny of the soul. They also sought to chart a third way between communism and capitalism.

Sölle, Moltmann, and Metz's work was in dialogue with and contributed to the emergence of Latin American liberation theology. Through that connection their work is woven into the emergence of contemporary academic political theology in the Americas, including the advent of feminist liberation theology, Black liberation theology, Latin American liberation theology, and recently, Native American liberation theology from the late 1960s onward. Exemplified by the work of Rosemary Radford Ruether, James Cone, Gustavo Gutiérrez, and George "Tink" Tinker, liberation theologies of the Americas seek emancipatory forms of social existence while questioning the ways in which fundamental aspects of modern, Western life—specifically its bourgeois, racialized, androcentric, or settler-colonial formations—were anchored in and sanctioned by theological frames of reference. However, the plot line that charts the intersections of reactionary and revolutionary forms of political theology masks a different trajectory, one that does not begin with a critical rejection of modern life. Instead, it starts with the question of how to defend and tend the human, forms of common life, and nature over and against their exploitation and degradation, whether within liberal capitalist, state socialist, or state communist regimes.

An alternative, more reformist narrative begins with the "discovery" of society in the nineteenth century as something distinct from the state and the market. Society and sociality are seen to exceed all modern forms of political economy yet to be existentially challenged by them through being commodified by capitalism and instrumentalized by the modern state (whether colonial, liberal, communist, or socialist). Aligned with the need to regenerate the quality and character of social relations is a concern for the natural environment in which social relations are enmeshed. This story looks neither to Schmitt and his interlocutors nor to the emergence of liberation theology in the Americas. Instead, it attends to the development of Christian *socialism*,

Catholic *social* teaching, the *Social* Gospel, and the turn to economic and political democracy as a way to respond to the rise of industrial capitalism, modern bureaucratic states, the destruction of nature, an atomized, mass society, and the formation of totalizing systems, whether these be Fordist or totalitarian. Democracy is a key focus in this stream of political theology, but not in a way that reduces it to statecraft. Rather, small "d" democratic politics is seen to include the formation and support of associations and nonstate- and nonmarket-based forms of corporate life and the relations between them. Figures like Jacques Maritain, Karl Barth, Jane Addams, William Temple, Reverdy Ransom, and Vida Scudder represent this strand of political theology.[13] In their view the state secures social justice through measures like social insurance or national healthcare, but, against Hegelian and Marxist visions of the modern state as the means of realizing human freedom and fellowship in history, it is the body politic or political society constituted through myriad forms of association that is the means of realizing freedom and fellowship, albeit in temporal, penultimate forms. This strand of political theology rejected a Hobbesian vision of sovereignty but did not thereby reject sovereignty per se. Rather, it developed an alternative, "consociational" or confederal conception of sovereignty that was at the same time aligned with a relational anthropology and a conception of property as a social, not a private, good. And like reactionary and revolutionary forms of political theology (aligned as these were with right-wing and left-wing social movements), reformist forms were aligned with a set of social movements, most notably the labor and civil rights movements.[14]

Combining an emphasis on liberation with the prioritization of the social over and against capitalism and modern statecraft, Latinx and Womanist Christian social ethics represent another, parallel route into the streetscape of contemporary political theology. This pathway begins with a turn to the quotidian, to popular culture, and to folkways as vital aspects of moral and political reflection, particularly when trying to discern what liberation for marginalized peoples and blighted lands might look like.[15] This is because the ordinary, everyday world is the site at which forms of domination, and the precarity and oppression they produce, are most acutely displayed. An example is Katie Cannon's contribution to Womanist ethics, which made the folklorist and anthropologist Zora Neale Hurston a key interlocutor because she used the ordinary and everyday as sites for generating moral and spiritual wisdom and liberation.[16] This move can also be seen as animating the work of agrarian thinkers such as Wendell Berry and the Argentinian "theology of the people" that informed Pope Francis's approach to Catholic social teaching.[17] The Mujerista theology of Ada María Isasi-Díaz develops one of the fullest expressions of such a move. Isasi-Díaz's conception of the common people as *mestizaje-mulatez* attends to the mixed ethnic, racial, and economic histories that inform the everyday experiences of Latinos/as living in the United States and elsewhere. Isasi-Díaz retains liberation as a normative criterion for evaluating whether something is good or bad, but rather than focus on structural problems—as the first wave of liberation theologians did—she focuses on *lo cotidiano* or quotidian experiences, particularly of "Hispanas/Latinas." She asserts, "*Lo cotidiano* situates us in our experiences. It has to do with the practices and beliefs that we have inherited, with our habitual judgments, including the tactics we use to deal with the everyday." *Lo cotidiano* is not merely the reproduction of habit, but experiences that have been analyzed to generate "folk wisdom" about how to survive and thrive amid daily struggles. And attention to *lo cotidiano* leads to questioning and even subverting established traditions and customs, especially when these reinforce structures of oppression, even as these traditions and customs are vital sources of wisdom.[18]

This focus on everyday life is also developed by the Jesuit priest and scholar Michel de Certeau, a figure whose work straddles the political and the theological without using the term *political theology*. De Certeau's investigations into the modern state explore how privileging writing and text over speech and bodily performance reconstitutes central features of everyday life. Scholars who are inspired by this line of thought, such as Silvia Federici and Verónica Gago, have explored how this shift in focus correlates with a shift in political economy toward private property and enclosure. These turns have historically informed the consolidation of the Catholic Church as a global empire and its complex and at times violent control over female, transgressive, and heretic bodies.[19]

While these threads in the political theology conversation attend to revolutionary possibilities, a different thread, emerging out of the heart of contemporary empire, develops from a decidedly reformist orientation. The term *public theology* was coined by the University of Chicago–based religion scholar Martin Marty in 1974. He used it as a way of talking about figures such as Reinhold Niebuhr and the American Roman Catholic John Courtney Murray and their influence on how churches—both Protestant and Roman Catholic—came to understand their role as constituent parts of American civil society. Public theology attempted to do three things: (1) justify theological claims and the role of the church beyond the private realm within liberal nation-states; (2) bring theological insight to bear on specific public policy questions such as immigration and nuclear weapons; and (3) justify theologically liberal nation-states as a form of political order to Christians. Public theologies that shared these aspirations came to prominence in other parts of the world at a later date. In South Africa, public theology supersedes liberation theology as a way to address questions of building a liberal democratic nation-state in the post-apartheid context.[20] In Germany and the Nordic countries, public theology is seen to supersede political theology in the post–Cold War, and then post–9/11, context as a way to address globalization and increasing ethnic and religious diversity.[21] However, whatever the context, the shared impetus for the development of public theology was the desire for Christians committed to liberalism to defend it as a political philosophy. In its initial phases, public theology sought to oppose communism while moderating the excesses of capitalism. In the current context, it is not communism that public theology opposes, but forms of ethnoreligious nationalism and reactionary forms of political theology marked as "fundamentalist."

Critics of public theology see it as forcing religiously motivated actors into the straightjacket of liberalism as a political philosophy and thereby subordinating religious belief and practice to being a good liberal (and beyond that, a good bourgeois, individual, autonomous, self-reflexive subject wedded to capitalism and the liberal nation-state as the primary public realities).[22] In contrast to political theology, public theology assumes that it is necessary to either translate theological concepts into the idioms and frameworks of liberalism or be bilingual on the assumption that liberalism is the determinative discourse shaping the public realm. Whether it is the political philosophy of Jürgen Habermas or John Rawls, it is liberalism that is assumed to set the terms and conditions of what constitutes the civil or public sphere within which religious discourse is articulated. In contrast, contemporary political theology asks fundamental questions about modern forms of political order, especially those governed by liberalism.

From its inception as a term, political theology has pointed to how modern sovereignty is grounded theologically and thereby articulates the role of theology in securing hierarchical systems of domination. As Bretherton notes in his essay, this dynamic is at work in the very first uses of *political theology* as a formal term in Mikhail Bakunin's 1871 treatise "The Political Theology of Mazzini and the International." Bakunin's essay points to how theology is transmuted into immanent political ideas and projects while at the same time providing the architecture for these political ideas and projects, as well as the terms and conditions under which they operate. In other words, modern immanent political projects are secularized versions of prior Christian ones. A particular focus of critical analysis in all forms of political theology since Bakunin is how, despite claims to the contrary, theology constitutes the liberal nation-state. In doing so, political theology is distinct and stands in opposition to most iterations of public theology that seek to defend rather than critique the liberal nation-state.[23] At heart the difference between political theology and public theology today is that the latter seeks to reclaim the role of theology in national and global public spheres, bringing to the fore the theological roots and possibilities of modernity; by contrast, political theology attends to the failures of modernity, with its collapse into forms of the will to power, while witnessing to the possibilities of solidarity—whether authoritarian or democratic—amid the catastrophes and ruins that modernization brings in its wake.[24]

As should be clear from the various story lines sketched here, *political theology* is a contested term. It attracts advocates of both hard-right and hard-left politics, fascist and radically democratic movements, and colonial and decolonial projects; as a discursive frame of reference, it trades and traffics among all of them. Moreover, any story we tell about the origins of political theology will bring to the fore certain actors and center particular geographies while marginalizing others. Yet telling origin stories can make explicit the shape of contemporary conversations about political theology and can help explain that shape. Telling certain stories is also an invitation to tell new stories that will further expand the conversation.

THE CONTOURS OF POLITICAL THEOLOGY

Having approached political theology through its history, we turn now to its subject matter. Political theologies come in many shapes:

1. Confessional theological reflection on social, economic, or political questions.
2. A mode of critique that unmasks the ways in which supposedly secular modern political thought and arrangements suspend or conceal religious frameworks. Conversely, political theology also attends to the legacy of and ongoing ways in which religious beliefs and practices are used as modes of political and economic "governmentality," whether for liberative or oppressive ends. Key here are the ways in which political theology desecularizes the immanent and secularized self-conceptions of left, liberal, libertarian, and other contemporary political frameworks while at the same time, and often in the same breath, disenchanting and historicizing religious and theological discourses by attending to how they function politically and economically.
3. Critical analysis of the structural and conceptual relationship between theological and political ideas and practices, asking

to what extent they are analogous or share a point of origin or intellectual history.
4. A critical hermeneutic of political life and thought that refuses the Weberian iron cage or immanent frame as determinative of reality and takes seriously the role of metaphysical, theological, and ontological claims as already present in politics. This hermeneutic might be put in terms of the reenchantment of politics (descriptively, critically, and normatively), or the refusal of the secularization thesis, or a focus on the inherently extramaterial, superorganic dimension of politics. Such reflection asks questions about the meaning and purpose of politics and the character and quality of political relations in either a normative or critical key, in a way that looks beyond what Pope Francis called the "technocratic paradigm."[25]
5. A hermeneutic of sacred texts that takes seriously the social, economic, and political contexts of their production, and in exegesis centers questions about how power dynamics are represented as well as how the text is taken up in different settings, whether historical or contemporary.

The characteristic foci of political theology stem from its most fundamental questions: What is the nature and metaphysical basis of modern forms of life? What orients the human practices through which a common life is negotiated and sustained? In asking these questions, political theology probes the crises and contradictions of modernity in terms aligned with and going beyond the problems of capitalism, colonialism, patriarchy, extractivism, and an anthropocentric relation to nature. Central to political theology as a critique of modern ways of being alive is how it, paradoxically, demythologizes modern structures of power and cultural systems by remythologizing politics over and against the ways in which modern political orders conceptualize themselves within what Charles Taylor calls "the immanent frame."

POLITICAL THEOLOGY DISCIPLINED

Political theology is not just what is downstream from its origins, nor is it wholly determined by a specific set of questions. Political theology also exists in the context of academic disciplines, with all their particularities and peculiarities. What political theology looks like in Christian theology can be quite different from what it looks like in political theory, continental philosophy, religious studies, Islamic studies, or anthropology. If our task is to open up the conversation in a way that cuts across these disciplinary divides, we need to first reflect on how political theology can inform and even reshape different disciplines.

Political Theory and Political Philosophy

Intellectual historians of political thought, political theorists, and political philosophers increasingly recognize the ways a secularization narrative has shaped the field's self-understanding and thereby generated a myopia about the religious dimensions of much political thought. Against the secularizing frameworks of such approaches as the Cambridge School of intellectual history and its particular way of conceptualizing political thought, there has been a push in the past twenty years to recover the theological backdrop and ongoing influence of theology in the historical development and contemporary articulation of political theory and political philosophy. This pushback ranges in scale from the macro to the micro. Examples of the former from European intellectual history are Michael Gillespie's work on the theological origins of modernity, Paul Avis's work on the role of theology in the Enlightenment, and Charles Taylor's work on the concept of the secular.[26] Examples of more specific or microscale interventions include work on the theological basis of both John Locke and John Rawls's political philosophies;[27] the theological and biblical basis of key political concepts such as tolerance and republicanism;[28] the constructive role of Catholicism in the development of existentialism, Marxism, and Negritude in the francophone world;[29] and the Christian origins of human rights discourse.[30] To ignore the role of theology and other religious discourses in modern political thought—whether viewed within a national, transnational, or global frame—not only is intellectually irresponsible and bad history but also cuts political theory off from a vital resource from which to do its work. A good example of how political theology can inform and shape work at the intersection of intellectual history and political theory is Alison McQueen's turn to apocalyptic discourses to make sense of political realism.[31] McQueen echoes an early generation of political theorists and intellectual historians who envisioned modern political developments such as fascism and communism in millenarian and apocalyptic terms.[32] Another example is the work of those like Hannah Arendt, Sheldon Wolin, and Michael Walzer who challenge liberal contract theory by drawing on the theological and biblical motif of covenant. These conversations in political theory are altogether different from debates about religion in public life that involve figures such as Richard Rorty and Jürgen Habermas. Political theology is interested in the way religion and politics are always entangled at multiple levels, not in how political institutions can manage an ostensibly self-evident phenomenon called "religion."

A further key contribution of political theology to political theory, political philosophy, and their intellectual history is the way it again brings into view movements that have been ignored by scholars but are central to the history of politics. One of the most successful political movements since 1945 in Europe is Christian Democracy. Yet the intellectual history and political theory of Christian Democracy are insufficiently researched in comparison to nearly all other equivalent and often less electorally successful political movements, such as libertarianism.[33] Political theology also helps address a further myopia: the ways in which social movements that self-identify as religious or that have major religious components are read in ways that take religion out of them. Examples include the civil rights movement, the sanctuary movement, and the environmental justice movement. Due to the legacies of the secularization thesis, religion tends only to show up as a factor in considering reactionary movements (for example, the Moral Majority in the United States). Even then, the theological conceptuality used within such movements is taken out of them. Rather than being causal or having conceptualities that need examining, religious frames of reference are reduced to ideological window dressing for what are judged to be solely materialistic ends. Political theology helps read theology and religious frameworks back into politics (and environmental and economic questions) in ways that help make sense of it and without which the theory and history remain incoherent.[34]

The need for political theory and intellectual history to incorporate and engage political theology in the postsecular context and in a nonsecular form only grows more urgent. Some facility with political theology is necessary to make sense of the political discourses that inform such developments as the Russian invasion of Ukraine, the dynamics within Israeli, Palestinian, and

American politics, the rise of ethnoreligious populisms around the world, Indigenous land rights movements, and the apocalypticism shaping so much environmental politics.

A parallel case can be made in the intellectual history of economics and the critical study of capitalism and globalization. Like work on political theory and political philosophy, such studies tend to operate within the confines of a secularizing framework that reads religion out of the picture. There is a growing body of work that reads religion back into the intellectual history of economics and that either envisages capitalism in religious terms or offers critical analysis that draws from economically oriented political theology.[35]

Continental Philosophy

European philosophers toward the end of the twentieth century grappled with the conceptual knot Carl Schmitt labeled "political theology." French political philosophers turning away from Marxism toward the political center, such as Claude Lefort and Marcel Gauchet, wrestled with the afterlives of the theological in search of a foundation for European liberal democracy.[36] This interest in grappling with the theological as a means to ask foundational questions about politics would be taken up again, toward the turn of the millennium, by a set of European philosophers who understood their politics to be more radical than liberal-democratic: prominent among these, Giorgio Agamben and Jacques Derrida, with Alain Badiou and Slavoj Žižek chiming in as well. Agamben's account of the *homo sacer*—a doubled figure, inside and outside society at once, sovereign and banished, eternal body and mortal body, human and animal—has been particularly generative for scholars across the humanities and critical social sciences, including in postcolonial studies (notably, as theorized by Achille Mbembe).[37] Recently philosophers in this tradition have broadened the palate of theological concepts under consideration while continuing to position political-theological reflection as a challenge to the liberal-democratic order, increasingly understood in terms of neoliberalism: Elettra Stimilli's incisive writing on the theological logics of the economy is exemplary in this regard.[38]

Parallel to these debates among European philosophers, anglophone aficionados of European philosophy (often located, institutionally, outside philosophy departments) echoed and applied the ideas developing in Europe. Political theology, for some, was the Next Big Thing, a contrarian challenge to the postmodern settlement that had started to appear uncomfortably aligned with neoliberalism. In conferences, edited volumes, and blog posts, a set of primarily United States–based, primarily male, primarily white "theorists" embraced political theology and articulated it with ecology, economy, materialism, multiplicity, and other trending themes—though their engagement with the rich textures of both religion and politics was rather limited. However, a number of scholars emerging out of this milieu embraced a curiosity and rigor that allowed them to make serious contributions to conversations in continental philosophy and in political theology.[39]

For readers versed and invested in discussions of political theology as they unfold in this vein of continental philosophy, the terminology in this book may seem familiar while its use may seem unsatisfying. We do not write as philosophers, concerned principally with clarifying and questioning concepts. While we do find increasingly subtle understandings of sovereignty and its family of concepts responsive to the contours of the world, our interest is in speaking to the world rather than to the realm of the conceptual. Put more simply, we each hold ourselves accountable to the world and see that relationship of accountability pulling forward our thinking. Moreover, each of us has commitments that precede any conceptual analysis of the theological and its family relations. While one way of describing these different commitments is in more or less disciplinary terms—Christian confession, left politics, and cultural anthropology—another way is in terms of attunement to the existential investment marked by the political-theological. Put simplistically, we are concerned with matters of life and death and also of life beyond death; the philosopher tends to fixate on the conceptual as a shield from the existential. Of course, that is uncharitable to the philosopher, and an exaggeration, but it points at the concerns that motivate us to take the approach to political theology that we do, both worldly and profoundly concerned with the end of worlds.

Religious Studies

On the face of it, religious studies would seem to be the natural home of political theology. The field of religious studies is interested in the travels and travails of religious concepts, in tracking the sacred, ritual, holiness, and much else across the globe and across time, unconstrained by the truth claims associated with religious traditions. Is this not also what political theology does, tracking the workings of the claims to the theological in domains of the political, across time and space? Yet political theology has not found a hospitable home within religious studies.[40] Beyond the unhappy coincidence that the word *theology* provokes allergic reactions in many religious studies scholars, these scholars sometimes find that the more critical and interdisciplinary conversations in political theology are deficient in terms of the depth of their engagement with religion. The bread and butter of religious studies is appreciating the complexity of religion in culture: the nuances and particularity of its history, thought, practices, affect, and power. In the way that political theology has been picked up in fields like literature and cultural anthropology, it can seem that religion is being flattened, that *religion* refers to little more than a gesture toward the transcendent. Moreover, on even more practical grounds, the lanes into which the discipline of religious studies is divided do not easily accommodate work in political theology: It does not fit with a world religion, it is not religious ethics, it is not comparative religion, and it is not tethered to a sacred text.

And yet, all three of us find ourselves drawn to religious studies and, in some instances, are more at home there than in other disciplinary spaces. We think religious studies is, at its best, a place where political theology could and should be welcomed. The sort of political theology that we experiment with in the chapters that follow is attuned to religion in culture, and it cares about history, thought, practices, affect, and power. While the three of us enter with distinctive academic formations and aspirations, religious studies is, if anything, welcoming of pluralism: it is a discipline composed of many methods and many motivations (explicit, implicit, and repressed). We hope that this volume can serve as an invitation to religious studies scholars to enter into the discourse of political theology, even as religious studies readers may productively challenge us to deepen our appreciation of the complexity of religion. We hope that, once and for all, religious studies scholars can set aside their prejudice about the word *theology* and appreciate that it is not a conversation stopper; it does not point to the unquestionable or irrational. Rather, engaging theology calls for distinctive resources and orientations. We are cemented in our conviction that a liberal-capitalistic and technocratic order is inadequate, that a more critical, imaginative, and wisdom-seeking approach to thinking (and living) is needed—all lessons we think the discipline of religious studies would do well to learn better.[41]

Interfaith Relations

This genealogy of political theology situates it primarily within a Christian-majority context. However, political theology is increasingly taken up as a term and mode of analysis within non-Christian religious traditions, particularly Islam and Judaism.[42] As Bretherton outlines in his essay, this adoption points to how political theology exists beyond a solely Christian frame of reference and is now a point of mediation between many cosmologies. Engagement with political theology beyond Christianity speaks to the capaciousness of *political theology* as a term and can be ascribed to three dynamics within political theology as a hybrid mode of analysis and point of mediation between multiple traditions.

The first dynamic concerns the histories that different religious traditions share, histories marked by both violent entanglement and cross-pollination. In the modern period, these are intensified by processes of imperialism, trade, and missionary endeavor. The meshwork of relations such encounters and entanglements produce can in turn generate hybrid forms of belief and practice. Political theology can be read as one such hybrid form and point of intersection. Three examples illustrate these possibilities. The first is how Gandhi drew on Jesus and the New Testament to inform his radically democratic vision of nonviolent resistance. Those who pioneered the civil rights movement in the United States in turn drew on Gandhi to shape their Christian understanding of radical democratic politics. Both the movement Gandhi led and the civil rights movement are hugely significant for how democratic social movements around the world operate today (even as there is a growing critical evaluation of Gandhi himself). This historical relationship is neither straightforward nor unidirectional. It involves a web of relations between different geographies, religious traditions, and conceptions of democracy.[43]

Another example emerges from within the context of the anti-apartheid struggle in South Africa. The movement brought together Christian and Islamic activists, generating intense exchange and the adoption of liberation theology as a frame of reference by Islamic thinkers such as Farid Esack who sought to conceptualize the struggle within Islamic terms.[44]

A final, parallel example is the emergence and development of Black nationalist thought in North America and how insights from its early Christian proponents such as Martin Delany and Marcus Garvey are incorporated in Islamic articulations of Black nationalism, as exemplified in the work of Malcolm X. In turn, Malcolm X is taken up as a key point of reference in the Black liberation theology of James Cone and Albert Cleage.

All these examples point to how political theology can function as a site at which to name and map these intersections, particularly as they emerge from shared democratic struggle and coalition building across diverse communities. Its focus on sites of struggle and formations of political order distinguishes political theology from comparative religious ethics and interfaith dialogue, as well as from the growing field of comparative political theory. To reiterate: political theology's methodology is not comparative but juxtapositional. It embraces and interrogates points of convergence and hybridity, centering questions of power.

The second way political theology names interreligious cooperation and conflict is by articulating shared discursive themes such as apocalypticism, mysticism, and prophecy, particularly as these intersect with formations of political economy and drive social movements. To take one example, prophecy has been a source of consternation and possibility in multiple traditions. It was the demotic license to speak freely and challenge authority, based on nothing other than personal revelation, that so worried the early modern Christian and Jewish political theologians Thomas Hobbes and Baruch Spinoza. In their critiques of prophecy, they point to how it threatens political stability. Yet its dangers are also the source of its democratic promise: Criticizing the status quo and prefiguring alternative possibilities are vital if there is to be movement from the world as it is toward a more generous and just one.[45] How prophets and prophecy shape politics, and how different traditions conceptualize the figure of the prophet while drawing on other traditions in their conceptualization, are but some examples of how political theology can operate as a site of exchange and mediation.[46]

The third way political theology articulates a shared space between multiple religious traditions, one that enables and produces cross-pollination, is through shared critical concerns such as secularism, nationalism, colonialism, racism, sovereignty, human rights, capitalism, and notions of historical progress. The question of secularism and secularity is a particularly formative site of exchange in the development of contemporary political theology, as illustrated by the work of Talal Asad and Saba Mahmood. Following from Asad's work there has been a debate about the degree to which conceptions of secularity and secularization are themselves Christian or, more specifically, Protestant ideas imposed through colonialism around the world.[47]

A parallel debate focuses on whether religion is a Eurocentric, colonial category that subsumes radically different phenomena within a largely Protestant framework.[48] This framework was born out of interactions between metropole and colony that generated a progressive and hierarchal view of religions, a view exemplified in David Hume's *Natural History of Religion* (1757). In Britain, Germany, and the United States, Protestantism (and its offshoots, including Deism) was the standard used to measure all other religions. That which did not conform to a tacitly Protestant conception of true religion was labeled primitive or in need of reform. Such a view can still be heard in contemporary debates about the need for Islam to undergo a "reformation": that is, become more Protestant and therefore "better."[49] Haunted by free-floating fragments of Protestantism, modern sociological concepts of religion took as definitional that religion is an assemblage of propositional beliefs, interior experiences, and social practices. Traces of this kind of approach are found in Robert Bellah's recent definition of religion as "a system of beliefs and practices relative to the sacred that unite those who adhere to them in a moral community."[50] Yet this definition could be applied as much to a graduation ceremony or political rally as to a worship service, so why it demarcates something called "religion" is not clear. Bellah is well aware of the problems of this definition and proceeds to question it. Nevertheless, it shapes his monumental analysis of the role of religion in human evolution. Such an account of religion is not neutral. What it does do, however, is homogenize disparate and arguably incommensurable phenomena, remaking different traditions into versions of the same kind of this-worldly thing called "religion."[51] This social scientific definitional move is then enlisted in secularizing political projects of governance—whether reactionary, reformist, or revolutionary—that seek to manage and contain something now separated out and demarcated "religion." The critique of religion and secularism points to how political theology as a critical project shared across multiple traditions unmasks how theological assumptions shape political life and formations of political economy. It also points to how political theology constitutes a point of mediation between and intervention within the fractious relationship between theology and religious studies by rendering them subject to critical reflection on how they both constitute configurations of power and privilege indexed to particular confessional commitments.

THE FUTURE OF POLITICAL THEOLOGY

We have traced where scholarship on political theology came from and where it stands today. Where should scholarship on political theology go in the years and decades to come? While we do not have a programmatic vision for the field, implicit in the three chapters of this book are a few orientations or "rules" that we believe should guide discussions of political theology. First, religions need to be treated in a way that is attentive to their complexity, particularity, and historical variation as well as in a way that avoids reductively collapsing God, the gods, or the spirits into the human realm. Second, political theology needs to operate with an open conception of politics, one that looks beyond statecraft or questions of sovereignty to how politics is the craft of forming and sustaining a common life over time with others in specific places. Third, political theology needs a nondeterministic, nonmaterialistic conception of the human and of human agency that emphasizes how human freedom and creativity generate shared worlds of meaning and action as well as uphold the intrinsic dignity of each person, no matter who they are or where they come from. Fourth, political theology is at its best when it remains sharply critical of secularism as an ideology entangled with liberalism, capitalism, and technocracy and attends to how secularism functions as a constraint on political imagination and action. Fifth, political theology fails unless it learns from, and holds itself accountable to, the crossing of the political and the theological at a microscale, in particular lives and bodies, especially those living under conditions of domination—all the while being cognizant of the ambivalent and often tragic nature of these crossings. Sixth and finally, we believe political theology will be relegated to the dustbin of passing fads, or of dusty, insular discourse, unless the field is animated by encounters across disciplinary boundaries, across theoretical and methodological orientations, and across lines of geography, history, and tradition. If these six rules are followed, political theology will be a site of intellectual effervescence through the next crises—which approach ever more quickly, ever more terribly. The chapters that follow exemplify and advance this agenda, each in different ways.

CHAPTER SUMMARIES

In what follows we argue that the only way to understand the meaning of the term *political theology* is to probe its multiple associations, how they put pressure on one another, and how they open up a fruitful way of understanding religion and politics and their intersections. To dramatize these tensions and possibilities, the following chapters answer the question "What is political theology?" from the distinct disciplinary perspectives of a Christian theologian, a critical theorist, and an anthropologist. In doing so, we make clear what the multiple conversations about political theology have in common while also underscoring open questions and debates around the concept.

In "Political Theology as Testimony," Bretherton maps but also reconfigures the Christian conversation about political theology. He reflects on the voice of the Christian theologian engaging in this conversation, theorizing that voice as "testimony," "witness," and "confession"—and demonstrating how that voice serves and is informed by rigorous, critical analysis. Bretherton weaves together key themes in the debates about political theology, such as the way political theology navigates questions of life and death as well as order and chaos, demonstrating how those themes fit within an overarching theological framework. Then, he sets out the four different meanings and uses of the term *political* in *political theology* and how each of these connects to the central topoi of Christian theology: creation, fall, providence, and eschatology. He also demonstrates how these theological reference points can in turn be located within conversations about political theology in the humanities. Finally, Bretherton describes how Christian political theology can avoid its capture by authoritarian and antidemocratic sociopolitical movements by drawing on theological, non-Christian, and secularized theoretical resources.

In "Political Theology from Below," Lloyd presents political theology as it emerges from social movements that are responding to perceived crises. He reflects on the period between the 2008 financial collapse and the 2020 pandemic and racial justice uprisings as a new time of perceived crisis that has generated political-theological responses among grassroots movements that call for analysis and that offer inspiration. Lloyd argues that such moments of crisis cleave leftist from liberal political outlooks, and political theology is an essential resource for understanding this cleavage. Proceeding through close reading and theoretical reflection, he asks what political theology would look like if it were grounded in the anticolonial writings of a figure like the Black Caribbean poet and politician Aimé Césaire instead of the Christian nationalist writings of Carl Schmitt. Lloyd argues that this new starting point allows political theology to appreciate and engage with new conversation partners at sites where secularized theological concepts are animating politics today—such as the new abolition movement.

In the final chapter, "An Anthropological Political Theology," Napolitano engages with the energetic, emerging conversation about political theology that has recently developed in the discipline of anthropology. Using ethnographic vignettes, Napolitano brings into focus the messy, lively, invigorating realities of political theology on the ground, practiced in the space between people and their environments. From Rome to Detroit to Indigenous communities in Latin America, Napolitano makes clear that political theology is at its best when it is understood as a coalescence of global and local exchanges. At the same time, she transforms political theology by bringing to the fore theoretical tools from new materialism, affect theory, Indigenous and migration studies, and across cultural anthropology. In the process, political theology becomes less about sovereign decisions and state power and more about vulnerability, uncertainty, negation, forms of life, and sensorial archives.

In a brief triptych that serves as an appendix, we each provide a roadmap, through a literature review, to emerging conversations in political theology from the perspective of our own discipline. We see this as a way to signal promising directions we see emerging and to mark our hope for the future of political theology.[52]

1

POLITICAL THEOLOGY AS TESTIMONY

LUKE BRETHERTON

My answer to the question "What is political theology?" is determined in large part by being someone who teaches and writes about it as a Christian. However, in making transparent the parochialism of my location, I am at the same time pointing to the inevitable contingency of *all* political theology. The contingency but also the truthfulness of political theology emerge from its being constituted by a testimony of faith. As testimony, political theology articulates a set of beliefs about the nature of the world as it is and a vision of the world as it should be. Another way of framing this duality is to say that political theology encompasses both a *via negativa* and a *via positiva*, an apophatic as well as a cataphatic way of seeing things. Its testimony "denounces" this world as well as "announces" a new one.[1] Things go wrong when this duality is lost.

By offering testimony, we become answerable for what we see and hear by making sense of and narrating it to others. In doing so, we make ourselves and others accountable. However, the testimony given by political theology is that of neither an impartial observer of a scientific experiment nor an expert in a court of law. Rather, it offers a declaration of belief. But as a statement of faith, political theology is not thereby reducible to either its contexts of formation or its creedal commitments. Nor is its testimony a bid for recognition from existing authorities. It does not seek inclusion into existing frames of reference as one more form of diversity to be treated with equity. Rather, as testimony, it bears witness to something that lies outside itself and is largely illegible within the terms and conditions set by dominant frames of reference. Like Augustine's *Confessions* or a tent revival testimonial, its testimony points beyond itself and the conditions under which it was uttered, challenging others to see things in a new way. Its testimony is a call to join the congregation of those charting a different pathway. As testimony, political theology is not therefore first and foremost an academic discipline or emergent field; it is a therapy for the ways we live. As noted elsewhere in this book, political theology is thus always having to negotiate the validity and authority of its pronouncements in relationship with a community of practice, whether that is a religious community, a social movement, or a society.

The testimony I give here is not an apology for political theology. I seek neither to justify nor to defend it. Instead, I offer a portrait that invites further reflection. Like a triptych, this portrait has three interrelated but distinct sections. I first describe how political theology is constituted through the symbiosis between talk of God and talk of politics. At this intersection, political theology constitutes a form of testimony to who God is and what it means to be human in the light of God's self-revelation in Jesus Christ. I reflect on how political life is determined by how one understands the relationships between life and death as well as order and chaos. As a mode of Christian testimony, political theology generates specific ways of framing relations between life and death and between order and chaos. In doing so, it conceptualizes the nature and meaning of political life (implicit here is the assumption that, say, Jewish, Islamic, or Buddhist testimony will configure political life differently according to how they conceptualize the order/chaos and life/death relations). In the second part I define what is meant by the term *political* in *political theology*, mapping four interrelated yet often conflicting uses of the term. And in the third part I outline how political theology is now a project of critique that confesses the characteristic sins and evils of modernity. This insight leads into a discussion of how political theology is now a discursive space through which are negotiated and refracted diverse cosmologies, both Christian and non-Christian, and their distinct social imaginaries for ordering life together.

POLITICAL THEOLOGY AS CHRISTIAN TALK

The interweaving and mutually constitutive relationship between talk of politics and theological talk is inevitable. Many of the terms Christians use to talk about who God is and who we are in relation to God are also political terms. Words like *ruler* and *kingdom* have obvious political overtones. But even seemingly churchy words like *liturgy*, *ecclesial*, and *bishop* are explicitly political in origin. The symbiosis between talk of God and talk of politics means that political concepts can illuminate but also be overidentified with theological ones, and vice versa. For example, when we talk of God's sovereignty, is that the same as talking about the sovereignty of a state? Or should we understand these uses of *sovereignty* very differently? The attempt to talk rightly about the interaction between Christianity and politics generates different schools of thought. For example, how Calvinists frame church-state relations (as involving a connected but mutually disciplining relationship) differs markedly from how Anabaptists understand them (as necessitating separation).

Embedded in the descriptive statement that talk of God and talk of politics are coemergent and mutually constitutive is a more substantive claim that politics is a crucial arena of human activity through which we come to grasp the truth of many theological concepts. It was not merely for convenience's sake that those who wrote the New Testament foraged Greco-Roman ideas about political life. The prevailing forms of political life were a crucible through which the New Testament writers articulated what it meant to be the church; for example, *ekklēsia* (church) and *leitourgia* (liturgy) are political terms turned to ecclesial ends. Early theologians continued this process of converting political categories into ecclesial ones and thereby reorienting and recalibrating them. A paradigmatic example is Augustine's reconceptualization of Cicero's definition of a people in his discussion of what it means to be the people of God.[2] The nature and form of political life were crucial to understanding something about the nature and form of divine-human relations. Conversely, participation in ecclesial practices enabled new kinds of moral and political judgment to be made, generating new understandings of what it means to be human. The symbiosis of talk of God and talk of politics is thus a seedbed from which *all* theology grows. Political life is therefore a fundamental basis for Christian talk, while in contexts where Christianity is a major influence, political life inevitably comes to be saturated with Christian beliefs and practices.

Born out of its position at the intersection of reflection on God and reflection on political life, political theology as Christian confession is bifocal. As one modality of Christian testimony, political theology articulates the nature, form, and purpose of political life in the light of the revelation of God given in Jesus Christ. At the same time, it attends to the historical realities in which that life is lived. Political theology discerns the consonance and dissonance between the way of life and form of rule incarnated and inaugurated by Jesus Christ and the social formations and authorities shaping this age between Christ's ascension and return. At times, it identifies how penultimate authorities and ways of life participate in Christ's way of being, while at other times it detects how they are anti-Christic. Political theology as a form of Christian testimony is thus a way of discerning how to act or conduct oneself appropriately in *this* time, in both its historical and eschatological registers. Its full realization is not therefore in a set of academic discourses but in a changed way of life.

Political Theology and the Relation Between Life and Death

As testimony to how all reality is determined by the life, death, and resurrection of Jesus Christ, Christian political theology foregrounds how all conceptions of political life are premised on a prior set of judgments about the proper ordering of the relationship between life and death.[3] While other cosmologies can frame this relationship in more harmonious terms, Christianity conceptualizes life and death as an antithesis, albeit one that resolves itself through the source of life swallowing death (1 Corinthians 15:54). The creedal confession is that death is ultimately determined by the human life of the Logos, Jesus Christ, the one in whom and through whom all things exist. It is Jesus Christ, not death, who has the last word. Jesus is the alpha and omega (Revelation 1:8; 21:6; 22:13). Now of course, as the Russian Orthodox political theologian Sergei Bulgakov notes, even in this confession, the relation between life and death is cast in paradoxical terms. As creatures we only know a *mortal life*: a life constituted by mortality and a mortality constituted by life. As Bulgakov contends, we experience this mortal life as a ceaseless struggle between life and death, in both an ontological and biological sense.[4] Our existence is made possible by a process in which life depends on death and death depends on life (for example, without something animal, vegetable, or mineral dying or being consumed I have no energy to live). But still, much follows from whether life precedes and is more basic than death or vice versa. If the former, then death does not exist except for a prior form of life; that is to say, creation is the condition and possibility for death and all that brings life to death. And in the wake of Jesus's life, death, and resurrection, death has lost its sting (1 Corinthians 15.35–58). Therefore, not only is there the possibility of life beyond death, but in this life, no place or people is godforsaken and so life can be renewed or healed no matter what the circumstances. What is accursed can become a blessing. What is a source of horror can be made holy. What is crucified can be resurrected. Where death reigns, the work of a faithful, hopeful, and loving politics is to witness to the possibilities of eternal life despite the power of death.[5] Or at least it should be.

Rather than testify to life stronger than death, some political theologies envisage death as stronger than life. Violence, terror, and horror are rendered the fundamental basis of shared existence. For example, the Nazi jurist Carl Schmitt, who is often read as a foundational figure of modern political theology, sees friend-enemy relations as the ground of politics, such that enmity and violence are foundational to all forms of shared existence. The condition of life for any given people is the need to render some other people as a threat to that life. "Our" way of life presumes the possibility that either "them" or "us" must die.

My contention is that to be a form of faithful, hopeful, and loving testimony, political theology should point to how no system of death is all-determining. Rather, it should proclaim that death is parasitic on and countered by the ways and means of life—ways and means that can be repaired or born witness to in the midst of death. On such a view, the carceral, for example, is not totalizing; life can be made present in its midst.[6] More controversially, according to this kind of theological account, anti-Black racism is not totalizing; Blackness as a cultural and political modality of life emerges in the crucible of slavery and is itself indigestible within and in excess of structures of death produced by racial capitalism. This is a point drawn from Frederick Douglass's autobiographical reflections on the role of the music and songs made by enslaved people. As Paul Gilroy notes, this music "was not simply a matter of African cultural life reasserting and renewing itself. For him, the music and the social relations it created supplied the favored means to assert and examine the humanity of the slave population that was being dehumanized by the government of the plantation."[7] For Gilroy, the spirituals embody a humanism that is counter to the form of humanity generated by the political economy of racial capitalism. The songs mark ways that systemic violence is both refused and metabolized into new forms of life, even in the wake of ongoing death.[8] Likewise, the Black liberation theologian James Cone sees the spirituals as a key form through which the enslaved resisted being defined by white supremacy and having their self-definition and way of experiencing the world determined by the trauma and oppression of slavery. Cone states that the spirituals are "the people facing trouble and affirming 'I ain't tired yet.' But the spiritual is more than dealing with trouble. It is a joyful experience, a vibrant affirmation of life and its possibilities. . . . The spiritual is the community in rhythm, swinging to the movement of life."[9]

In this age before Christ's return, the mechanisms of shame and death will continue to assert themselves and often seem to have the last word or be all-determining. But as Scripture testifies, what is intended to shame and demean—in this instance, the designation *Black*—can become a source of wisdom and glory (1 Corinthians 1.27–29). Desmond Tutu articulates this dynamic in his reflection on the crucifixion in the context of the anti-apartheid struggle and his own call for a "politics of transfiguration":

> Well, look at the cross. It was a ghastly instrument of death, of an excruciatingly awful death reserved for the most notorious malefactors. It was an object of dread and shame, and yet what a turnaround has happened. The instrument of a horrendous death has been spectacularly transfigured. Once a means of death, it is now perceived by Christians to be the source of eternal life. Far from being an object of vilification and shame, it is an object of veneration.[10]

Political theology as *Christian* testimony witnesses to the ways the forces of death can be eschatologically metabolized into eternal life, albeit still bearing the marks of death: Christ's risen body is inscribed with the scars of the very same crucifixion by means of which he defeated death.

Alongside naming the possibility of life in the wake of death, political theology also testifies to how death is at work but falsely named as life. This is the work of ideological critique. Ideology, as defined here, does two things. First, it naturalizes and universalizes contingent and contestable concepts and visions of how to order and organize life, generating the sense that certain oppressive ways of doing things are simply the ways things should be and everyone should conform to them without asking questions. When the contestability and contingency of a particular policy or way of doing things are hidden, the existing modes of exploitation, domination, and unjust hierarchies of value written into that way of doing things are thereby normalized and reproduced. For example, within white supremacy as an ideological framework, racial distinctions and stereotypes are taken to be "natural" rather than constructed through particular modes of economic, cultural, and political production. Their "naturalness" in turn justifies further violent and discriminatory behaviors and policies, both to those doing the discriminating and to those discriminated against.

Second, ideology turns things upside down, justifying the opposite of what is happening by inverting what is really going on in order to direct attention away from the question of whose interests are being served. For example, in mainstream economics, *security* now means risk, *credit* now means debt, and *trickle-down economics* is said to "lift all boats" and thereby serve the interests of everyone when in actuality it concentrates wealth and political power in the hands of existing elites. In the words of the prophet Isaiah, bitter becomes sweet and sweet bitter, evil is called good, and good evil (Isaiah 5:20). As a form of false testimony, ideology simplifies our understanding of reality, masks what contests it, directs our attention elsewhere, and renders invisible or illegible what is really going on in order to delegitimize other ways of doing things and further entrench an unjust status quo. In contrast to the witness of a Christ-focused political theology, ideological ways of seeing are a form of *unwitnessing*. They make invisible what is going on and unmake the social and material conditions of truth telling.

Part of the therapy political theology offers is to expose the mechanisms of ideology. Theology thereby becomes the poultice by which to unblock ears, open eyes, and unseal mouths, even as theology is at the same time being used ideologically. Marx's critique of capital is a case in point. He critiques the ways that religion legitimizes capitalism while simultaneously using religious and theological concepts to make visible and legible the ways that capitalism redefines what brings death as something that brings life.[11] The Christian theological claim is that because of the revelation of Jesus Christ we can now see and hear how the world is *not* as it should be. Sin and evil can be named. Moreover, after Pentecost, the Spirit is now poured out on all flesh. Anyone and everyone may now offer prophetic, Spirit-anointed speech and in doing so dissent from the dominant consciousness and critique the existing authorities and systems. In other words, the Spirit makes possible the social and material conditions of truth telling. And such speech is divinely sanctioned and ordained. It was this demotic license to speak freely and challenge authority based on nothing other than personal revelation that so worried Baruch Spinoza and Thomas Hobbes—figures foundational to early modern political theology. In their critiques of prophecy, they point to how it threatens political stability. Yet its dangers are also the source of its democratic promise: Critiquing the status quo and prefiguring alternative possibilities are vital if there is to be movement from the world as it is to a more generous and just one.

There is, however, an internal contradiction at work in the ways politics is constituted by the life-death relation. Most of politics is taken up with prudential judgments about better and worse ways of doing things, as well as the compromises necessary to sustain forms of shared life. When politics is collapsed into a binary, existential choice between life and death, politics as the negotiation of a common life becomes impossible. Everyone must line up behind one position or another, with both sides claiming to represent the forces of life and oppose the forces of death. The abortion debate in North America is a case in point. To compromise or draw equivalencies on existential questions is seen as signing a death warrant for someone. Refused is the reality of what Gillian Rose called "the broken middle," where negotiations of life take place and shared action amid trauma and tragedy is risked because life must go on.[12] Instead, an absolute binary forces an either/or choice. Increasing numbers of issues, from the environment to sexuality, are framed in existential terms so that politics becomes a zero-sum game: life for us means that this other way of life must die or be abolished. Yet for any form of ongoing life to be possible, negotiation and compromise are necessary. There can be no human, let alone humane, life without them. The alternatives to forming a common life through negotiation and compromise with others I disagree with or whose ideologies I find deplorable are to kill, dominate, and persecute them, none of which generate forms of shared existence.[13]

Political Theology and the Relation Between Order and Chaos

Sutured inside the distinction between life and death is the distinction between order and chaos. Conceptualizing the nature and proper form of political order is a central concern of Western political theology. This point is made by Eric Voegelin in his magisterial, multivolume work of political theology, *Order and History* (1956–1985). Voegelin sees order primarily in terms of sovereignty, law, and governance (with their cognate significations of stability, organization, hierarchy, sequence, regularity, classification, discipline, and institutional arrangements). But political theology also reflects on order understood in terms of right relation (love, freedom, justice, solidarity, and communion) and how order as right relation disrupts and contests order as determined by sovereign structures and systems of government. Chaos emerges at the point of intersection and contradiction between these two conceptions of order. Chaos is also a way of naming the inherent instabilities, fissures, and conflicts that constitute all forms of order. But the ways in which the order-chaos relation frames any form of political life is not straightforward.

Many top-down political theologies presume an identification between order as right relation and order as sovereignty. To put this another way, sovereignty is indexed to ontology (or ontotheology). This identification is exemplified by integralist visions of political order in which the individual, the household, and political structures cohere into a uniform and seamless hierarchy. Integralist visions draw an analogy between soul, polity, and universe that emphasizes uniformity over plurality. While exemplified in Plato's *Republic*, that analogy is common within the Christian tradition, one often derived from a doctrine of God that emphasizes the oneness, omnipotence, and transcendent lordship of God over the universe. By extension, there is said to be but one king governing the polity, one father governing the family, and reason governing the actions of each soul. God is the archetypal sovereign, and human sovereignty—in all its forms—participates in the various attributes ascribed to God's nature. This is the basis of Schmitt's conception of sovereignty. Anything that opposes this order is then read as a chaotic element that must be expelled, suppressed, or destroyed in order to maintain the true and good political order that itself accords with the true and good order of being. The alternative to this order is moral and political chaos.

In his biting critique of the political theology of the nineteenth-century Italian revolutionary leader Giuseppe

Mazzini, the anarchist Mikhail Bakunin captures the logic of this integralist position:

> If there was no God-the-creator, [Mazzini] says, the world with all its wonderful laws could not have existed, or else would be nothing but a dreadful chaos, in which all things would be governed not by a providential and divine purpose but by the frightful chance and anarchic collision of blind forces. There would be no purpose in life, and everything would be material, brutish and accidental. For without God there would be no coherence in the physical world and no moral law in human society; and without moral law, no motherland, no Rome, no Italy, for if Italy exists as a nation it is only because she had a providential cosmic mission to fulfil, and she could only have been charged with this mission by God.[14]

According to this logic, action that inhibits or expunges chaos is good and loving because it maintains the true order of being. This logic is reflected in conceptions of political order that reject democracy in favor of authoritarian regimes. Democracy as rule by the many, with "the many" envisioned as a lawless mob, is inherently chaotic and so must be resisted or suppressed.

Contrary to the integralist view, bottom-up strands of political theology argue that established forms of order are usually what the twelfth-century prelate Rufinus of Sorrento called "the sleep of Behemoth." When disturbed, Behemoth reveals its beastly nature by turning on those with the temerity to challenge its disordered and unjust tranquillity.[15] However, the formation of even a modestly just earthly peace requires agitating the monster rather than leaving undisturbed a subjugated quiescence that dresses up compliance as harmony. Echoing the prophets, nonintegralist or insurgent political theologies point to how the established form of rule is misrule and how those upheld as paragons of virtue are really hypocrites who cry peace when there is no peace (Jeremiah 6.14). Alongside unjust orders that produce peace for some through terror and precarity for others, there are situations where too much control, too much order, too much of the puritanical in the political generates its own kind of corruption and disorder. This is a central theme of Mikhail Bakhtin's conception of the carnivalesque and is exemplified in Shakespeare's *Measure for Measure*. The chaotic topsy-turvy world of the street and the brothel ensures the bawdy comeuppance of injustice and hypocrisy by those with power and enables justice tempered by mercy to prevail.

At the intersection of chaos and order is the question of the exception so central to debates about sovereignty. If, as Schmitt contends, the sovereign is the one who decides the exception, then the sovereign can suspend order yet not induce chaos. Sovereigns suspend the existing order so as to establish a (putatively) better order. They declare an emergency and thereby suspend the rule of law in order to bring order to the chaotic conditions of emergency (whether caused by a natural disaster, political crisis, or the advent of war). But who declares the exception? Who declares the emergency? Who decides when to suspend the rule of law? Who or what determines when order has become chaos and disorder is needed to reestablish order? Does the declaration come from above or below? Is it determined by the sovereign or the subject? The ruler or the revolutionary? The slaver or the abolitionist? Pilate or Jesus? For liberation theologies and various millennial movements, it is the latter. For Schmitt and conservative political theologies, it is the former: The sovereign is the *katechon* who holds back chaos (of the Antichrist as well as the anarchist and the eschaton).

A further question that arises at this point for political theology is whether, in an unjust and fallen world, chaos is a necessary principle of order and order inherently the progenitor of chaos. Much contemporary political theology answers this question in the affirmative. Flesh, carnality, pleasure, transgression, fluidity, subversion, syncretism, hybridity, and the monstrous are the means of being good and harbingers of life and fecundity. By contrast, law, government, order, hierarchy, sovereignty, harmony, purity, and the like are portrayed as the means of generating domination and death. This would seem to be an inversion of the pathway to morality that existed for millennia within Christianity. Dionysius is now to be favored over Apollo. Still other political theologies envision the relation between order and chaos in dyadic terms. The recent work of Giorgio Agamben is but one example. For Agamben, there cannot be freedom without domination, the livable without the unlivable. Order for some is *always* premised on chaos for others. A kernel of abjection and horror *necessarily* lies at the heart of civilization, anarchy at the heart of governance. There is neither progress nor decline, only ever-changing, always-becoming assemblages of chaos and order. But the interaction and paradoxes of order and chaos are not so clear-cut within Christian moral and political thought and practice down the ages.

These conceptions can be contrasted with a more dynamic understanding of the interplay of chaos and order in Christian cosmology. Theologically understood, the noneschatological order is a deeply ambiguous one in which the world is complexly faithful and unfaithful, loving and idolatrous, saved and sinful. It is a time in which political authorities may both participate in the reordering of creation to its true end and become anti-Christic: that is, utterly opposed to God's good order by leading creation to chaos and thence nothingness. The scriptural language of *empire*, *Antichrist*, *demons*, and *principalities and powers* is language that reckons with the capacity of political, ecclesial, or any authority to act in wholly malevolent ways, with the idolatrous cultural forms and regimes of governance that are something more than simply a distortion of a gift (or more properly something *less*, if, following Augustine, we take evil to be a privation of the good). A Christian conceptualization of cosmos—an order at once metaphysical and moral that simultaneously contains the possibility and moments of its own inversion and dissolution—helps capture the ambiguity of our participation in any form of earthly, political order.[16] It allows us to see "the earthly city" as having intrinsic value as part of the noneschatological order of things in which we can perform the gift and vocation of being creatures but, at the same time, not be naïve about how we are simultaneously participating in worldly systems that can utterly desecrate this gift and vocation. Enabling life in the earthly city to be an arena in which this gift and vocation can flourish rather than be distorted entails ensuring that the prevailing social, political, and economic orders are neither made to bear the full weight of the meaning and purpose of being human nor divested of any meaning and purpose and thus rendered a nihilistic vortex of dominatory relations.

Christians confess that Christ is ruler over the whole cosmos. In this conception, Christ's rule extends beyond the church and changes the nature and form of all being. Therefore, political theology as Christian testimony is not ecclesiastical house rules. It testifies to the proper shape of all forms of shared existence. The theological claim is that all forms of existence are relativized by the way of being a creature revealed in the incarnation of Jesus Christ. The true order of being and becoming is given in Christ and only available to human creatures insofar as they participate in Christ through the Holy Spirit. The eschatological dynamics of participation in Christ mean that no earthly form of political economy can be wholly identified with or analogous to the kingdom of God. Rather, all earthly polities are subject to judgment by the Lamb on the throne. At the same time, any form of existence may now participate in Christ, whether explicitly identified as Christian or not. The therapy that political theology offers, therefore, should not be about either Christianizing the world or turning it into the church (both temptations to which the church repeatedly falls prey). Rather, it is to testify to how the world may be truly itself. In theological terms, this is to testify to how the world may once more be an arena of creational flourishing through being healed and renewed in Christ.[17] The measure and mark of what that flourishing looks like in practice are whether it recapitulates the life, death, and resurrection of Jesus Christ.[18] Yet any such form of life, however Christ-like its manner and mode of life, is only relative to the ultimate fulfilment of all things at the end of history. In other words, all political orders are penultimate and subject to judgment by the ultimate and true order of being revealed in Christ.

The formation of a meaningful and penultimately good political life in this age before Christ's return entails the disruption of two very different kinds of disorder. The first that need upending are totalizing, Babel-like systems that demand unquestioned uniformity and claim that they are the only true and good order of being (that they and not Christ are the end and fulfilment of history). The second are systems that disaggregate and dissolve any form of common life, working on the premise that there is neither meaning to history nor any moral life possible within the existing order of things: All is chaos, all is death, Christ was not resurrected. In addition to discerning what needs disrupting, participating in Christ entails prefiguring forms of life that witness to Christ's order of being as the true order of the cosmos—even if such prefigurations appear to be chaotic within and disruptive of the present, earthly order of things. For some, such as Walter Benjamin and in premillennial eschatology that talks of a rapture, the messianic age only becomes possible with the destruction of this world. However, in the view set out here, the new can be prefigured within the terms and conditions of the old order. It does not require the abolition or ending of the old before the new can emerge. Rather, it looks to the *conversion* of the old through the inauguration of the new in its midst. Like the resurrection, the miracle of new life is possible within this age in a way that anticipates and bears witness to the age to come.[19]

PART 2: CONCEPTUALIZING "THE POLITICAL" IN POLITICAL THEOLOGY

The life/death and order/chaos distinctions set the metaphysical terms and conditions for the fourfold meaning of the term *political* in *political theology*. Implicit in my argument is how the life/death and order/chaos distinctions determine the temporal and spatial orders through which political life is constructed. That said, a fully orbed political metaphysics would entail an account of history (understood as progressing, regressing, cyclical, linear, or something else) and what spatial form determines the normative shape and scale of political order (city-state, nation-state, empire, or something else). As will be seen, different conceptions of political life lend themselves to different temporal and spatial orderings.

Each of the following interrelated yet often conflicting conceptions of political life is an attempt to answer the questions that the life/death and order/chaos distinctions raise. The first question is: What makes life possible? As animals, we are interdependent creatures who need the care of others to live, let alone live well. This care can be organized at various scales and enacted through myriad means, but some kind of shared life or life-in-common is a material and social condition for the care needed to make human life possible. Without it we die. Political theology addresses this question by describing what it means to form a common life.

Intrinsic to this first question is the second question: How should we relate to those who are not part of "our" common life? How should our own roots, our sense of what counts as home, identity, or belonging—that is, our way of life, our distinct and particular way of doing a life-in-common—be coordinated with and ordered alongside those we find strange or who don't share our beliefs and practices or are not part of "our" shared life? In political theology, this second question is framed in terms of the friend-enemy relation and the ways in which those we find strange are seen as a threat to what makes "our" life possible. As a chaotic element that disrupts or jeopardizes our common life, they are rendered "other" and thereby marginalized within or excluded from the circle of care.

The third question asks, How should a common life be ordered so as to prevent either the death of those we care for or the collapse of our common life into chaos? At the heart of this question is the question of how power is organized and ordered among these people in this place so as to enable this form of life to go on. Political theology frames the answer to this third question in terms of sovereignty. However, modern forms of sovereignty entail coercive uses of power and a monopoly of violence. Domination by the modern state and a political life structured by enmity and violence give rise to a final set of questions: What would a political life look like that is free from enmity, chaos, and modes of domination and exploitation? Is such a realm possible here and now? And what is the role of existing forms of politics in realizing such a realm? Driving this last set of questions is an eschatological longing for a peaceable kingdom and a time and place without suffering or division.

In perhaps too neat a move, a Christian conception of political theology can organize each of these four characteristic uses of the term *political* within a broader dogmatic framework: namely, that of creation, fall, providence, and eschaton. Political life figured within the doctrine of creation is about life-in-common; political life understood as fallen attends to the ways sin and idolatry produce injustice, exploitation, and enmity; political life conceptualized within the doctrine of providence points to how sovereign authorities generate order amid fallen life by inhibiting evil and enabling some kind of modestly just and generous form of common life. Finally, political life situated within eschatology opens up the possibility of a common life without the chaos produced by domination, enmity, injustice, or violence—in other words, a redeemed or liberated world freed from sin and idolatry.

Creation: The Political as Constituted by Life-in-Common

The first conception understands the political as that which pertains to how all creaturely life is a life-in-common as well as how human life itself is a commons. In this conception, politics is the means through which humans build up and sustain a shared world of meaning and action that make life possible through forms of mutual care and the pursuit of goods in common. This shared world of meaning and action constitutes a distinct common life or polity. According to Aristotle's succinct formulation, humans are political animals, which is to say, humans are animals who cannot survive, let alone thrive, without some form of common life.[20] A particular common life through which a life-in-common is cultivated and negotiated is the condition of human life itself. And beyond mere survival, flourishing depends on being embedded in just and generous forms of common life. Politics in this creational register is the work of forming, norming, and sustaining that common life. Alongside the term *political life*, other terms for this common life include *commonwealth*, *commonweal*, and *public life*, or *res publica*. To pursue this common good, politics must be directed to the flourishing of the whole rather than the part, the common rather than either a factional or private interest. When political life serves only the interests of the one, the few, or even the many, rather than what is common or shared, then politics is corrupted into a form of tyranny such as plutocracy, oligarchy, or majoritarianism. For Aristotle, all such forms of tyranny are catastrophic failures of what it means to be a human because they fail to uphold the material and social conditions of what it takes to thrive as a human animal.[21]

Politics as the way human creatures organize and sustain care for one another through forms of ongoing association is thus not reducible to the exercise of unilateral, dominatory forms of power. Rather, it is more fundamentally about how we love and desire one another. Of course, this truth raises questions about who is loved and desired (and who is not) and what the character and form of this love should be. These questions, as well as a conception of political life that centers love and desire, are at the heart of Augustine's political theology, which itself casts a long shadow over all subsequent political theology in the West. For Augustine, conflict and domination are not part of creation but are an inherent part of all earthly forms of political life east of Eden. However, these conflicts center on what is loved, while domination emerges from who is loved and how our loves are ordered. Is love of God the fundamental orientation of the political community, or love of self? If the latter, then political relations will be characterized by the *libido dominandi*, a "lust for the domination" of not only others but also of ourselves. But whatever the character of the polity, for Augustine, all forms of political life are a response to a prior act of love, namely, creation (as Creator, God is the source of all that exists). Moreover, the proper end of all politics is the city of God, a political community based on the right ordering of its loves. Bad politics arises from loving the right things the wrong way.

Taking their cue from Augustine, a number of recent political theologians argue that politics is a realm for the cultivation of both civic and theological virtues.[22] The assumption in such work is that since politics is a social activity through which humans form a common life, it depends on the quality and character of the interpersonal relationships through which politics is conducted at least as much as, if not more than, it depends on systems and structures. Change the character of the relations and the character of the politics follows. In these accounts, forging a freer, more equitable, and just society is never solely a matter of changed structures. Neither is it merely a question of changing the identity or status of who holds power. Real change requires changed hearts and minds. The virtue of faith illustrates this dynamic. Faithfulness is vital to developing any kind of common life and to dismantling corrupt or oppressive structures. Faithfulness denotes reliability, commitment, and trustworthiness. Without it, promises are broken and relations of trust dissolve, undermining our ability to deliberate and act together. The fruit of faithlessness is that the long-term, collaborative relations needed to sustain the kinds of social practices and solidarity vital to struggles for a freer, more equitable, and just society become impossible. Alongside faith, other virtues, notably tolerance and hospitality, are crucial for navigating plurality in a way that cultivates a common life as opposed to killing or coercing those with whom we disagree.[23] The logic here is that the formation of virtuous relationships between people enables new and better forms of shared action.

Alongside the cultivation of virtue, building and sustaining a shared life as creatures also requires institutional forms that enable the pursuit of association amid disagreement and diversity. These institutions take the form of laws, constitutions, and the means of governance (e.g., bureaucracy) and legitimation (e.g., electoral systems). As a name for the institutions of a polity, politics is a synonym for statecraft: that is, the exercise of sovereignty and the governance of state apparatus. And so this first conception of the political incorporates the third use of the term, outlined in the following paragraphs.

Within this first conception, alongside and (more often than not) working as a counter to statecraft, what is political also refers to the participatory and collaborative social practices through which a common world is cultivated. As Hannah Arendt puts it: "The political realm rises directly out of acting together, the 'sharing of words and deeds.' Thus, [shared] action not only has the most intimate relationship to the public part of the world common to us all but is the one activity which constitutes it."[24] Politics as an informal, relational craft takes place in multiple settings and is not coextensive with control of the state or even dependent on there being a state at all. Nomads in the desert outside of any formal state structures still generate a rich form of political life through customary practices of hospitality, greeting, and so forth that sustain a common life based on shared goods (e.g., access to water). Elders and pastors negotiating changing service times in a church are practicing the craft of politics. Neighbors sorting out complaints about noise between themselves without calling the police are likewise doing politics in this informal, relational register. Politics in these instances is the art of association. And this association is the ground from which modern statecraft can be resisted. As Milinda Banerjee and Jelle Wouters put it: "Let us be clear. To resist state and capital, we need solidarities. For solidarities to be viable, some enduring sense of community is needed."[25]

A vital and ancient mode of politics as a participatory and collaborative social practice independent of statecraft is "commoning." Commoning is the formation, organization, and sustaining of a commons. A commons is a shared social and material good (a mountain pasture), a human community (shepherds and the villages of which they are a part), and a set of formal and informal customary practices, rules, processes, and priorities for governing and administering that good (practices for rotating access to the pasture between shepherds). A commons is produced through the interaction of human cooperation, nonhuman ways of being alive, and material processes. Each commons is distinct and adapted to specific conditions, such that the moral and social norms for managing a commons cannot be easily transferred (e.g., a forest commons in Germany will be different from one in Indonesia). There are three basic types of commons: the natural commons of fisheries, forests, watersheds, irrigation systems, and the like; the cultural and knowledge commons of a community's language, ancestral wisdom, stories, scientific techniques, rituals, modes of association, and cultural practices such as games; and now, the digital commons of open-source software, information, and technologies (e.g., Wikipedia, Linux, and TCP/IP protocols). Each type of commons embodies a noncentralized authority structure, with its form and character determined by the many rather than the one or the few. As a way of provisioning human needs and constituting a form of life-in-common, it is distinct from either state or market processes and entails highly participatory, self-organized, and distributed forms of peer-to-peer governance. Human life as such is a commons made possible by ongoing forms of human, nonhuman, and divine cooperation and negotiation within the context of a particular polity or form of common life.

The enclosure of the commons and its consequences have consistently generated radically democratic movements and political theologies in response. An early modern example is the seventeenth-century Diggers, who made reclamation of the commons the building block of their understanding of salvation.[26] At St. George's Hill in Surrey and a number of other locations around England, communities of Diggers occupied and started cultivating land they claimed as a commons. They took this work of cultivation to presage the return of Christ, "the true Leveller," who would bring about the restoration of creation.[27] Building on Genesis and Acts 2–4, they explicitly rejected wage labor and advocated holding all things in common as a means of restoring mutual fellowship and properly ordered relations with creation. And like other radical reformation groups before them, such as the Mennonites, they advocated nonviolence as the primary means of bringing about social transformation and bearing witness to the coming kingdom of God. Their experiment in radical democracy was short-lived. However, it anticipated a number of developments that would become central to Christian responses to modernization and the dislocations it wrought. Moreover, the Diggers' political theology is but one iteration of a long-standing and global phenomenon of agrarian radicalism and peasant millenarianism, which constitutes an underexplored stream of political theology "from below." These agrarian and millenarian radicalisms believe that when political life is enclosed, life itself becomes unsustainable. Political life is enclosed when it is no longer understood as a commons but is reduced to the aggregation of self-interests, a means of extracting value for private gain, a mechanism for managing populations, or a social contract between autonomous, property-owning individuals who are envisaged as sharing nothing but contractual or commercial obligations.

As the example of the commons illustrates, in this first conception, the political is not war by other means. The bullet and the ballot box are mutually exclusive routes to solving shared problems.[28] At a basic level, politics as a means of negotiating conflict is the alternative to unrestrained violence and cycles of revenge. Politics entails a commitment to conditions in which worlds of shared meaning and collaborative action—and thence mutual care—can be created or sustained. By contrast, the proactive use of physical violence—beatings, kidnapping, torture, bombing, and the like by state and nonstate actors—represents the destruction of the institutions, customs, practices, and habits that enable communication and reciprocal relationships to be sustained over time.[29] Within this first conception, it is inappropriate to use *politics* as a synonym for talk of power understood as a wholly negative, unilateral, and inherently violent phenomenon.[30] Alongside unilateral power, the political is also constituted through "relational" and "soul" power.[31]

If politics is the way we constitute a common life, then it is not only the alternative to war. It is also not a zero-sum game. Rather, it presumes difference and diversity, as well as the need to compromise. This first conception begins from the assumption that we are all complex bundles of competing, often contradictory loyalties and loves, whose personhood cannot and should not be reduced to a singular set of commitments or beliefs. No one is reducible to being either a friend or an enemy. No one can be essentialized as wholly determined by this or that identity. Rather, in the midst of competing interests, conflicting visions of the good, intersecting identities, and active disgust or scandal at the lifeways of others, a shared world of meaning and action can still be discovered. Everyone, everywhere, at any time is a creature made in the image of God participating in creation.

In this first conception, plurality, complexity, and contingency are enabling conditions of political life. Latinx political theologies articulate compelling accounts of how plurality and difference-in-relation constitute us as humans by drawing on such notions as *mestizaje-mulatez*, *mezcolanza*, and the Nahautl term *nepantla*, meaning "to be between" or "torn between ways."[32] Antipolitical ways of ordering life with others are attempts to overcome or repress these conditions and deny how we are all torn between ways. Rather than see plurality and hybridity as an inevitable and welcome feature of political or common life, these antipolitical perspectives pathologize and try to suppress difference. In the name of purity of identity or ideology, they refuse to listen to, compromise with, or conciliate different interests and ways of being alive, thereby reifying difference and refusing the possibility of a common life constituted through difference-in-relation. By contrast, as Bernard Crick puts it, in this first conception of the political,

> the political method of rule is to listen to . . . other groups so as to conciliate them as far as possible, and to give them legal position, a sense of security, some clear and reasonable safe means of articulation, by which these other groups can and will speak freely. Ideally politics draws all these groups into each other so that they each and together can make a positive contribution towards the general business of government and maintaining order.[33]

Alongside Crick, modern exponents of this conception of politics include Hannah Arendt and Sheldon Wolin. Martin Luther King Jr.'s political theology articulates a powerful version of this first conception of the political. For King, challenging injustice and seeking to convert enemies into friends through nonviolent direct action is a way of witnessing to the creation and reconciliation of all things in Christ, a deeper reality than the violent enmity that opposes it.

King's political theology is but one example among a broad swathe of Christian political theologies that take as basic this first conception of the political and turn to democracy as the primary means through which to enact and embody this vision. These theologies include Catholic social teaching, the North American Social Gospel, as well as European Christian socialism and Christian Democracy as political movements. Each takes up and redefines democracy as the form of politics that best honors the dignity of each person while also ensuring that everyone is able to participate in forming a common life and so realize their personhood. Rather than be acted on and having their world determined and controlled by the one or the few, a participatory, small "d" democratic politics enables everyone to have agency in cultivating and contributing to shared worlds of meaning and action (life-in-common). Democracy thereby provides the conditions and means through which the *imago dei* of each person is actualized in and through free and mutually responsible relationships with and for others.[34] It makes provision for each and every person to have a hand in determining their living and working conditions and benefit from the material and social goods generated through that common life.

A conception of the political as pertaining to that which forms and sustains life as a commons stands in direct contradiction with the second definition of the political at work in modern political theology, to which the following section turns. But this contradiction is internal to this first conception. A consequence of politics as constituted through a common life is the way politics generates distinctions between those who are loved and cared for because they are counted as part of "our" common life (friends) and those who are unloved and marked as outside of or beyond a specific community of care (strangers, others, or enemies).

Fall: The Political as Constituted by Friend-Enemy Relations

The second conception of the political used in modern, Western political theology speaks to the fallen nature of political life and the ways it is structured by sin and idolatry. It is set forth in what is often taken to be a foundational text of modern political theology, Carl Schmitt's *The Concept of the Political*. Schmitt conceives of the political as determined by the friend/enemy antithesis. As Schmitt puts it:

> The political enemy need not be morally evil or aesthetically ugly; he need not appear as an economic competitor, and it may even be advantageous to engage with him in business transactions. But he is, nevertheless, the other, the stranger; and it is sufficient for his nature that he is, in a specifically intense way, existentially something different and alien, so that in the extreme case conflicts with him are possible.

Otherness, for Schmitt, represents a latent threat to one's own way of life because it signifies a form of life that can replace or supersede one's own. This threat becomes operative when the other becomes an adversary who "intends to negate his opponent's way of life and therefore must be repulsed or fought in order to preserve one's own form of existence." His conception of the friend-enemy relation builds on a conception of original sin: "The fundamental theological dogma of the evilness of the world and man leads, just as does the distinction of friend and enemy, to a categorization of men and makes impossible the undifferentiated optimism of a universal conception of man."[35]

Schmitt names a foundational aspect of political life east of Eden. For example, in the Greco-Roman world within which Christianity was birthed, those judged to be outsiders or non-citizens, whether resident within the boundaries of the polity or living elsewhere, were potential, if not actual, enemies. Their way of life threatened the very existence of the polis. And since the physical, moral, and spiritual existence of the individual citizen was coterminous with the flourishing of the city, this meant that outsiders to the life of the polis were necessarily either potentially seditious (if they were resident aliens or denizens) or a threat (if they were foreigners). It was necessary to guard against alien forms of life, and if they disturbed the peace, they were either repressed (if inside the walls) or repelled (if outside). In the New Testament, violent reactions against Paul's preaching and miracles in cities like Philippi and Ephesus exemplify these responses (cf. Acts 16:12–40; 19). Internal and external "others" were also a means by which the common life of "our" polity came to be defined and understood. "We, the people" were not like "them," and all that the other was imagined to be (effeminate, uncivilized, treacherous, cruel, etc.) was all that "we" were not (virile, loyal, brave, honest, rational, etc.).[36] Consider, for example, numerous ancient Greek depictions of the Persians.

That city-states such as Athens or nation-states like France generate friend/enemy distinctions seems intuitive. From Diogenes the Cynic onward, the proposed antidote to this dynamic is often some form of cosmopolitanism, that is, a universal claim that we all share a common humanity irrespective of where or how we live. Talk of humanity as such thereby contests the boundaries of citizenship or a circle of care by challenging who is considered a friend and who an enemy. Yet on Schmitt's account, whether it is Stoicism, Christianity, liberalism, Marxism, or Islam, all universalizing discourses that posit a shared humanity establish friend/enemy distinctions. What is human is defined according to a particular conception of the universal human that includes some and excludes others. Cosmopolitan citizenship is no less premised on the friend/enemy antithesis than the citizenship of city-states and nation-states. Divisions between saved and unsaved, rational and irrational, civilized and savage, bourgeois and proletariat, and so on have distinct temporal and spatial divisions built into them that create different formations of the political. For Schmitt, such was the world as it should be. However, as the Caribbean critical theorist (and occasional political theologian) Sylvia Wynter argues, as a means of securing a way of life for "us," these friend/enemy distinctions produce brutality and exploitation for those marked as "other." As Walter Benjamin puts it: "There is no document of civilization which is not at the same time a document of barbarism."[37] Or as Frantz Fanon states in more pointed terms: "When I look for man in European lifestyles and technology I see a constant denial of man, an avalanche of murders."[38] In Augustinian terms, all claims to be civilized are deluded claims to self-righteousness.

For Wynter, as for Schmitt, all universals generate friend/enemy distinctions. In her account, the European context generates different versions of these universalizing frameworks and their friend/enemy distinctions. They evolve from the saved/unsaved distinction of the late medieval world, extend through the rational/irrational distinction of the early modern period (what she calls Man1), and culminate in the "evolved/nonevolved" or "selected/dysselected" distinction of the modern colonial, bourgeois, and racist representation of the true human (Man2).[39] Wynter points to how Christian "civilization" has imagined itself over against different internal and external others. Each way of constituting the enemy as other is built on different provincial representations of the fully human being that claims for itself a false universality (and a false righteousness). These provincial universals—which reify the interests of a particular ethnoclass—justify the subjection and exploitation of those who do not conform to the universal "us" and are in turn designated as the unfit, not-fully-human "them." To be designated as the other (unsaved, irrational, and dysselected) is to be consigned to what Wynter calls an "archipelago of Otherness," characterized by poverty and degradation.[40] Politics for Wynter requires recognition of the friend/enemy distinctions in play, even as it entails a struggle to become otherwise: that is, to become wise and insightful about those who act or live differently but with whom a fruitful common life is possible and necessary. Wynter thereby advocates for what David Scott calls an "agonistic humanism," one born out of spiritual, moral, and political struggle to realize forms of shared life that are both heterogenous and free from domination.[41]

The contradiction at work within conceptions of political life as constituted through friend-enemy relations is that naming humans as enemies depends on recognizing them as human. To be named as a real enemy depends on identifying a form of shared life—which is to say, a form of political life—that is recognizably other to one's own way of life and a possible threat to it. In that very act of recognition, another way of being human is named. To be designated an enemy is therefore to be recognized as the kind of animal that forms itself into moral and political communities that might pose a threat to my way of life. However, to name others as enemies and therefore human can in turn lead to their exploitation as humans. For example, as Jonathan Tran notes, modern, racialized chattel slavery depends on recognizing others as humans with the skills and capacity to do the work for which they are enslaved.[42] This form of slavery then entails an ideological system that renders certain bodies exploitable in their humanity. Wynter also makes this point. It is not that the enslaved are not human; it is that they are the wrong kind of human. As unsaved, irrational, or dysselected, this kind of human is rendered available for domination and exploitation. Moreover, this domination and exploitation constitute a form of care that is selected by the saved, rational, or selected for the unsaved, irrational, or dysselected. Schmitt recognized this contradiction, contending that friend-enemy relations rest on a prior commitment to a shared humanity.[43] But, for Schmitt, this shared humanity can only be realized dialectically through friend-enemy relations, which always and everywhere presuppose the possibility of war between friends and enemies.[44] My own work is an attempt to testify to an alternative to Schmitt's vision of political theology: The dialectic can only be realized through an agonistic yet nonviolent democratic politics in which enemies can become neighbors and a prior and deeper form of shared existence—and thus shared humanity—can be discovered.[45] The theological confession is that, after Christ, enemies can be loved as neighbors, not treated as threats. Such is the witness of the Good Samaritan parable: The circle of care can now be extended from all peoples to all peoples, *especially* the afflicted, the oppressed, the stranger, and the enemy.[46]

PROVIDENCE: THE POLITICAL AS CONSTITUTED BY SOVEREIGNTY

The third meaning of *political* is its current, ordinary use as that which pertains to the state and the operations and administration of government (referred to hereafter as statecraft). This is how most dictionaries now define the term, and it largely determines the contemporary philosophical and social scientific study of "politics." Within political theology, the focus on statecraft circulates around the nature and legitimation of sovereignty and the role of theology in determining it. Much contemporary political theology seeks ways beyond or outside of statecraft, even as it centers questions of sovereignty when conceptualizing the political. In a theological register, sovereign or public authorities are a providential good ordained by God to restrain evil and enable good order. But while providential, sovereign authorities are still fallen, and the order they generate produces sin, idolatry, and evil.

The ways in which sovereignty produces both order and domination in the same gesture are exemplified in the production of welfare by ancient and modern states. Inherent to the conception of political life as a condition for the cultivation of mutual care is a claim that the duty of the sovereign and a central task of statecraft is to sustain life through the exercise of pastoral power. The Bible picks up an image from the ancient world to portray this duty by depicting the sovereign as a shepherd caring for the flock.[47] Early theologians developed the figure of the shepherd as the model for political rule. For example, in his *Church History*, Eusebius casts the role of the Emperor Constantine as being like a bishop, thereby at once affirming and limiting the emperor's role: While divinely anointed, the emperor is neither a god nor an autocrat but rather has a duty of care for the people like a shepherd. Evidenced here is a line of thought that was to be developed by Gregory I and Isidore of Seville in which the episcopate, as the office charged with pastoral care, becomes the model of good rule within Christian society. Foucault's analysis of pastoral power outlines how this logic continues in our day, albeit under conditions where it has become "no longer a question of leading people to their salvation in the next world but rather ensuring it in this world. And in this context, the word 'salvation' takes on different meanings: health, well-being (that is, sufficient wealth, standard of living), security, protection against accidents."[48] However, even as the "secular" sovereign assumes the mantle of care, an insight central to Augustine's political theology presses in, namely, that an order of love can at the same time be a regime of domination. This insight is also at the heart of much contemporary political theology that, echoing Foucault, critiques sovereign structures for offering care that sustains and protects life (for example, through educational, medical, security, and carceral systems) while simultaneously using these regimes for governing populations in ways that produce domination and death.

Within modern, state-centric conceptions of the political, focused as these are on questions to do with sovereignty, politics becomes about identifying and pursuing the interests and reasons of the state. Whoever can capture the mechanisms of the state determines whose interests it serves. Politics within this framework is a zero-sum game. Whether through democratic means or the use of revolutionary violence, politics is a battle for sovereignty and thence the ability to control the apparatus of the state so that the interests of one's own party or group prevail. These interests can be either ideological or material, but never moral. This view is articulated in Malcolm X's 1964 "The Bullet or the Ballot" speech. Malcolm X was in many ways a political theologian par excellence, but in this speech at least his conception of the political was state-centric. Whether through the bullet or the ballot, Malcolm X insisted that the political philosophy of Black nationalism (as distinct from its social and economic philosophy) and the political struggle to end white supremacy must involve taking control of the state, either locally or nationally. This step could entail appealing to a higher legal sovereign authority—specifically, the United Nations—to intervene in the American nation-state on behalf of the human rights of Black folks. But this was still a form of statecraft.

Within a state-centric, sovereignty-focused conception, the primary concern of politics is the use of unilateral, command-and-control forms of power, not the fulfillment of moral goods or the cultivation of human flourishing. On this view, to pursue moral goods through politics and insist that politics is a realm for the cultivation of virtue either corrupts politics or is simply naive. Hence Malcolm X's derision of Martin Luther King Jr.'s advocacy of building a beloved community through nonviolent politics in which moral means are used to achieve moral ends. Malcolm X's "realism" is echoed in many forms of modern political thought, from the revolutionary to the reactionary. For Lenin, revolutionary change demanded the suspension of the ethical, while in scientific and deterministic Marxist accounts, morality was understood to be merely an expression of ideology, used to regulate and enhance relations of capitalist production.[49] Likewise, on the opposite end of the ideological spectrum, Schmitt held that the exercise of sovereignty could not be constrained by moral norms and that virtue was a private matter that had no place in defining political relations.[50] And while social democracy is motivated by moral commitments to equality and social justice, from the Fabians onward, governmental operations are envisaged as an amoral, bureaucratic exercise in technical rationality.[51]

Within this usage of the political, the advocacy of moral ends and means in politics is subject to a hermeneutics of suspicion because, echoing Nietzsche, ethics is itself a form of the will to power, and so the pursuit of moral ends is merely another form of the "political" in the technocratic, immanent sense of the term.

This third conception of the political can be productively framed within a view of politics as a tragic endeavor.[52] A tragic vision of politics foregrounds how political life must balance the pursuit of justice with the need for order if the world is not to collapse into violent chaos through the settling of scores. Sovereign authorities provide order in the face of impending chaos. Moreover, they enable life to go on amid suffering, loss, the randomness of evil, intractable injustice, and the fragility and folly of life with others. A tragic orientation looks at political life and sees that, to quote Henry James, "life is, in fact, a battle. Evil is insolent and strong; beauty enchanting but rare; goodness very apt to be weak; folly ever apt to be defiant; wickedness to carry the day; imbeciles to be in great places, people of sense in small, and mankind generally unhappy. But the world as it stands is no narrow illusion . . . we can neither forget it nor deny it nor dispense with it."[53] My source for this quotation is Saul Alinsky's *Rules for Radicals* (1971). Alinsky is one of the founding figures of broad-based community organizing, a highly participatory form of explicitly faith-informed democratic politics.[54] Using Alinsky as the source makes the point that a tragic view is neither pessimistic nor quietist. Alinsky's realism is couched in a hope that radical change is possible. But he eschews utopian or apocalyptic dreams of a final solution that is realizable by political means here and now. Like Augustine, Alinsky enacts a penultimate politics that is shorn of both messianic pretensions to solve everything all at once and a demonic despair that thinks no change for the better is possible.

A tragic view involves a certain realism about what can and cannot be achieved through earthly politics. It calls for judgments and institutional arrangements that restrain evil and either uphold or move toward a more equitable order, but in ways that forgo sweeping programs of social engineering. A classic, twentieth-century articulation of this tragic register is Reinhold Niebuhr's conception of Christian realism and his distinctive rearticulation of an Augustinian conception of political life.[55]

There is an internal contradiction that haunts all conceptions of political life as constituted through sovereignty. The contradiction is that although the sovereign somehow precedes and stands over and above the society that is governed, the sovereign has no existence apart from the society of which it is a part. Hobbes, Locke, and other social contract political theorists resolve this contradiction by positing an imagined moment of founding when sovereign structures come into existence based on mutual agreement and consent. Thereafter, society is enclosed within the structures of sovereignty. The reality is that, as per the first conception previously outlined, some form of common life precedes and constitutes the basis of sovereignty. Conceptions of sovereignty are internal to and preceded by a particular form of life-in-common.

ESCHATON: POLITICAL LIFE AS A REALM WITHOUT SOVEREIGNTY, SUFFERING, OR ENMITY

The fourth use of *political* in *political theology* is paradoxical in that it signifies a postpolitical form of life; that is, it names a form of existence without conflict, domination, injustice, and sovereign structures because it seeks to inhabit a truly peaceable kingdom. In other words, it is an attempt to envision and enact a form of common life without sin. In this use, doing politics is about generating a mode of life that is free from friend-enemy relations (the second conception) and that can dispense with the need for sovereign authorities (the third conception). Forms of millennialism illustrate this fourth conception of the political as denoting a non- or postpolitical realm.[56] For example, the millenarian Anabaptist Thomas Müntzer (c. 1489–1525) understood that he and his followers were already living in the end of days when earthly sovereigns were overthrown and relations of enmity superseded because all things were to be held in common. Numerous modern revolutionary programs echo such millennial expectations. They reject the existing liberal capitalist system *tout court* and envisage themselves as vanguards ushering in a new age. For some the connection is explicit: In *The Peasant's War in Germany* (1850), Friedrich Engels interprets Müntzer as a protocommunist revolutionary; likewise, in *Thomas Müntzer als Theologe der Revolution* (1921), Ernst Bloch envisages Müntzer as embodying an anticipatory utopian consciousness that finally comes to expression in Marxism. An alternative form of millennial expectation can be overheard in Walter Benjamin (1892–1940), who combined Marxism with Jewish mysticism and for whom the messianic provides a critical horizon that interrupts and calls into question all historical political projects. These appropriations provoked a theological response. Martin Buber saw them as forms of "dispossessed Messianism."[57] Henri de Lubac, in his two-volume work *La postérité spirituelle de Joachim de Fiore* (1979–1981), explored in detail the connections between medieval millennialism and modern political thought, while Jürgen Moltmann, in his extensive analysis of the interaction of Christian millennialism and politics, reads modernity itself as a form of millennialism.[58]

In terms of Christian political theology, millenarian or apocalyptic movements tend to echo—intentionally or not—the eschatological framework of Joachim of Fiore (c. 1135–1202). Joachim broke with the mainstream Augustinian view in a number of ways, one of which was that he saw human history as the arena through which the new Jerusalem would be made fully manifest through immanent developments. Joachim divided history into three ages: the age of the Father, which refers to the period of the old covenant; the age of the Son, which began with the period of the New Testament; and the final age, the age of the Holy Spirit, which was imminent. The reign of the Antichrist and a period of persecution would precede this last age. At the same time, an outburst of renewal would anticipate the age of the Spirit. In his context, Joachim identified various forms of monasticism as the renewal that presaged the age of the Spirit.[59]

In Christianity, a Joachimite approach tends to hold that the new Jerusalem can be experienced in human history and that the direction of history and the legibility of divine action in history are clear if one has the right spiritual insight and way of reading the Bible. It is on this basis that such approaches are ready to pass definitive judgment on the worth or otherwise of present political arrangements. By contrast, a more Augustinian approach holds that the new Jerusalem is an irruption of the divine from outside human history. By implication, we can never be certain what direction history is going in, and so an Augustinian approach is more open-ended and less absolutist in its judgments on present political arrangements. The Augustinian tradition is ready to see both good and bad in any polity yet at the same time to pursue change and be open to the Spirit's work here and now. By contrast, the Joachimite tradition tends to be more radical and revolutionary: A polity is either for or against the end of history it confidently predicts. However, both see a direct link between eschatology and present political arrangements: The end times determine judgments about the proper shape and order of political life here and now.

Christian millenarian movements, and the politics they enact (whether prefigurative, revolutionary, or quietist), identify themselves as inhabiting the age of the Spirit, with those who oppose them depicted as agents of the Antichrist. Alongside the already mentioned Thomas Müntzer are attempts by Anabaptists and others to establish the new Jerusalem in Münster, Germany (1532–1535)—an episode that ended in its violent collapse and suppression. The contemporary equivalents of the citizens of Münster are less the pacifist Anabaptists influenced by Menno Simons (1496–1561) than groups such as the Branch Davidians in Waco, Texas (an offshoot of the apocalyptic-focused but quietist Seventh-Day Adventists). That said, the radical reformation does inform the work of postliberal, ecclesial-centric political theologies that envision the church as a prefigurative community bearing witness to the age to come here and now. Such a political vision is exemplified by the work of Stanley Hauerwas (b. 1940). A vocal critic of contemporary forms of liberal democracy as a mode of statecraft, Hauerwas calls on "the church" to embody the peaceable kingdom of God through the radically democratic social practices of nonviolence and patient, noncontrolling, place-based ways of building relationship together.[60] Such ways of building relationship form a people with the character to inhabit the love and justice of God in a violent world. What it means to be the people of God in this way is exemplified for Hauerwas by the L'Arche communities, which he calls a "peace movement."[61] L'Arche displays what it means to inhabit a truly peaceable way of life that can bear the name *Church*.

A very different outworking of a Fiorian eschatological conception of political life can be seen in various eighteenth-century

Enlightenment figures. Gotthold Ephraim Lessing appealed to Joachim of Fiore to argue that humanity had come of age, while Kant drew on a millenarian schema to frame what he saw as a transition of ecclesiastical faith into the universal religion of reason.[62] In the nineteenth century, this Joachimite tradition informed the postmillennialism of Walter Rauschenbusch (1861–1918), who saw in modern scientific, economic, and political developments, and the reform they enabled, the heralds of the last age. In the twentieth century, Ernst Bloch and Jürgen Moltmann both claim Joachim as an ally for their differing conceptions of a politics of hope, while Eric Voegelin interprets modern political phenomena such as Marxism and Nazism as gnostic political religions that draw on Joachimite impulses in their attempts to build the new Jerusalem now.[63]

The zealous fervor of millennial movements must be set against those who dreamed of Cockaigne—another example of the fourth conception of politics. Cockaigne was a paradisiacal land in which all social, political, and economic problems dissolved because every individual was satisfied and every need was met.[64] Pieter Bruegel the Elder's *Land of Cockaigne* (1567) depicts such a dreamworld in which eggs have legs and walk to you, roasted pigs amble around with carving knives strapped to their back, and fowl lie down on a silver platter ready to be eaten. The point of interest here is not that Cockaigne is a land without labor, production, or conflict, but that it requires no governing authority: It is a spontaneous order of plenty.

Libertarian economics echoes the notion that the best of all possible worlds is an apolitical socioeconomic realm that spontaneously organizes itself. It envisages material prosperity as flowing spontaneously out of the voluntaristic decisions of individuals. Johann Kaspar Schmidt (1806–1856), whose nom de plume was Max Stirner, explored these themes. He was a one-time associate of Engels and a "individualist anarchist." The former student of Ludwig von Mises, Murray Rothbard (1926–1995) also elaborates these ideas. He coined the term *anarcho-capitalism*. The analogue of this *pro*-capitalist, antistatist, libertarian vision is the *anti*-capitalist and antistatist vision that rested on a parallel notion of spontaneous order and an equally voluntaristic anthropology. It is a position exemplified in the anarcho-syndicalism of Pierre-Joseph Proudhon (1809–1865) and Georges Sorel (1847–1922). They looked to the abolition of the state because any need for coercive power and centralized coordination would disappear within a decentralized and federal organization of *syndicats* or occupational associations, which in turn would give rise to a spontaneous order of transactions and exchanges. The administration of things would replace the government of persons, and a new polity, one founded on the workshop and not the state, would be created. In such a polity, the advent of technocratic self-government would eradicate the need for any kind of coercive political order and overcome divisions between people (whether based on class, nationality, and so forth). Myths of spontaneous order and the overcoming of friend-enemy relations through the advent of a new, enlightened (or woke) consciousness continue to reverberate through contemporary insurgent political theologies that posit forms of polity without sovereignty, ways of life without hierarchy, modes of organization without structure, and autonomy without association (and the time-bound, place-based patterns of loyalty, trust, and cooperation that just and compassionate association entails).[65]

Cockaigne and millennialism are postpolitical political visions that presume a world without sin. The negotiation of a common life in the face of immorality, competing and conflicting interests, different visions of human flourishing, and the unequal distribution of resources is dissolved because either all needs are satisfied

(Cockaigne), or justice is achieved through the return of the true king who vindicates the virtuous and removes the vicious, turning the existent world upside down in order to establish what is true and good (millennialism). However, we do not have the agency to achieve these forms of spontaneous order, and they exist beyond any actual spatiotemporal realm. They are either sheer fantasy or the result of an apocalyptic event (whether revolutionary or divine). Modern utopian thought is another example of a postpolitical conception of political life, but one that centers human systems and structures. For example, Thomas More's *Utopia* (1516) is premised neither on a notion of spontaneous order erupting through an apocalyptic event nor an alternative reality through which to render contingent and satirize present conditions. Rather than existing outside of or beyond history, More's utopia is designed as a blueprint and intended as a guide to action in history. More's ideal commonwealth issued not from the actions of a prince or parliament but from technocratic procedures. Its founder, Utopus, is not a lawgiver appointed by God after the model of Moses, but a systems designer and bureaucrat. Neither revelation, nor nature, nor immemorial custom forms the basis of his laws. They are a work of technique. More's utopia is entirely different from Cockaigne, where the lawgiver is unnecessary because everyone is a law unto themselves; or the millennium, where the law is divinely inspired and written on the heart rather than coercively imposed.[66] *Utopia* presents a postpolitical regime in which we see foreshadowed all attempts to supersede the need for sovereign authorities and a movement beyond friend-enemy relations through a rationally and scientifically administered state. Yet for all their technocratic, secularized reasoning, such utopian postpolitical political visions are haunted by an eschatological longing for a world without sin.

In contrast to the previously described conceptions of political life, this conception tends to adopt an apocalyptic rather than a tragic stance. *Theologically understood*, an apocalyptic orientation is neither pessimistic nor optimistic, nor does it represent a form of catastrophizing. Rather, it entails trusting that history is open to change, that a new creation is coming, and that the Spirit can bring into being a radical, surprising, and unanticipated newness, often in response to the cry for justice and love by those on the underside of history. In Christian political theology, an apocalyptic register is born out of a revelation of what is really happening from a heavenly perspective and a discernment of the active and living presence of God here and now. An apocalyptic register also sounds a note of judgment on the present order of things, making clear that the world is not as it should be, and so we should repent and humble ourselves. It demands reckoning with how our lives now are subject to the judgment to come and understanding that we live in a time when the kingdom of God is coming into being, creating moments of transformation and rupture. New beginnings are possible, and so established ways of doing things need reevaluating. It is not good enough to simply go with the flow because the messianic age is dawning; we must act now as if the present order of things does not have the last word and is coming to an end. This apocalyptic orientation calls for judgments that both provide prophetic critique of current arrangements and imaginatively proclaim as well as prefiguratively embody new visions of what flourishing could mean for these people here and now in the light of the end of *this* world—that is, the form of life we currently inhabit. As Lloyd's essay indicates, abolitionism exemplifies how political theology can operate in an apocalyptic and tragic register simultaneously.

Theology Is Political Theology; Political Theology Is Theology

Properly understood, political theology trades in all four of these meanings of the political. A brief case study of James Cone's early work illustrates how these uses rotate and often conflict. Cone does not reference Schmitt, but in both *Black Theology and Black Power* and *God of the Oppressed*, Cone generates a consciousness of friend-enemy relations. Blacks must recognize that whites are their enemy, while whites, despite professions to the contrary, treat those judged Black as enemies to be repressed and exploited at every turn. Cone condemns bothsiderism.[67] One must pick a side: Either one is for Black life (and so a friend of God who in Jesus Christ identifies with the poor and oppressed) or one equivocates, in which case one is an enemy of both God and Black life.

> Accordingly [theology] cannot avoid taking sides in politics, and the side that theology must take is disclosed in the side that Yahweh has already taken. Any other side, whether it be with the oppressors or the side of neutrality (which is nothing but a camouflaged identification with the rulers), is unbiblical. If theology does not side with the poor, then it cannot speak for Yahweh who is the God of the poor.[68]

Theology here is inherently political in that it is determined by God being the enemy of the oppressor and friend of the oppressed. As Cone puts it: "The doing of theology, therefore, on the basis of the revelation of Yahweh, must involve the politics which takes its stand with the poor and against the rich."[69] But alongside the political being defined by friend-enemy relations, Cone also consistently talks of such things as "political structures," "political interests," "political consequences," and "political involvement," by which he means the interests, consequences for, and involvement in the structures of the state and the ordering of power through state mechanisms. "Political" in this respect is distinguished for Cone from social and economic structures. To be liberated is to be set free both from oppression by the state *and* to be no longer governed by racist social systems regulated by friend-enemy relations as determined by the Black/white distinction. Yet in Cone's work, these different uses of the political are never defined, and there is constant slippage between them. And in contrast to the Black liberation theology of J. Deotis Roberts, Cone—at least in his early work—lacks any conception of politics as the cultivation of a common life between friends and enemies.[70] According to the early Cone, politics as the negotiation of a common life exists only within the Black community. It is needed to overcome internal divisions and form a cohesive people who can exercise self-determination/ Black Power. As Cone puts it: "In this context, reconciliation *precedes* liberation. For unless we are reconciled with each other and begin to join hands in the struggle of black freedom, we black people will not be able to survive in this troubled world."[71]

As Cone observes, theology is inherently political. More precisely, theology is constituted through all four conceptions outlined previously. Theology is about both divine and human forms of sovereignty. And it can be used to legitimize or contest existing forms of statecraft, even as it makes use of the terms and material conditions of statecraft to reproduce itself. For example, in its declaration of Jesus Christ as the Lord of the cosmos, the Council of Nicaea questions the sovereignty of the emperor even though the creed is as much as a product of Roman imperial statecraft as it is a fruit of theological deliberation. Theology is also political insofar as it is a means through which a common world of meaning and action is generated—between humans, between humans and nonhumans, and between creatures and creator. And theology is inherently political insofar as it participates in and reproduces friend-enemy relations. Again, these relations can be between different human communities (church-world) or between humans and God (for example, in how sin and idolatry place us in enmity with God). Finally, theology in its focus on soteriology, providence, and eschatology is political in that these doctrines center questions about what God has done in the past, what God is doing for us now, what we should do in response, and how the last things affect the present age. These are the backdrop against which to make any form of judgment about political life.

Beyond the ways in which theology is constituted through politics and is itself political, there is also the way in which theology reflects on prevailing forms of political order. In recognizing that all forms of political life east of Eden are inherently ambiguous and contested, political theology as a reflection on political life should move back and forth between the aforementioned conceptions while attending to the contradictions, paradoxes, and tensions they produce. My constructive claim is that a properly theological account of politics needs to keep in play each of the four meanings if it is to be doctrinally coherent even as different emphasis can be given to one over the others in any particular rendition of political theology. My own work illustrates this point in practice.

My position is that politics is existentially and normatively about forming a common life through which human life as a commons is cultivated and sustained. This normative and given nature of politics has two dimensions. The first is that political life is born out of discovering a basic and shared creaturely existence—a life-in-common—in specific times and places (and so formations of political life are always contextual and contingent and thereby under constant negotiation). The second is that formations of political life can anticipate and bear witness to the healing and eschatological fulfillment of life together in a fallen world (the fourth conception). However, in the earthly city, some kind of statecraft is a providential necessity for restraining evil and sustaining forms of common life, even as statecraft itself is a fallen endeavor that needs to be restrained and held accountable. But forming and sustaining a common life under fallen conditions are not exhausted by statecraft. Indeed, the conversion of political life as overdetermined by statecraft (third conception) takes place through the expansion and prioritizing of politics as a practice of association (first conception). By building up and extending how a common life is formed and sustained through multiple forms of association, which are themselves primarily organized through the exercise of relational rather than unilateral power, the political is reconstituted so that it ceases to be overdetermined by top-down modes of either governmental or corporate administration. Yet, as fallen, political life—even in its associational modalities—also manifests and is often constituted by friend-enemy relations of one kind or another (second conception). But friend-enemy relations can be converted when enemies become neighbors (thereby fulfilling the command to love enemies). A faithful, hopeful, and loving politics is then a process of neighboring that itself entails a nonviolent, democratic struggle. This struggle enacts a form of agitational solidarity through an ongoing dance of conflict and conciliation by which a common life between friends and enemies is discovered and maintained. In my view, politics—understood theologically—therefore involves forming, norming, and sustaining some kind of life-in-common amid asymmetries of power, competing visions of the good, and feelings of fear or aversion without killing others, dominating them, or causing them to flee.

The four conceptions of the "political" outlined here, and how these frame theology as itself political, shape the ways in which political theology can be taken up as a mode of critique.

PART 3: POLITICAL THEOLOGY AS CRITICISM OF MODERNITY

There is a central, if mostly unacknowledged, paradox driving contemporary political theology—Christian or otherwise. On the one hand, Christianity in the West is seen as having overturned itself (or been overturned) through a process of secularization whereby it loses its political significance. On the other hand, Christianity continues to set the terms and conditions for political life in and beyond Western nations. This paradox is in play from the very first uses of *political theology* as a formal term. An early use of *political theology* as a critical term appears in Bakunin's 1871 treatise "The Political Theology of Mazzini and the International." His usage was anticipated by another founding figure of anarchism, Pierre-Joseph Proudhon. In his *Confessions of a Revolutionary* (1849), Proudhon contends that theology is the foundational basis of political life.[72] This insight is echoed by Carl Schmitt, who holds that "all significant concepts of the modern theory of the state are secularized theological concepts."[73] Bakunin, Proudhon, and Schmitt all point to how theology is transmuted into immanent political ideas and projects, while at the same time providing the architecture for these political ideas and projects, as well as the terms and conditions under which they operate. In other words, modern immanent political projects are secularized versions of prior Christian ones. For Bakunin, this truth necessitated a relentless attack on theology in order to free revolutionary politics from its grip and move beyond a form of life determined by sovereign power. Yet at this point Bakunin resorts to a kind of antitheological political theology in order to extirpate God from politics and thence overthrow the existing structures of sovereignty.[74]

To use the analogy of a play, it is as if the players of Christianity are removed from the stage. Other actors come in to occupy the theater. They undertake various performances, but within a space, time, and sequence all determined by the prior play, set, props, and stage directions. These players think they are doing something new, something now freed from the superstitious fantasies of religion. Yet they are simply reenacting a performance without its original purpose. They have the speech without the meaning of it, the ritual without the cosmos within which the ceremony made sense. Christianity haunts the stage, for even in its absence it determines the means and modes of representation.[75] In this account, modern political theories and projects do not supersede Christian ones.[76] Instead, they are a palimpsest: a text written over the original but at the same time copying its form, tone, and order.[77] But the fact that modernity is simultaneously Christ-forgetting and Christ-haunted is no cause for celebration.

Echoing Bakunin and Proudhon, to critique modern structures and systems of oppression entails identifying and critiquing the underlying theo-logics at work within them. Thus, for example, Foucault's account of the government of populations entails a genealogy of its formation by Christian practices of confession and pastoral power. For Foucault, "Western man has become a confessing animal."[78] Lynn White's seminal analysis of the environmental crisis identifies the roots of the crisis in particular readings of the Bible. In White's view, for all the talk of living in a post-Christian age, "we continue today to live, as we have lived for about 1700 years, very largely in a context of Christian axioms."[79] At the very point of being rendered inoperable as the means of constituting political life (whether as the basis of a common life, as determining friend-enemy relations, or as a justification for sovereignty), Christianity reappears as a prevailing power in need of abolition. But at this precise juncture, paradoxically, theology reasserts itself as both a resource for critique and a means of repair. Political theology as a form of modernity criticism is born at this nexus point.

POLITICAL THEOLOGY AS A THERAPY FOR TECHNOCRACY

Political theology contests the ways in which political life is said to operate in what Max Weber called a disenchanted iron cage. Within the iron cage, modern political life is wholly determined by immanent juridical, technical, economic, and bureaucratic rationalities. Confined to the iron cage, the political is thereby seen to be enclosed within a "secular" space and time, and thus, by definition, it excludes any form of the "sacred" or transcendence. Pope Francis called this framework the "technocratic paradigm."[80] For Francis this paradigm is a primary obstacle to overcome in order to properly participate in creation as the human creatures we are. As a framework, the technocratic paradigm has its roots in Thomas Hobbes's conception of the state as an artificial machine, and thus the state—and thence sovereignty—as the only proper subject and telos of politics. As a way of imagining and narrating politics, the technocratic paradigm suffers from what Schmitt called the pathos of objectivity; that is, it assumes it can do without normative and metaphysical points of reference.[81]

Modern political theology points to the contingency and insufficiency of nonreligious ways of conceptualizing the political. In doing so, it rejects the technocratic paradigm, contending that any account of politics must reckon with how, alongside legal, economic, and bureaucratic processes, politics is a rich semiotic and symbolic realm suffused with ritual, passions, and metaphysical commitments. To use Hobbes's terms, the mortal god of the modern sovereign is only conceivable in terms of the immortal God of theological description.

In rejecting a technocratic paradigm for understanding statecraft and sovereignty, political theology unmasks the ways in which supposedly secular modern political thought and arrangements suspend or conceal religious frameworks. Conversely, it also attends to the legacy of religious beliefs and practices and the ongoing ways in which they are used as modes of political and economic "governmentality," whether for liberative or oppressive ends.[82]

In part, then, political theology can be understood as a protest against how politics is narrated and imagined within a wholly technocratic, "immanent frame" and its accompanying rationalism, functionalism, empiricism, and aligned notions of inevitable technological and social progress (with their accompanying salvation narratives and divisions between sheep and goats or who is or is not on the "right side of history"). The critique of technocratic conceptions of political life is increasingly indexed to a critique of dominant, Hobbesian conceptions of sovereignty. Likewise, it interrogates a Lockean conception of property and how the ideal citizen is thus imagined in enclosed, territorialized, and bounded terms as a property-owning, autonomous, individualized, rights-bearing subject. The critique of a Hobbesian conception of sovereignty, a Lockean conception of property, and aligned conceptions of the individual property-owning citizen undergirds how political theology—particularly in its apocalyptic modes using the fourth conception of political—questions the nation-state as the locus of political agency and the inter*national* Westphalian system as the basis of a universal political order (exemplified institutionally in the United Nations and philosophically in Kant's cosmopolitanism). This critique goes along with a quest for alternative conceptions of political subjectivity or "citizenship" and non-national modes of solidarity. Constructively, it articulates non-state-centric, non-enclosed, and non-property-based conceptions of political agency and how the communal and cooperative aspects of life together exceed and cannot be subsumed within existing forms of political economy, even as social existence is instrumentalized by state processes and commodified by capitalist ones. These alternative conceptions of political agency are often premised on the excess and indigestibility of othered, marginalized ways of knowing and being within the existing political order of nation-states and a globalized capitalist economy. Such othered, marginalized forms of life seed and prefigure alternative modes of political agency (conception four). These modes include Black life, Indigeneity, queerness, forms of spontaneous, transnational working-class solidarity (as in the alter-globalization vision of the Zapatistas), and advocacy of the commons as a modality of mutual, self-generating social life outside the state-capital nexus (the premise of many anarchist visions from Peter Kropotkin on). They can also include the forms of life that emerge in the kinds of borderlands spaces that Valentina Napolitano discusses in her essay. All these forms of social existence represent alternative imaginaries and practices beyond the existing order. Recent work on subaltern political theology in India and the call for multispecies democracy exemplify this dynamic.[83]

Political theologies that prioritize patterns of social cooperation and community over and against state sovereignty and capitalist modes of economic production constitute a fundamental refusal of a Hobbesian conception of the political (and thus the enclosure of politics and of human life as a commons). For Hobbes, the Leviathan of the state secures and preserves life. Outside its domain, life is nasty, brutish, and short. Likewise, the capitalist economy, which is secured by the Leviathan of the state, holds that outside its orbit, scarcity and thence death prevail. Prioritizing the social over and against the economic and political thus conceived refuses this dichotomy by showing how, rather than sustaining life and abundance, a sovereign nation-state and aligned forms of capitalist political economy actually embody what the francophone, postcolonial theorist Achille Mbembe calls "necropolitics." Mbembe draws on as well as critiques Christian theology to argue that national forms of sovereignty and capitalistic forms of economy hoard life for some by requiring the living death of others to make that life possible.[84] For example, enslaving Africans and enclosing Indigenous lands through colonization make a particular construction of modern life possible for Europeans (a theme in Black liberation and post- and decolonial theology). Mbembe thereby echoes a point made earlier by Wynter, Benjamin, and Fanon.

Beyond naming the evils of slavery and colonialism, the concern is that the aligned duopoly of the modern nation-state and racial capitalism, wedded as these are to a technical rationality and the enclosure of the commons, does several things at once. It alienates humans from being attuned to nonhuman forms of being alive, establishing a solely extractive relationship with nonhuman life; it atomizes humans into individualistic units of biological production and administration so as to commodify and exploit them; and, lastly, it does all of this in the service of idols that humans now serve to their destruction, namely, the state and money. Thus the dominant political imaginary and its violent foundations were, as Marisol de la Cadena puts it,

> shaped not only by distinguishing friends from enemies among humans but also by the antithetical separation of "Humanity" and "Nature." Together these two antitheses—between humanity and nature, and between allegedly superior and inferior humans—declared the gradual extinction of other-than-human beings and the worlds in which they existed. The pluriverse . . . disappeared. Instead a single world made its appearance, inhabited by many peoples (now we call them cultures) more or less distanced from a single "Nature."[85]

This secularized, denatured, enclosed, commodified, and racialized form of political existence, imagined and narrated as unfolding in a single, progressive history, fed on the social death of some while simultaneously rendering their brutal exploitation illegible or invisible.

One insight to be drawn from contemporary political theology—particularly in its decolonial modalities—is that radical change is not about overthrowing one state system and replacing it with another (the primary concern of the French, American, Russian, and Chinese revolutions). Rather, it is about cultivating forms of life undetermined by the modern state-capital nexus, even as this nexus is strategically engaged with. Particular formations of ecclesial and social life may thereby provide resources to engage not in mere resistance to oppression (political theology in its apophatic mode) but in a creative process of what Adolfo Albán calls "re-existence" (political theology in its cataphatic mode). Against modes of unwitnessing, a politics of reexistence names the "mechanisms that human groups implement as a strategy of questioning and making visible the practices of racialization, exclusion and marginalization, procuring the redefining and re-signifying of life in conditions of dignity and self-determination, while at the same time confronting the bio-politic that controls, dominates, and commodifies subjects and nature."[86]

As already indicated, from its inception, the critique of prevailing structures of sovereignty goes along with an attempt to imagine and put forward alternative ways of living together (the fourth conception) outside of existing forms of a state-capital sovereign order (the third conception) and beyond friend-enemy relations (the second conception). Since the end of the Cold War, the turn to theology as a means of repair is taken up with greater urgency in response to the failures or collapse of immanent emancipatory projects—notably, scientific Marxism, state-centric socialism, and nationalist postcolonial struggles. Political theology becomes part of a search for both new resources for critique (apophatic mode) and ways of framing redemptive and liberative political possibilities (cataphatic mode).[87] The heart of the challenge thus wrestled with is this: If one cannot turn to the state, the nation, parliamentary democracy, the market, a revolutionary vanguard, or a singular subject of history as the means of ushering in liberative change because their modern instantiation all perpetuate systemic forms of injustice, where does one turn? To the surprise of many, religion has become one port of call. Jürgen Habermas is but one example of a contemporary philosopher who now recognizes the importance of religious categories for the development of normative political thought that is able to address central dilemmas of contemporary human existence. Slavoj Žižek, Giorgio Agamben, Alasdair MacIntyre, and Charles Taylor are others.

Marisol de la Cadena's work is a good example of the interrelationship between the critique of Western modernity, dominant conceptions of sovereignty, and an attempt to imagine forms of political life beyond both. She focuses on mountains as other-than-human "earth beings" involved as political agents in Quechua struggles over land rights and mining access in the Andes.[88] Cadena develops an ethnographically driven conception of "cosmopolitics" that disrupts modernist, technocratic conceptions of politics, whether of the left or right. Her work is at the same time a testimony to Quechua struggles to preserve their Indigenous way of life in the face of extractive mining companies enclosing and destroying their land, a struggle that straddles a number of nation-states and enacts nonsovereign and non-property-based forms of communal political agency. Cadena's work also points to how political theology as a form of modernity criticism now travels beyond a Christian consciousness. The question her work raises is whether political theology is always in some way indexed to a form of Christian testimony.

ONE AND MANY: POLITICAL THEOLOGY AMID A PLURALITY OF COSMOLOGIES

Political theology as a field of scholarly and critical endeavor now encompasses a wide range of moral and political traditions and is fed by multiple methods and academic discourses. As an approach to critically analyzing the intersections of religion and politics, it is taken up within, among others, Buddhist, Islamic, Jewish, and Hindu studies. This adoption points to how political theology exists beyond a solely Christian frame of reference and is now a point of mediation between many cosmologies. It thereby corresponds to a world in which many worlds exist.[89]

The discourse of *buen vivir* prefigures and illustrates the possibilities of political theology within the context of multiple cosmologies (and the multiple modernities these generate). *Buen vivir* is the Spanish translation and some would say political and philosophical elaboration and hybridization of the Quechua and Aymara words *Sumac kawsay* and *Suma qamaña*.[90] According to Pope Francis's "Querida Amazonia," it is the term used by the Indigenous peoples of the Amazon region to "express the authentic quality of life as 'good living.'"[91] Rooted in reflection on quotidian, lived social practices and cooperative forms of life, in its most general sense, "*buen vivir* denotes, organizes, and constructs a system of knowledge and living based on the communion of humans and nature and on the spatial-temporal-harmonious totality of existence—that is, on the necessary interrelation of beings, knowledges, logics, and rationalities of thought, action, existence, and living."[92] Similar notions exist among other Indigenous peoples in Latin America: notably, *Ñandereko* (Guarani), *Shiir waras* (Ashuar) and *Küme Mongen* (Mapuche). These Indigenous concepts broadly converge on the idea that the good life is one lived in convivial, reciprocal relations and mutual care between human and other-than-human beings (including spiritual beings), rather than in pursuit of some combination of capital accumulation and the technocratic administration of life.[93] In other words, cultivating a common life between human and nonhuman is the basis of a shared existence (first conception) rather than either friend-enemy relations (second conception) or structures of sovereignty (third conception).

As a conceptual frame of reference, *buen vivir* emerged in the 1990s, after the end of the Cold War. It can be identified as part of a shift in discourses of liberation from decolonization, which still had in view the formation of sovereign nation-states, to what Walter Mignolo identifies as a turn to "decoloniality" and an intensification of attempts to uncouple South American patterns of development from European and American templates.[94]

Buen vivir points to a nonsecularizing, nonprogressive paradigm in which there is a "pluriverse" of different cosmologies within which multiple visions of human flourishing arise. Crucially, it seeks to generate prefigurative alternatives that contest dominant technocratic, extractivist, and state-centric processes of modernization.[95] *Buen vivir* also represents a move beyond an emphasis on critique, instead it bears witness to the need for more cataphatic visions that embody meaningful and purposeful forms of life in the midst of present and emerging catastrophes. In doing so, it articulates a fourth conception of the political over and against existing second and third conceptions. Translocal, Indigenous movements are envisaged as occupying a new political space of self-determination and communal landholding beyond the state and the market and in ways that reconcile humans with humans and with nonhumans.

The point of intersection with political theology as a form of Christian testimony is not only Pope Francis's invocation of *buen vivir* in his 2020 apostolic exhortation "Querida Amazonia" but also Enrique Dussel's role in its formal conceptualization.[96] Dussel is one of the foremost thinkers in Latin America working at the intersection of Christianity and Marxism and a major influence on both Latin American liberation theology and decolonial thought. A central concern of both "Querida Amazonia" and Dussel's work is an "integral" understanding and embodiment of spirituality, ecology, ethics, and politics as a necessary condition for untethering a conception of creational flourishing from dominant Western visions and processes of modernization. This connection is in keeping with the aspirations of what advocates for *buen vivir* seek, which is for its discursive frame of reference to enlarge current debates and enable the emergence "of novel conceptions, institutions and practices through collective learning."[97] The resonances between *buen vivir* and

Francis's interpretation of Catholic social teaching also point to a theological claim: that attunement to and reflexive participation in creation—particularly as this participation is articulated through negotiating a common life amid asymmetries of power and divergent conceptions of the good—is a necessary condition for the emergence of transformative ways of imagining and enacting forms of life that transcend the terms and constraints of the earthly city.

Buen vivir embodies a form of politics that seeks a humanism determined by neither the representation of one ethnoclass over and against all others nor a formation of the human set over and against the nonhuman. *Buen vivir* also recognizes how formations of the human exist at the intersection of multiple cosmologies and how, rather than this interrelation collapsing into some form of friend-enemy relation, it can be constituted through a dialogue of wisdoms about the nature and form of human and nonhuman flourishing as part of an ongoing work of cultivating a life-in-common.

Political theology as a pluralistic venture does not negate how it came to be shaped by Christian commitments. Rather, this process of expansion and adoption bears witness to how political theology as a form of Christian testimony can incubate and contribute to the emergence of a "pluriversal" dialogue of wisdoms about human flourishing between multiple traditions.[98] In turn, the current ontological and epistemological plurality of political theology forces its Christian articulations to reckon with their own contingency and historical formations through being contested by other cosmologies and their respective visions of the meaning and purpose of life together. My theological claim—no doubt scandalous to some—is that this pluralistic form of political theology, and the ways it renders Christian testimony epistemologically contingent, are themselves made ontologically possible and testify to the cosmic Christology previously outlined.

Listening to and learning from the plurality of political theology offers testimony to the need to unsettle existing ways of being Christian and thereby discover how to participate faithfully, hopefully, and lovingly in Christ. As finite and fallen creatures, we can only access the truth of who and what we are in Christ through a shared struggle toward cultivating a common life with near and distant neighbors. This struggle also discloses what it means to be human by embodying and revealing the ways and means of forming relationship with and for others over time and in specific places; that is, the formation of a political/common life is the way to realize both a human life and a Christian life. Conversely, as numerous non-Christian historical figures such as Gandhi attest, political theology can be taken up in myriad contexts and traditions to contest the boundaries of who is considered fully human as part of the negotiation of political life.

CONCLUSION

Political theology takes as its object of study political life, contending that politics is a religious matter and religion (however conceived) a political one. The symbiosis of religion and politics is born out of how any form of life entails answering two existential and metaphysical questions: How are life and death related? What are (named as) order and chaos? Political theology reveals how any given form of political life constitutes a way of answering these questions. In doing so, it examines how particular forms of common life are the way human life itself is cultivated and sustained as a commons (the first conception of what constitutes political life). Any such analysis entails assessing how, on the one hand, all forms of common life respond to those outside its circle of care (the stranger, the enemy, the friendless); and, on the other hand, how that common life is ordered and organized through structures of sovereignty and systems of government (the second and third conceptions of what constitutes political life). Political theology also provides a therapy for the world as we find it by providing resources of critique and repair by means of which this world can be converted into some form of the world as it should be, a world no longer ordered by violence, alienation, and friend-enemy relations (the political in its fourth conception). As a form of modernity criticism, political theology witnesses to the legacies and ongoing impact of Christianity on every dimension of human life today, acknowledging that even accounts of politics as secular owe a debt to Christianity and the cultural revolution it enacted. As Christian testimony, political theology witnesses to how this world to come is revealed and made possible first and foremost in the life, death, and resurrection of Jesus Christ. And this very testimony must at the same time confess the need for a common life—which is to say, a political life—with other cosmopolitical visions if it is to be faithful, hopeful, and loving.

A final reflection. In all its modes, whether as Christian theology, modernity criticism, or political reflection at the intersection of multiple cosmovisions, political theology is not just testimony; it is also a kind of confession. It is a way of telling the truth of the matter while also recognizing that any such declaration should be an act of penitence, as it is bound up with identifying what is wrong with the world. In a confession, a truth claim is stated, and praise offered, but that claim is never simply an articulation of what is going on. It is also a statement about our sins. In addition, it is a plea for and a celebration of a way of life unmarked by sin. As confession, political theology demands an unsettling of this world in pursuit of a world to come. And here

Michel Foucault's analysis of confession hangs over this essay. For Foucault, confession is not only a primary technique through which Western societies produce truth (through legal testimony, inquests, interrogation, tribunals, etc.) but also a way that religious and then political authorities establish their power to govern how life is conducted.[99] This power is legitimated by these authorities' claim to offer a release from sin and a cure for the soul. As a mode of confession in the Foucauldian sense, therefore, all political theologies inhabit a contradiction. In an effort to produce truth about the world and a therapy for the world as it is, political theology identifies what needs to be repented and also points to new worlds, even as it is bound up with and reproduces that which it calls others to renounce. This essay embraces this contradiction, taking it to be a condition for doing political theology and central to how political theology constitutes a form of testimony.

2

POLITICAL THEOLOGY
FROM BELOW

VINCENT W. LLOYD

Talk of political theology begins in moments of crisis. When the ordinary, worldly resources for addressing a problem seem inadequate, we reach for extraordinary resources that originate beyond the world—the tools of political theology. In Weimar Germany, economic and political tumult fueled the career of Carl Schmitt, whose name remains essential to political theology.[1] In 1960s Germany, revolutionary energies at home and in the Global South gave rise to a group of Christian theologians writing under the banner of political theology.[2] In 1980s and 1990s France, the apparent collapse of Marxism as a viable political project brought a group of secular philosophers to engage with political theology.[3] And after the attacks of September 11, 2001, cultural studies scholars and theorists in the United States gravitated toward political theology and toward the generations of European thinkers who had turned to the field in the preceding decades.[4]

The 2010s was also a decade of crisis. In the United States, the first Black president governed, but racism was not over. New technology circulated images of police officers harassing, injuring, and killing Black Americans, and the Black Lives Matter movement was born. So were a host of other social movements:

#MeToo gave new life and focus to feminism; Standing Rock and Idle No More drew attention to the continuing violence of settler colonialism; teenage climate change activists interrupted their education and interrupted public life to call attention to the impending end of the world; and socialism went from eccentricity or hollow shell to vibrant, rapidly growing political formations. Each of these movements grew out of crises that participants had long identified, and felt bodily, but that had been largely overlooked by mainstream discourse.

All of this social movement energy and innovation in the 2010s followed from the crisis that launched the decade: the 2008 financial crises, the Great Recession. The sense of economic comfort and predictability that flowed to a generation of the North Atlantic middle class since the end of the Second World War, only mildly disturbed by the oil shocks of the 1970s, suddenly vanished. For young people previously insulated from financial pressure, the future grew dark; it no longer looked as though their standard of living would match, let alone exceed, that of their parents. A generation was primed to appreciate, and in some cases join, insurgent social movements.

Social movements were gaining steam because of the failures of existing political institutions to manage economic, cultural, and ecological crises. Neither government bureaucracy nor elected officials seemed able to respond to the gravity of these problems. From the Right, authoritarian and protofascist movements were attracting increasing support and visibility, and they captured the White House. This development only raised the stakes for justice-oriented social movements: If they did not succeed, lives were at risk, and nations were at risk of succumbing to full-blown fascism.[5] As if the pressure were not high enough, the decade was capped by the 2020 pandemic, which exacerbated existing inequalities, licensed even more illiberal instincts, and pushed the high-stakes framing of politics—a matter of life or death—into mainstream discourse everywhere, for everyone.

These crises of the long 2010s, this decade of crisis, had powerful effects on the academy, particularly in the United States. The Great Recession served as an excuse for states to dramatically reduce funding for public higher education. Both public and private colleges and universities rapidly increased their tuition, and student debt loads ballooned—further dampening a generation's anticipation of future prosperity. Many universities pushed hard to shift from an academic labor force of permanent faculty to contingent instructors. This change not only reduced job prospects for doctoral students but also created a population of young students and scholars with one foot inside and one foot outside the academy. Aided by social media, these university insider-outsiders circulated academic discourse in nonprofit and activist spaces, and they helped bring the concerns of insurgent social movements into the academy. The academy was not insulated from crises; the academy was among the sites of crisis.

In short, the stage was set for another turn to political theology, with all the ideological ambivalence that entails—for political theology has been a discourse of the Right (Schmitt), the Left (German Christians of the 1960s), and liberals (French political theorists of the 1980s and 1990s). The conditions in 2010s North America were quite different than the conditions in 1920s Weimar or 1960s West Germany. After decades of neoliberalism, the state had shrunk, multinational corporations had grown mammoth, and mainstream discourse had become allergic to Christianity, with spiritual-but-not-religious the fastest-growing religious identity in the United States. In these conditions, if political theology were to respond to the moment of crisis, its ambivalence was all the deeper. It could be a right-wing discourse about the theological significance of the state or about how Christians ought to approach national politics, approaches championed by Christian nationalists and their intellectuals (or pseudo-intellectuals). Or political theology could be found in the practice of social movements grappling with the existential stakes of their activism. If we are drawn to the latter and critical of the former, we need to develop a hermeneutics that attunes us to political theology from below.

To take a first pass: Such an orientation to political theology would shift our attention away from the state's secularized theological concepts and toward the secularized theological concepts found in the practice of social movements. If, in the long 2010s, crisis is articulated among those marginalized by the state, those for whom the state is unredeemable, captured or displaced as it is by corporations and ideologies of domination, it is going to look quite different from crisis articulated at the level of state power. The affect of crisis may remain the same: an overwhelming, a deluge of surprises, the urgency of response, the sense that response will necessarily be inadequate. But now the epicenter of the crisis is no longer out there, with effects here; it is right here, felt immediately, bodily, among me and my people. A political-theological response is not abstract theorizing about the concept of the state. It is a call to action for us, a call to be swept up in the movement of the people.

The social movements of the 2010s brought with them distinct, and seemingly incommensurable, theoretical frameworks. Together with each crisis grew sophisticated theory: Black Lives Matter was accompanied by accounts of anti-Blackness associated with Afropessimism and Black feminism, for example; Standing Rock and Idle No More were accompanied by theories of settler colonialism; intersectional accounts of feminism that identified the depth and power of patriarchy grew up around

#MeToo. Each seem different; none seem closely related to political theology.

Yet consider this sentiment, put forward by trans activists Morgan Bassichis, Alexander Lee, and Dean Spade in 2011, capturing the mood of the moment: "Impossibility may very well be our only possibility. What would it mean to embrace, rather than shy away from, the impossibility of our ways of living as well as our political visions? What would it mean to desire a future that we can't even imagine but that we are told couldn't ever exist?"[6] Across movements, there is a sense of impossibility, a sense of stuckness. The horizon of possibility does not include anything remotely resembling justice, on any of the many fronts where marginalized communities are mobilizing. The proper response, Bassichis, Lee, and Spade hint, has an existential dimension: We must lean into impossibility. We must acknowledge that the world as it is, our social practices and norms, need to come to an end. We also must acknowledge that the just world we hope for is blocked from coming into existence. We are stuck between an impossible present and an impossible future. Impossibility here is not merely theoretical. It means the negation of the conditions of life; put simply, it means death. And yet we desire life, we desire a future of flourishing, even as there is no plausible path from here to there. In their reflections, Bassichis, Lee, and Spade invoke hope, faith, desire, and the unknown. In their diagnosis of our political moment, these authors offer language that is deeply resonant with a theological imagination, with a political theology.

To echo Antonio Gramsci, the old paradigm for addressing social injustice is falling away. A new paradigm has not yet taken shape. The stakes are life-or-death. In the long 2010s, as in the 1920s, the times call for grappling with forms of theological imagination, and with the way the theological and the political are entangled.

Political theology is politics tethered to ultimate concern. It is politics shaped by the sense that something deep and powerful is at stake, something connected to life itself, to questions of life and death. It is politics fueled by the existential.

In the sections that follow, I first examine the tensions and connections between contemporary left politics and political theology. Both grapple with the existential dimension of politics in a way that liberalism does not. Then I examine what it means to develop political theology from below, using Aimé Césaire as an example of both practitioner and theorist, labels that barely hold. Finally, I turn to the abolitionist framework undergirding many contemporary social movements. I argue that grappling with the questions and approaches put forward by political theology from below helps to bring coherence and orientation to these movements. In contrast to political theology as an enterprise of Christian confession or political theology as a matrix for cultural analysis, this chapter explores political theology as political practice, as the practice of movements for justice.

LEFT POLITICS, POLITICAL THEOLOGY

Ultimate concern is also what distinguishes left politics—today, and as a tradition. Leftists see politics as rooted in matters of life and death, of *my* life and death. Today, now, my life is threatened, perhaps quashed: working conditions, low wages, and degrading treatment make it as if I am not living, only barely surviving. Each decision I make and each bodily action I take are shaped by the need to survive: to earn enough to scrape by, achieved through aligning my body with the forces of production and reducing thought to the minimum needed to satisfy those forces. Turning from old Left to new, we might say that racism, patriarchy, homophobia, and transphobia put my body under threat, forcing me to perform for survival, to direct my intellect toward preserving my life with little extra to spare. It is only by naming the systems that threaten my life and joining with others in struggle against those systems that I can imagine truly living. And it is in struggle that I live. In collective struggle, I no longer fear death, and in the life of struggle, I experience a foretaste of the promised life of the future, the life where all forms of domination are no more.[7]

Ruth Wilson Gilmore's influential definition of racism, grown out of her own years organizing for prison abolition and now circulating widely in both activist and academic spaces, captures well the existential dimension: "state-sanctioned and/or extralegal production and exploitation of group-differentiated vulnerability to premature death."[8] What motivates the struggle against racism, at least among those most affected by it, is not some notion of racism's wrongness. It is fear of premature death and the living-death that such vulnerability produces. Similarly, the three cofounders of #BlackLivesMatter announce, in their "Herstory" of the movement, that the struggle against racist violence entailed by their work "is an affirmation of Black folks' humanity."[9] Circulating in movement spaces is talk of putting bodies on the line, of survival, and of the joys found in everyday struggle.

Today's racial justice movements closely track the political outlook announced in 1977 by the Black lesbian-feminist Combahee River Collective, as Keeanga-Yamahtta Taylor has lucidly demonstrated. Often understood as a precursor to intersectionality analysis, the collective argues in its statement that "the major systems of oppression"—racial, sexual, heterosexual, and class—"are interlocking." The "conditions of our lives" are determined by those combined systems. The result has been that Black women have waged a "continuous life-and-death struggle for survival and liberation." Systems of oppression are death-dealing. Avoiding death—that is, living—requires struggle. The collective offers concepts for what had long been felt by Black women: "the threat of physical and sexual abuse by men." Those concepts are tools for naming systems of domination; without them, Black women may feel "craziness," attacked by apparently mysterious, unnamed forces.[10] Sanity is restored, and life can be lived, once the struggle is embraced—at both an intellectual and a bodily level. The world denies the value of Black women's lives, but Black women's experiences of themselves motivate struggle for a world without racial, gender, and class domination, where that value is recognized by all. A longer story could be told about the way such existential concerns animate threads of decolonial and anticapitalist politics, how there is a tradition of the Left with its own exemplary figures, narratives, and habits that centers the threat of death and the affirmation of life—a new humanity, as Frantz Fanon and, more recently, Sylvia Wynter call it.

Certainly, the everyday practice of left politics is at a distance from existential concerns. Politics is a technical activity involving analysis of a context and how power is distributed in that context, of interventions that can transform a context and redistribute power, and implementation of those interventions with all that entails: rhetoric, negotiation, judgment, alliance, imagination, adjustment, and new analysis.[11] Leftists, at least those who are serious about politics, do all of this just like other political actors, but leftists are fundamentally motivated by the ultimate nature of the stakes: life or death. Politics may be a technical activity, but if it fails, the consequences are personal: I will be at risk of death, or my life will be a living death.

For the centrist technocrat, politics is about managing a heterogeneous and dynamic population, creating efficient institutions to address all contingencies. Thoughtful liberals talk about principles. Commitment to certain principles guides the liberal's political practice. The leftist's motivations run deeper. It is not that equality is a principle guiding political practice; it is that poverty means death, racism means death, and patriarchy means death. Eruptions of left social movements are often triggered by these confrontations with death: racist police violence, misogynistic or homophobic sexual violence, and dehumanizing or death-dealing working conditions. Incidents of public death that capture the public imagination focus our attention on the systems of domination that work so hard to conceal themselves, to naturalize themselves, and yet on a daily basis attack life. The elementary form of left politics, organizing, means cutting through the manufactured fog that cloaks systems of domination through collective consciousness-raising and through confrontation with the forces of domination—for nothing reveals the viciousness of those forces like naming them and challenging them. The energy of social movements that infuses the infrastructure of organizing is a bridge between the existential root of left politics and the technical activity that is political practice.

Politics may be about navigating our shared life in pursuit of the common good, but the leftist adds: I must be able to live before I can think of life together. It means nothing to talk of our shared life today when my life is threatened, when my life may be a living death. If we are to talk about pursuing the common good, it must be in the mood of uncertainty and wish. We may imagine a future of shared flourishing, and that image of the future may strengthen our political resolve in the present, but there is no knowable path from here to there, from our present world suffused with systems of domination to a future world of shared flourishing. When the leftist speaks in the indicative, she starts in the first-person singular: I am threatened by death. Then she speaks in the first-person plural: we must work together to remove this threat, and that requires investing time and energy in the technical practice of politics. Dreaming of shared flourishing is, at most, a tool for reminding us of the existential root of politics: *that vision is so beautiful, but it is impossible because I live under threat of death, or in living death.* In contrast, for the technocrat and the liberal, navigating our shared life dictates political commitments and practices in the present: tinkering with or reforming institutions so that they, supposedly, yield more shared flourishing.

(For those on the illiberal Right, politics is also often framed in existential terms. But in that case the existential is part of an economy of rhetoric and affect that manufactures anxiety and a subsequent desire for order that serves the interests of the few.)

We are in a political moment of surging leftist energy: in social movements and in organizing, and also in the technical practice of politics, including in electoral politics and in policy work. While the general public is starting to sense the difference between liberals and leftists (a novel development in post–McCarthy era US politics), there is little clarity on what defines this difference, in part because the narrative is rarely controlled by the Left. From the perspective of technocrats, liberals and leftists are just principled political actors. From the perspective of liberals, leftists just have principles that fall farther along a spectrum than those of liberals: charitably, they are more *progressive*, more concerned with *social justice*. In contrast, from the perspective of leftists, there is a qualitative difference between leftists and all other political actors, a difference that grows out of the existential concern that defines left politics. Only for leftists is politics rooted in matters of life and death, of ultimate concern.

Liberal political theorists refine principles that can inflect the practice of politics, for example, by clarifying concepts like justice, legitimacy, and equality on which principles are based.

(Technocrats do not need theory.) Some political theorists have found this project confining and have sought ways of pushing beyond a frame defined in technocratic or liberal terms. One favored technique is distinguishing politics from *the political*.[12] The former has to do with governance, with the state and its institutions and with the principles that guide them; the political deals with something more fundamental. On one account, the political has to do with the amorphous power of a collective before that collective is disaggregated and defined as individual subjects by the state: *constituent power*, the power of the multitude.[13] Such amorphous power is never fully contained by the apparatus of the state, and it occasionally erupts and interrupts, causing a reconfiguration of the terrain of politics (including political principles).

Another approach to the political, one made infamous by Carl Schmitt, defines the political by a distinction between us and them, friends and enemies.[14] While Schmitt's formulation of this position privileges homogeneity in defining *us*—we pure Germans—more recent political theorists such as Chantal Mouffe and Jodi Dean have taken that *us* to be dynamic, its identity constituted in political action without compromising its fundamental significance.[15] *We* could be the 99 percent, the disenfranchised, an alliance of the variously powerless, but defining that *we* remains essential, a question of the political that is the prerequisite to the practice and principles of politics.

Whether the political points to constituent power or antagonistic relations, the difference between politics and the political is derived from analysis of collective life. The intuition here is that the practice and principles of politics cannot exhaust the force latent in our life together. That force, however it is understood, is concealed by the claims of politics to exhaustiveness. Some political theorists aspire to provide a framework for understanding and guiding the Left by drawing attention to the political, as a location for revolutionary energy or as a site for playing out socialist strategy, guiding the work of marshalling the forces of the disempowered. But such efforts depart from the self-understanding of social movements and leftist organizers, and they are often at odds with the best theoretical accounts of systems of domination (e.g., Marxist theory, critical race theory, radical feminist theory, queer theory). Leftists and those organic intellectuals accountable to leftist movements are motivated by existential questions, by life-giving collective struggle confronting death-dealing forces of domination, whether that struggle takes the form of protest or refusal, aesthetic production or bodily pleasures.

While Carl Schmitt at times distinguishes the political through an examination of its social logic, at other times he turns in an existential direction. Indeed, Richard Wolin locates Schmitt in an early-twentieth-century German tradition of *Existenzphilosophie*, an embrace of life itself motivated often by the confrontation with death that so many Germans had experienced during the First World War.[16] Wolin associates Schmitt with Ernst Jünger and Oswald Spengler, and he sees Schmitt's "political existentialism" developing in parallel with the existential concerns animating Martin Heidegger's philosophical project. Law is a prime site at which the fundamental tension between the abstract and the concrete manifests, and for Schmitt, understanding law in purely abstract terms was unsustainable. There must be a moment of return to the concrete, to the personal, to real life: the moment of decision. Unlike abstract rules that are mechanically applied in courtrooms, the sovereign is he who decides on the exception. As Schmitt writes in *Political Theology*, "In the exception the power of real life breaks through the crust of a mechanism that has become torpid with repetition." Indeed, Schmitt announces his project as one offering "a philosophy of concrete life," and it is because of that interest, he claims, that he turns his attention to the exception.[17]

Wolin condemns Schmitt for his existential concerns, seeing them as authorizing Schmitt's embrace of dictatorship and ethnic cleansing in the interest of producing homogeneity. Furthermore, Wolin draws attention to Schmitt's attraction to war. Schmitt writes that in war "the exceptional case has an especially decisive significance in which the inner meaning of things is revealed. For only in actual battle is the most extreme consequence of the political grouping of friend and enemy shown."[18] Elsewhere, Schmitt proclaims, "Politics means intensive life," and he suggests that the concepts of friend and enemy "receive their real meaning precisely because they refer to the real possibility of physical annihilation."[19] The aspects of the political that are located beyond or beneath politics for Schmitt, deciding on the exception and the friend/enemy distinction, are moments when life and death, respectively, are tapped.

Schmitt's existential moments can appear in tension with his interest in Christian theology. It seems quite different to say that the importance of deciding on the exception is establishing a connection with concrete human life and to say that its importance is establishing a structure that parallels religious beliefs about God's power to suspend the laws of nature and perform miracles. Indeed, these instincts seem to be pulling in opposite directions: toward the concretely human and toward the abstractly divine. There may not be an easy resolution to this tension in Schmitt's writings, though there is an obvious theological point that could be made, about Jesus as quintessentially human and fully divine. Those who focus on Schmitt as a theorist of political theology tend to overlook his political existentialism, and those who focus on Schmitt as a theorist of the political tend to overlook the personal, human dimension of his existential commitments, instead emphasizing the conceptual edifice he constructed. My contention is that connecting political theology with political existentialism offers a way to align political theology with left politics.

Many scholars and activists gravitating toward political theology are already doing so in the service of left politics, and they share intuitions about political existentialism with left politics, but these intuitions are rarely fleshed out. Why? Some who gravitate toward political theology approach from the direction of continental philosophy and particularly care about the foundational issues opened in that field: in this case, the possibility of asking questions about the political rather than merely about politics. For them, the theological is a lever to move from questions of politics to questions of the political. But in these discourses engaged with continental philosophy, there is little talk about existentialism: That is what structuralism superseded, before structuralism was itself superseded by poststructuralism.[20] Others who gravitate toward political theology approach from the direction of Christian theology. For them, political theology means something negative and something positive. It means challenging the alignment of political power with religious commitments and practices (a typically conservative move), and it means mobilizing religious resources to challenge the political status quo (whether in a reactionary or revolutionary direction). From this perspective, there may be an existential root associated with faith, but religious engagement in politics brackets that existential root and instead turns to elements of a religious tradition as resources rather than to the nexus of faith and existential concern.[21]

Part of the issue here has to do with the particular shape of the Left in the United States. There continues to be a gap between the concerns of leftist political theorists located in the academy and leftist political actors. Whereas the latter are necessarily grounded in social movement activity and organizing and sometimes in electoral politics and policy, and therefore easily align with the existential concerns at the root of left politics, ever since the McCarthy era scholars in the United States who advertise leftist identities rarely have experience with the practices that are the essential components of left politics.[22] Moreover, for those approaching from within US Christianity, there is an additional layer of blurriness between liberal and left politics. They are inclined to a posture of non-partisanship, and they must communicate with audiences—congregations—that have liberal and left, and sometimes conservative, inclinations. There is also the pervasive "social justice" framing found in liberal-left US Christianity that attempts to pivot away from a charity frame by claiming to address structures of domination—but usually does so from a position of privilege rather than one of existential threat.

What results is the current state of political theology in the academy: an awkward assortment of effectively secular aficionados of continental philosophy who profess leftist convictions and a miscellany of Christian social justice advocates straining toward a left politics that slips through their fingers. There are also a few others from religious traditions beyond Christianity and from theoretical currents beyond the continental. Adjacent to and sometimes encompassed within political theology, and notable because of its wide uptake in and beyond anthropology, is the secularist critique of secularism associated with Talal Asad and Saba Mahmood that professes left politics. This is the past and present of the field, but there is a new future emerging amidst the motley present. Instead of flowing from continental or Christian streams, increasingly there are voices from Black,

Indigenous, feminist, queer, and decolonial studies guiding conversations around political theology.[23] In these fields, scholarship and political commitment have always run together; a commitment to their alignment defines each field. This commitment has to do with the straightforward connection often found in these fields between individual experience and scholarly interest, but it also has to do with the fields' origins in political struggle and the continuing struggle needed to keep them alive in often hostile institutional contexts. When the meaning of political theology is shaped by Black, Indigenous, feminist, queer, and decolonial studies scholars, there is necessarily a sense that political theology addresses matters of life and death, that political theology ought to be part of a struggle against death-dealing forces in the interest of bringing about new life—and that a foretaste of that new life is available in the practice of collective struggle.

In other words, just as Schmitt's generation was attracted to political theology because their lives and their loved ones' lives had been on the line in the First World War, because they had waged a life-or-death struggle, the emerging generation of political theology scholarship is bringing to their work a sense that their life is on the line and that they are engaged in struggle, sometimes on a daily basis, for survival. Schmitt's generation, of course, slipped into false consciousness: What appeared to be an obligatory life-or-death struggle was actually crude nationalism, and this nationalism presents an important note of caution for those of us today who are contemplating the future of the field.

Since 2016, the contours of left politics in the United States have shifted rapidly and dramatically.[24] From the early 1970s to the early 2010s, left politics was marginal to public discourse and often operating on a tiny scale.[25] But in recent years a Left has reemerged that is quite different from the old, labor Left of the early twentieth century and also from the new Left of the 1960s social movements. While the old Left, the new Left, and today's Left are all driven by existential concern and fueled by a vulnerability to death, they have changed not only in content but also in form. Protest and organizing characterize each of these, as does a spirited youth leadership. But the contingencies of early-twenty-first-century culture and media have amplified the energy and visibility of certain struggles in the United States: around prison abolition, around anti-Black violence, and around socialism.

These struggles pivot away from liberalism, by which I mean a particular disposition toward politics (distinct from neoliberalism, a mode of governance). Today, simply naming liberalism as an antagonist of the Left is novel, at least within public discourse. Previously, leftist academics would attack liberalism and tiny, fringe revolutionary groups would attack liberalism. Liberalism's primary antagonists were from the Right. Today's leftist energy is concerned with uprooting systems of domination, and liberalism is said to lack the resources for such deep transformation because it is too invested in preserving the status quo. The institutions that supposedly made progress possible, such as congresses and parliaments, courts, and government bureaucracies, in fact impede structural change—even when they mouth the words *structural change*. Along with naming and challenging liberalism, today's Left names and challenges reform as the path toward justice, though "revolution" is not always or even often positioned as reform's opposite. Furthermore, respectability has become suspect. In cutting cultural analysis and critique, leftist movements name the temptation to affect change by putting on a show, in words and bodies, that comforts the powers that be. But when interlocking systems of domination fully contaminate the status quo, any effort to perform that is responsive to the desires of those with power is counterproductive, distracting from the possibility of radical transformation.

As we saw in Schmitt's work, and as the political theorist Robyn Marasco has pointed out in her feminist reading of that work, Schmitt pivots away from liberalism by taking very seriously, as foundational, a vulnerability to death.[26] For Schmitt, it is the sovereign, in that figure's likeness to the Christian God (a God who is human and, in a sense, vulnerable), that provides a starting point for thinking the political beyond liberal politics. In today's leftist political movements, sovereignty is anathema, but there are other theological concepts that open and secure the turn away from liberal politics. The prison abolitionist requires faith in immediate action that runs counter to a rational analysis. The opponent of anti-Black racism tells a story about the fallen nature of the world, so wide and so deep that it will only be overcome at the world's "End." And the socialist imagines a world overturned, with the last first and the first last, all united in shared life, and looks to sample a foretaste of such a world in the present. These are unmistakably theological habits of thought. (I will remain agnostic on whether they are specifically Christian.) If they do not require an image of a divine sovereign, that may be because such a sovereign is an idol. But while Erik Peterson and the German theologians who made claim to a "new political theology" in the 1960s and 1970s sought to pluralize the Christian tradition, finding resources for radical politics not in the singular, transcendent God but in Trinity or Spirit, liturgy or prayer, a leftist political theology embraces the obverse of divine sovereignty. Instead of searching for correlation or aiming to make available religious resources, leftist political theology at its best aligns ungraspable power with the negative. The world is deeply fallen, with domination all-pervasive, and it is only a theological vocabulary that can adequately speak to this context—and theological forms of practice and imagination that flow from that negativity.

Even as the popular imagination often associates liberalism with an uncritical faith in progress, talk of fallenness has been the domain of a particular, influential strand of liberalism, the liberalism of Reinhold Niebuhr, Isaiah Berlin, and Raymond Aron. Because everything does not fit together perfectly, because of our individual and collective finitude and fallibility, this strand of liberalism charges that we must be savvy and humble analysts, choosing the better rather than the best, resisting fantasy, nostalgia, and fixation. In our tragic world, we must persist knowing we will fail often, but never blocking from view the world's complexity: This is the liberal ethos as developed in the twentieth century and recently synthesized by Joshua Cherniss.[27] At first, this seems like a quite different liberalism from the one Schmitt took to be his opponent—overconfident, managing plurality, accepting a diversity of goods—but perhaps the tragic liberal ethos is but the flip side of liberal governance. Schmitt sought to break with liberalism from above, as it were, by means of sovereign power tethered to existential concerns. Today's left-aligned political theology would seek to break with liberalism from below, arguing that liberals who supposedly embrace fallenness do not go far enough.

Domination means constructing false gods, elevating an earthly object or person to the position of lord over another. Systems of domination naturalize idolatry, attaching to white people, or men, or heterosexuals, or police officers a godlike aura. If it is true that systems of domination interlock, and if it is true that they go back centuries, perhaps to time immemorial, shaping our metaphysics, our concepts, our language, our perception, even our feelings, then we must either succumb to idol worship or embrace a political-theological vocabulary that starts with this context. From the leftist's perspective, the liberal succumbs to idol worship. Swimming in the waters of the tragic, accepting the inescapability of imperfect decisions while at the same time striving for ever-greater complexity and nuance in political analysis: This simply naturalizes domination, excuses idolatry. Believing that there is another option takes something like faith. When it seems that everything is contaminated, every river is polluted, every institution and individual and even my self are shaded by domination, and still to believe that domination does not have the last word, it is unclear what else could motivate such a commitment. Call it faith in God beyond the world, or call it faith in life itself, with the sensuousness of living offering evidence that domination is not the end of the story.[28]

Put another way, the project of political theology aligned with left politics today starts with the ruled rather than the ruler. It takes the dynamics of ruling, and so politics, to exist outside of formal political institutions. But whether political theology is approaching from above or below, the crucial claim is that ruler and ruled do not form a closed system. The dynamics of master and slave do not exhaust the world. An End of the world is possible, a world beyond this world. A miracle. The proposal here is not to pluralize miracles and discover them in the realm of quotidian political life, as Bonnie Honig suggests, or to find the unmaking of sovereignty in a vernacular political theology of the subaltern, as George Shulman suggests.[29] Rather, it is to embrace the defining features of the Left, which necessarily thinks on a scale both personal and grand: existentially motivated urgency, a refusal to tolerate domination even one more day, a realization of the depths of that domination, and an imagining of a world wholly other, with no discernable path from here to there.

FROM BELOW

Within Christian theology, liberation theology names theology from below. It names the ways of talking about God that are found in marginalized communities, addressing the dynamics of marginalization. Latin America and Black America are sites where liberation theology has been particularly well thematized, and in such contexts, talk about God necessarily involves talk about domination. It necessarily involves talk about the imperial context in which Jesus was crucified, and the way that forces of colonialism, white supremacy, and patriarchy continue to cloak themselves with the divine. And it invokes God as an ultimate guarantor of and guide to justice, even when justice is horribly obscured by the forces of domination. Liberation theology grew out of and supported communities of Christians struggling for self-determination, and in the Latin American context this took institutional form as "base communities" of Christians self-consciously committed to justice.[30]

A particular strand of German Christian theology that emerged contemporaneously with liberation theology in the 1960s called itself "political theology" and is sometimes referred to as the "new political theology."[31] Involving both Protestants and Catholics, this scholarly conversation developed as left-wing Christians in West Germany entered into dialogue with humanistic Marxists in East Germany. Marxist analytical tools including ideology critique entered the West German theological guild, and they informed a reading of Christian scripture and tradition that took a central component of Christianity to be its attack on false gods, including nationalism, militarism, capitalism, and colonialism. At the same time, a group of younger West German theologians were proximate to or participants in leftist social movements, including movements against the Vietnam War and Western imperialism around the world, against nuclear weapons, against environmental devastation, and against patriarchy.[32] This fusion of theory and practice yielded a set of sophisticated theological projects that often directly or indirectly addressed the social movement landscape of the day—while also implicitly challenging Carl Schmitt's capture of the term *political theology*. These German theologians were in dialogue with proponents of liberation theology in Latin America and Black America, but they saw their project rather differently. From the perspective of these German theologians, liberation theology was the voice of the poor and marginalized, whereas political theology spoke out as an immanent critique of the West that, at the same time, championed the voices of the West's victims. Put another way, liberation theology was theology from below while political theology was self-critical theology from above.

While these Christian theological debates are at a significant remove from debates in political theory, and even more so from political practice, the instinct animating liberation theology is important to remember. It takes seriously the religious worlds of the marginalized. It finds in these worlds, composed of symbols, images, practices, histories, and forms of imagination, implicit or explicit critiques of domination: colonial and postcolonial domination and racial domination but also, in later iterations of liberation theology, domination along lines of gender and sexuality.[33] In fact, German "new political theology" would seem to add little to this project: The critique of ideology, often using Marxist tools, is already baked into the project of liberation theology.

What makes liberation theology seem rather quaint from the perspective of current discourses in critical theory is its reluctance to interrogate what counts as religion. Among the most powerful innovations in twenty-first-century critical theory is the careful analysis of secularism, understood as the ideological project that excludes from public discourse or manages what counts as religion in the interest of the state or, more broadly, the wealthy and powerful. Indeed, critics of secularism charge that the religious and the secular cannot be taken as self-evident; they are filtered through the ideology of secularism, and this ideology is itself entangled with ideologies of colonialism, racism, patriarchy, and capitalism.[34] Secularism erases religion in some places and makes religion hypervisible in other places. As a tool of the ruling class, secularism particularly targets religion among marginalized communities, filtering through law, policy, education, and social norms how such religion is perceived and how it appears in public discourse. As a critical project, the analysis of secularism demonstrates the ways that religion is disfigured in the interests of the ruling class.

In short, liberation theology points to the political import of religion found in marginalized communities, while critics of secularism point to the likelihood of misrepresenting such religion. What is now called *political theology*—a critical discourse in the humanities, distinct from the earlier German Christian tradition—at its best attempts to reconcile these two competing instincts. Political theology attends to the worlds of the marginalized as they struggle against domination and to the ways secularism disfigures religion in those worlds. Put another way, if political theology for Schmitt is about analyzing secularized theological concepts that circulate among political elites, political theology as it is emerging today, political theology from below, is about analyzing secularized theological concepts that circulate among communities struggling against domination. That means that while sometimes political theology focuses on explicitly religious language, at other times it focuses on forms of theological reasoning, feeling, or imagining that are no longer marked as religious, having undergone a process of secularization that is managed by the ideology of secularism. Political theology from below, then, is at once descriptive and normative. It calls our attention to particular sites, and it asks about the operations of secularization there. It does so in the interest of garnering resources for struggle and exposing the machinations of the powerful. Political theology from below need not be and should not be exclusively Christian, but it must bring to its analysis a deep knowledge of the religious context of the sites it examines. Furthermore, political theology from below need not take the form of scholarly prose. Interrogating secularism in spaces of domination happens naturally to those experiencing domination, and it finds expression not only in scholarship but also in political writing, religious ritual, and various forms of aesthetic production.[35]

The Black poet, playwright, and politician Aimé Césaire is not a canonical figure in Christian political theology or in continental philosophy. However, he may become a canonical figure in the field of political theology as it is emerging today. Born in the French colony of Martinique in 1913, Césaire expressed a deep suspicion of Christianity. At points in his writings, he dismisses Christianity with Marxian flippancy as something like an opiate. Indeed, in his acclaimed and widely circulated political essay *Discourse on Colonialism*, Césaire describes the French prime minister as "looking like a communion wafer dipped in shit"—an evocative reversal (or complication) of the Schmittean identification of God and sovereign.[36] And yet Césaire ends his most famous book-length poem, *Notebook of a Return to a Native Land*, with several pages of prayer. He confesses his inadequacy. He surrenders his mind and body, and voice. Finally, he enumerates and commends the virtues, culminating with a promise of something like resurrection. "Rise / rise / rise," Césaire repeats in the final stanza.

The child and grandchild of teachers who enjoyed a relatively privileged status, Césaire excelled in his studies and traveled to France to continue them, eventually entering the famed École normale supérieure. There he was influenced by Bergson's thought and the vitalist movement in the years before the Second World War. He encountered and was inspired by the surrealist movement. But, most importantly, in Paris he discovered other Black men and women from the Caribbean, the United States, Europe, and Africa with whom he shared experiences—and who were each discovering France's unacknowledged investments in whiteness and in racial and colonial domination. While still a student, Césaire made possible collective reflection on these experiences by cofounding a Black literary magazine and fostering a sense of intellectual community that would eventually result in the multiple manifestations of the Negritude movement. After returning to Martinique, Césaire became involved in electoral politics while continuing to write poems and plays.[37]

Following his self-description, Césaire is almost always read as a secular figure, and Negritude is read as a secular movement. Recent work by historians has begun to change this. For example, Elizabeth Foster helpfully reminds us that one of the central figures in Césaire's world, and the world of Negritude, during the 1940s was the Senegalese intellectual Alioune Diop. Diop was a friend and collaborator not only of Césaire but also of Popes John XXIII and Paul VI and an important figure in the Second Vatican Council. As Foster pointedly asserts, "It is not merely that scholars have tended to discount or disregard the Catholicism of leading lights in the black cultural movement... but also that they have ignored explicitly Catholic engagement with pan-Africanism and colonialism." She identifies a strand of the Negritude movement, "Catholic negritude," that "became explicitly anticolonial, insist[ing] on a 'de-occidentalization' of the Catholic Church."³⁸ The writings of Césaire and his colleagues were disseminated not only to fellow Martinicans but also through Catholic ecclesial channels in France and throughout Africa.³⁹

The lengthy *Notebook* was first published in France in 1939, when Césaire was but twenty-six years old. He took the connotation of "notebook" seriously: Césaire would continue revising it, expanding it, and republishing it over the next two decades. As Césaire engaged more deeply with surrealism, the poem took on additional surrealist features in the 1940s. As his political engagement deepened—he was for a time a member of the Communist Party, then left the party—explicitly political elements took a more prominent role in the poem in the 1950s.

The poem involves a fairly straightforward narrative progression. At first, it features vivid examples of colonial and racial oppression, focused on the Caribbean but referring beyond the islands as well. The first-person narrative voice, returning from schooling in France, realizes that he has adopted the perspective of the colonizers as he looks at his own people. He then transforms his perspective, identifying with the colonized masses and calling for an overturning of values, a liberation from colonial rule. There is then a moment of antithesis to colonial rule in which the narrator embraces Africa and the attributes that he associates with Africa. In a final, synthetic move, the excesses of that African embrace are incorporated into disciplined political commitment.

Much attention has focused on the poem's moment of antithesis, its valorization of all things African. In that section, Césaire puts the term *negritude* into circulation and names a perspective that was picked up widely by his Black contemporaries in the francophone intellectual world. But for Césaire at his best, negritude is not the end of the story; it is a moment in a narrative. Indeed, even more important than the grand narrative of the poem is the phenomenology of domination that Césaire offers.[40] He traces how domination contaminates life, he showcases attacks on systems of domination, and he names the promise of life free of those systems.

What does life under colonial domination look like, according to Césaire? Reason and exchange go haywire in the colonial context; in the metropole, dominated by scientism, reason and exchange are fetishized. Those who suffer do so in vain; as Césaire puts it, martyrs "do not bear witness" (13). Césaire's narrator notices "an aged life mendaciously smiling, its lips opened by vacated agonies" (13). Here we see emotion, too, distorted by colonial domination. Smiles do not indicate happiness, not even in elders. Rather, they indicate lies. Why? Because of "vacated agonies," the pains of domination that have not been given a name and processed, and that cannot be. Domination not only inflicts suffering, but it also imposes a regime of suffering that forecloses language to express that suffering, creating second-order, and recursive, suffering. There is hunger, poverty, and anger, but none of these can be expressed. People speak, but they are "strangely chattering and mute," exchanging words in a way that bears little relation to life, individual or collective (15). Colonial officials, teachers, and priests do their best to make islanders speak, but all they can elicit are echoes of what the officials say, another kind of muteness. There is no way of making things right; those who live under colonial domination are "vexed no matter what" (13).

Césaire introduces us to his parents, or his narrator's parents, and they represent two forms of life distorted. The father alternates between "melancholy tenderness" and "towering flames of anger," emotional circuitry gone awry (23). The mother is emotionally stable, it seems, but only because she has no time for emotion. Her life is consumed by work, day and night, at a sewing machine, her body having been consumed by its rhythm.

For Césaire, in the world under colonial domination, individual life, social life, and life in the natural world are all at odds with one another, with the result that life is threatened. The poem is full of imagery of the physical features of the Caribbean and its natural life, but early in the poem such imagery represents a threat. The island where the poem takes place is "in breach of its fauna and flora" (15). Those emotions that could not be expressed under the regime of domination were displaced, sometimes to the natural world. "Fears crouched in the ravines," "fears perched in the trees," "fears dug in the ground" (15). These lines suggest broken relationships with the natural world, wrongly incorporated into the human world and ascribed with the emotions that could not be properly directed against agents of domination because the regime of domination permits no language that could name those agents. Similarly, life under domination is a river that flows improperly, "hesitant," "pitifully empty" (23). In this imagery, which is at once nature broken by domination and a metaphor for life under domination, we find "the stagnant air unbreeched by a limpid bird" (23).

No matter how powerful the regime of domination is, it leaves those dominated unsatisfied. This idea is represented by Césaire at both a physical level and a deeper level by "hunger." Colonial subjects hunger for food, and they hunger for something that they cannot name, that a surfeit of food cannot satisfy—"hunger buried in the depths of the Hunger" (17). Life is not reducible to a list of necessities: food, water, shelter, and so on. When life is denied through domination, Hunger arises. It may attach to particular objects—for example, offices or other rewards presented by the colonial regime, or fine food and drink—but such objects will leave Hunger unsatisfied. That Hunger motivates nostalgia and optimism, and it motivates a search for moments of ecstasy. In Césaire's presentation, this is precisely what colonial Christianity offers: "the bread, and the wine of complicity" (19).[41] The climax of the first part of the *Notebook* is Christmas, a moment of joy, of kinship, of desiring and preparing, of tasting and dancing. For a moment, fear transforms into hope, but both are equally products of the Hunger created by colonial domination. Then Christmas is over, and ordinary life under domination, ordinary suffering, resumes. With Christmas over, islanders are left with "life prostrate." They "don't know how to dispose of... aborted dreams" (23). Just as misdirected fears unexpressed compound into new fears, misdirected dreams aborted compound, pulling tighter the knot of affective energy that is continually missing the mark.

The *Notebook* is one of return, from the metropole to the colony, and the return occasions a new sort of distortion of life. The one who returns imagines that he knows life rightly, that he can identify the distortions of life to be found in the colony, among his community, and among his family. The one who returns aspires to speak about such life and to improve it. "My mouth shall be the mouth of those calamities that have no mouth, my voice, the freedom of those who break down in the prison holes of despair" (27). However, Césaire observes, "life is not a spectacle," and the one who returns treats it as spectacle (27). Subject is detached from object; immanence is refused. This embrace of the subject is underscored by the first-person singular, "I alone," that speaks the narrative voice.

With the antinomy of the one who returns, life becomes death—and Césaire maps the problematic of a Left that resists liberalism. The narrator catches himself, beginning to say, "this life," then correcting himself, "this death, this death" (27). What seemed like life is actually death—both life on the island, under domination, and the life of the one who returns, living in a world of abstractions and distance. Life is "without meaning or piety," so it is now death—filled with "dazzling pettiness," "hobbling from pettiness to pettiness" (27). The world of the island is a world of bureaucrats and rules, implementing domination on a day-to-day basis. They generate activity, but this activity has no meaning. It is hollow. Those who perform it, and live in its world, take on a zombie-like status, the living dead. The island is now seen as the place "where the apocalypse of monsters cavorts" (27). This sense of the apocalyptic does not mean that Césaire is calling for the end of the world; rather, he observes, phenomenologically, what it means to live under domination, where we can see vividly what life is not, what deserves the label *death*. This image of death in life, as with so many of Césaire's images, equivocates between the metaphorical and the literal. Domination operates precisely through this equivocation. It means the pettiness of bureaucrats, but it also means the living-death, and blood, of slavery. It means "marshes of putrid blood," "land red, land sanguineous, land consanguineous" (29). This does not mean that life can be better understood, or lived, by remembering the past, by remembering the death of ancestors. Living-death does not illuminate the life of others; it is mute, dark, blood without meaning.

In Césaire's account, Europe suffers from similar pathologies of reason and emotion as the colonies: both dominator and dominated have life distorted by domination. But Europe copes differently: it conceals its pathologies through excessive self-confidence. Because life is understood in the negative, as only accessible through negation, those who have been colonized must enact a sort of jujitsu to gain the tools of negation. This is what negritude, Césaire's positive program, borrows from Europe: "I summon this beautiful egotism," he writes (31).

Embracing that egotism, new negations proliferate. The poem's narrator proclaims that his life cannot be characterized by a nationality. It cannot be measured by a craniometer, reduced to the size of his head.

At the same time that borrowed egotism is fueling negation, reflection leads to submission. "My heroism, what a farce!," the narrator proclaims. "My soul is prostrate. Prostrate like this town in its refuse and mud" (39). Here again we encounter ambiguity, equivocation. The town is prostrate because of domination, whereas the narrator is prostrate as a mechanism for negation, as an ascetic practice into which he has been propelled by the previous moment of negation.[42] From this perspective, the narrator is able to see life anew, unexpected. Even as the natural world pains—"lands explode in accordance with the fatal division of rivers" (39)—and even as domination distends bodies—"our limbs vainly disjointed by the most refined tortures" (41)—life becomes evident. This is life without features, the bare fact of life, life defined by a double negative. It arises without reason, "impetuously springing up from this dunghill" (41). The appearance of life, under this sign of double negation, is not premised on an end to domination. There are still bodies tortured and rivers that kill. But it is life that becomes visible as domination is attacked, as new techniques of negation are deployed. When life appears, it is because the attempts to define life have proven hollow. "Sacred maxims" have been "trampled underfoot," and "pedantic rhetoric" has been exposed as "hot air" (41). As the narrator finally, fully owns his new voice, he uses it to reject what could make his life count: ancestors who invented electricity, money, or conquest.

As the poem approaches its finale, the register shifts to that of prayer. There is life, but it is imagined. It exists eschatologically, expressed aesthetically in the present, not directly producing imperatives for life in the present.[43] It is in this register that "negritude" appears, summoned in prayer. Here, in the eschatological register, there are people living in right relationship with one another and with the earth. As Césaire puts it, the "earthiest about earth ferments and ripens" (43). Yet even here, what we find is not conceptual clarity, systematic organization, or perfect harmony. In this world of negritude, there "is neither tower nor cathedral" (43). Instead, land, sky, and human life are in relation to one another, attending to one another, growing with one another. Indeed, in this eschatological register, harmony is so great that life is unconstrained, even by the laws of nature, by the domination that nature can impose on human, animal, and plant life. At this point, "the sun turns around the earth," Césaire proclaims, and "every star falls from sky to earth at our omnipotent command" (55).

But this engagement is not exhausting in the way that Césaire says engagement with the people and the natural world is exhausting in contexts of domination. In the white world, "rebellious joints" are "cracking under the stars" and "blue steel rigidities" are "piercing the mystic flesh" (45). In contrast, in the genre of prayer, the world of negritude is one of "perfect circle" and "concordance" (45). Without effort, unquenchable, distorted Hunger is removed, along with pathologies afflicting the emotions. "Eia for joy / Eia for love," the narrator exclaims (47). What remains is sweetness and intimacy, like "the succulence of fruit"—once again, the natural world and human life mixing freely (49).

The genre of prayer is crucial here. It involves envisioning a just future and asking for assistance. This assistance is not to bring about specific features of the world envisioned, a world that remains in the eschatological register, but rather to attack domination in the present world. What are needed are resources for the struggle: "grant me the courage of the martyr / grant me the savage faith of the sorcerer / grant my hands the power to mold / grant my soul the sword's temper" (47). Necessary for this struggle is the capacity for reason and emotion to be rightly oriented—in other words, it is necessary to struggle against the forces of domination that distort reason and emotion. Part of the prayer is to be sheltered from the temptation to excess anger, to be freed from resentment. Finally, struggle is motivated by hunger and thirst, but it is motivated by these imperatives now rightly directed. These are hunger and thirst not tethered to a need for food or drink, not motivated by the forces of colonial domination (or capitalist domination), but "universal hunger" and "universal thirst," which are to be summoned "free at last" (49). Once again, we have a sense of political theology tied to universal, unequivocal demand—a left-not-liberal, and certainly not right, political theology.

Here is the final step in Césaire's analysis of what life is not. It is not joy and love, not all succulence and sweetness. It is not a perfect circle and concordance. We can vision those qualities, paint those in brackets at the eschatological horizon, but we should not strive to achieve them. Life, for Césaire, is struggle against domination, where the world makes struggle difficult but prayer (in its practice, its performance, and its literariness) makes struggle easy. The governing metaphor is the "proud pirogue," the traditional canoe used by Indigenous people in the Caribbean. The pirogue is a small boat in a giant, unyielding ocean. Yet it stays afloat by attending to that ocean, even in the ocean's turmoil, "rising and falling on the pulverized wave" (49). It "rears under the attack of the swells, deviates for an instant, / tries to escape, but the paddle's rough caress turns it" (49). This is attention without a desire for conquest or domination, but it is still "playing the game of the world," engaged in the fray of collective life, within and beyond the human (45). The world remains full of domination, and responsiveness to that domination, to those giant waves, requiring skilled maneuvering.

The final stanza of the poem explains how to gain aid in this struggle. It is not gained through human effort but through ascesis, through surrender. Surrender happens during dance: surrender of the body in "fleshy rhythm" (61). It also happens by attacking instincts to describe and control, to react and to argue. The narrative voice, speaking in the second person to the world, but the world as life—perhaps Life, perhaps a site of auto-affection in the terms of Michel Henry or vitalism in the anticolonial tradition identified by Donna Jones—asks to be "bound" "to the very navel of the world" (61).[44] This is an imperative to negate all that would run counter to life, not once, but again and again. For this binding process must be imposed on oneself, and the only mechanism by which it can be imposed is through self-criticism of thought, practice, and desire. What remains after negating the negation is life, participation in Life, being bound to life—life in life, as life.[45]

At this point death-in-life becomes life-in-death.[46] Césaire meditates on the image of a slave ship, the paradigmatic site of domination, of one human transforming another into a nonhuman through the arbitrary exercise of will, backed with violent force, on the body of another. He tells of a captain who, out of boredom, decides to kill his largest slave. But in the process of dying, on the way to death, this enslaved African experiences life. Leaving the hold of the ship, he *stands*—a verb Césaire repeats thirteen times in the stanza. Standing is living, and standing is struggling. The enslaved African stands and then walks to the deck. He feels the wind and the sun. He feels his own blood. He is dying, but he is free. The world may always be characterized by domination—at the very least, by the domination of death, faced by all—but there can be life in death if we follow the pedagogy outlined by Césaire.

Césaire rejects Christianity as a tool of colonial domination only to return to Christianity in his finale. Death-bound-life is resurrected, and eternal life is realized, unfreedom overcome if only for an instant, perhaps an eternal instant. But if this is secularized Christianity, or spiritualized Christianity, it is the negative theological variety. Césaire's focus is on false conceptions that need to be purged, false conceptions that lead to wrong actions—actions that perpetuate systems of domination.

We can now return to Césaire's curious reversal of political theology. Rather than identifying God with a political leader and reflecting on the form of sovereignty common to both, Césaire describes the French political leader's appearance as that of God defiled, a "communion wafer dipped in shit." It is tempting to read this as a flippant dismissal of Christianity, to see Césaire depicting both Christianity and French rule as ugly, aesthetically as well as morally. But we might just as easily read Césaire as again engaged in negative theology. The Body of Christ is degraded when it is identified with political rule—specifically, here, colonial and white rule. But the ideation is genuine: the desire for the communion wafer, the longing for participation in the Body of Christ. Césaire, then, would be urging us to hold together these negative and positive moments: the moment when we critique idolatry and domination, and the moment when we recognize our longing for something more that cannot be fulfilled by grotesquely deformed political structures—the longing for new life.

At the root of things, for Césaire, is the sensuous engagement with the world that constitutes life and that is deformed but not eliminated by colonial and racial domination. Amidst the living-death of such domination, there remain traces of life that motivate politics: first, the critique of domination; then the collective organizing and social movement work that necessarily follows; and then the technical practice of politics, the business of elections and parties and power, of imagining new structures and manipulating old ones. Indeed, Césaire served as the mayor of Martinique's capital, Fort-de-France, for almost all of the period 1945 to 2001, and he was active in anticolonial alliances. As Gary Wilder's incisive study of Césaire demonstrates, his interventions in the domain of technical political practice were not always successful, but they were rooted in the lived experience of the death-dealing powers of colonialism and racism, and they were motivated by an imagined future without domination, a future of new life.[47]

ABOLITION

Political theology from below means attending to secularized theology in its richest sense, affective and embodied, at work in the political practice and cultural production of marginalized communities organizing against domination. It means starting in the Caribbean instead of Germany, in poetry instead of prose. It means appreciating a figure like Césaire not simply as an example of political theology or as a writer who applies the insights of political theology, but as a theorist of political theology—offering one among the myriad alternative origin points for theorizing political theology from below.

If Césaire provided an opportunity to ground political theology in cultural production, this section will ground political theology in political practice, specifically, the political practice of the long 2010s. With the mushrooming movements of these years, it might seem hard to know where to start looking for political theology from below, for organizers who are themselves theorists of political theology. But what if there was a common grammar to the social movements of this decade?[48] There are already hints at this: Themes of healing, self-care, interlocking systems of oppression, urgency, and the end of the world are found, in various ways, across these social movements. Yet we are often entranced by the theoretical heavy machinery involved and the debates they provoke. Should we be talking about Afropessimism or racial capitalism? Black feminism or settler colonialism? Anarchism or syndicalism? Labor and class or prisons and police? What if we bracket these big theories and look closer to the ground, at what social movement organizers are feeling and saying on a daily basis? This is a necessarily speculative exercise, and my purpose is not to persuade the reader that each movement can be lined up with a common grammar but rather that a common grammar is plausible and would entail certain commitments—to political theology.

A couple generations ago, it would have been natural to label insurgent social movements *revolutionaries*. The *revolutionary* label that was, in the 1960s and 1970s, claimed by social movement leaders ranging from Black Panthers to Marxists to feminists, sounded quaint in the twenty-first century—and then was tainted by its association with the class-first, identity-later electoral politics of Bernie Sanders.

There was, however, a political identification that, by the end of the 2010s, was starting to circulate across the divides between social movements: "abolitionist." While it originated in the movement to end human caging and quickly expanded to include movements against policing as such, in both cases drawing on analogies and genealogies that pointed to nineteenth-century movements to abolish slavery, the language of abolition soon circulated widely and loosely, as an unqualified identity of individuals and organizations. It pointed to shared dispositions, shared ways of seeing the world, and shared styles of organizing. In other words, the vernacular theory of abolitionism started to explicate the grammar shared by this family of social movements.

Abolitionism deploys, in grassroots political organizing, concepts whose provenance is in the theological realm. Moreover, the logic of theology that undergirds abolitionism is essential, not incidental. The distinction that matters the most to abolitionism, its contrast with reformism, falls apart if we forget the political theology at play. Political theology makes abolitionism left, not liberal. My suggestion here is in one sense descriptive, that we notice political theology in the social movement grammar marked by abolitionism, and in another sense normative, that abolitionists ought to better appreciate political theology lest they risk losing the coherence of their political project: lest they turn away from justice, becoming disoriented, perhaps committing injustice in the name of justice.

These two claims are not intuitive because of secularism—the secularism that pervades mainstream U.S. culture and the particular species of secularism that pervades social movement culture. In the former, secularism involves the careful management of religious pluralism, permitting some types of religiosity while muzzling others. The effect is that social movements can be perceived either as having nonviolent Rev. Dr. Martin Luther King Jr. clones as leaders (Rev. Dr. William Barber, II) or as renouncing religion altogether. Within these social movements, an allergy to Christianity—often motivated by churches' racism, sexism, and homophobia—blocks movements from seeing just how religious, and particularly Christian, they really are. It blocks inquiry into political theology, sometimes replacing it with a sort of political spirituality that introduces the New Age vice of too much acceptance, too little judgment—a mismatch for the quite judgmental work of social movement organizing.[49]

When abolitionism is theorized, it is often with the hope that it will be adopted, that readers will be persuaded to take on the identity of abolitionist. In other words, abolitionism is often presented as apologetics. My interest is in abolitionism as dogmatics, as movement grammar. The nod to theological categories here is intentionally evocative. In a sociological sense, there is something quite religion-like about how the language of abolitionism is used. Because taking on an identity as an abolitionist involves taking on an unpopular, even demonized viewpoint and joining a new community of those who share that viewpoint, it involves something like a leap of faith. The reaction to professed abolitionism—say, at the bus stop or at the parent-teacher association meeting—is usually some version of "you couldn't *really* believe that." For these reasons, abolitionists are disposed to focus on persuasion, on making their views plausible to nonbelievers so that they might take the leap and join, or at least so abolitionism is not a conversation stopper. But this disposition results in accounts of abolitionism that overlook or underplay the features that are, from the internal perspective of an adherent, the most important. To explicate this latter perspective is to do political theology.

Approaching from this dogmatic perspective, we can identify several key features of abolitionism. They have to do with what is to be abolished, the possibility of abolition, the practical implications of abolition, and what happens when abolition fails.

Abolitionism is about eliminating something very bad from the world, about purging a moral abomination. This was the idea with slavery, and this is the power of the analogy with slavery: If the prison is seen as a moral abomination, it ought to be ended. So, too, with policing. Various theories can be put forward for what slavery, prisons, and policing have in common: theories of anti-Blackness, racial capitalism, settler colonialism, patriarchy, or some combination of them. But we need not be bogged down in such theories. The insider's language that describes such systems is "carcerality." It points to a certain phenomenology of control. Sometimes this is state control, and sometimes it is present in para-state institutions like child welfare offices and foster care programs. Moreover, what the state once did directly are now habits that nonstate entities have picked up themselves, forming cultures of carcerality, to the point that individuals impose carceral habits on themselves.[50]

While the analysis of carcerality developed in a particular corner of the social movement landscape, around prison and police abolition, it was quickly embraced by other social movements of the 2010s. Feminists sought to distinguish the sort of justice-oriented feminism that grows out of grassroots organizing from the "carceral feminism" that is found among feminist elites and among those whose feminist activism flows from social media rather than from hands-on organizing.[51] An analogous move was made around racial justice organizing: A carceral approach demands the arrest, conviction, and incarceration of, say, a police officer caught on video assaulting a Black motorist, but some social movement organizers have sought to imagine alternative, noncarceral responses to police violence.[52] As the abolitionist law professor Allegra McLeod observes, "Prison abolition . . . is an aspirational ethical, institutional, and political framework that aims to fundamentally reconceptualize security and collective social life, rather than simply a plan to tear down prison walls."[53]

By the start of the 2020s, "abolition" had transformed from a political project, once aimed at slavery, then at prisons and policing, to an ethical stance and identity. Activists identified themselves as abolitionists to signal a posture that could be taken toward any issue, including prisons and policing but moving far beyond them.

Within contemporary social movement discourse, there is an often-unmarked ambiguity around where political energy ought to be directed, around what ought to be torn down, abolished. Is it authority that we need to abolish, or is it domination? Is the world we seek a world without authority or a world without domination? As anarchist, Marxist, feminist, and decolonial streams of political thought mix together, each understanding these terms in different ways and putting forward different accounts of justice, everyday social movement language related to goals and aims becomes increasingly murky. When no distinction is made between domination and authority, it becomes difficult for movements to organize themselves, let alone their communities. Organizing requires engaging with authority, creating structures that bound authority inside and outside of a group, and targeting figures of authority to advance the interests of a group. When all authority becomes suspect, when all authority is treated as domination, social movements turn in on themselves, self-immolating with suspicion.[54]

This is a place where political theology is clarifying. The intuition behind suspicion of domination is that human beings ought not act like gods. Specifically, humans ought not have the capacity to arbitrarily rule others, to impose their will without reason. While humans naturally desire to dominate, and domination generates pleasure that motivates further domination, we are also capable of envisioning a world without domination. And we are capable of working toward that world. In contrast, authority is a much more mundane phenomenon: It is a necessary aspect of our world. Our expertise is limited, so we defer to specialists, trusting that their decisions are reasonable and that they are in a better position to judge than we are. We defer to dentists as authorities on our teeth, to our coaches as authorities on sports, and to architects as authorities on home design. The deference in such cases is pragmatic, limited to a specific domain of life to advance our interests. There is always the danger that an individual who is treated as an authority will forget that the deference they are accorded is limited in scope and provisional rather than absolute. We all know dentists, coaches, and architects who slip from wielding authority to dominating, enjoying the deference they receive and acting as if they are entitled to arbitrarily exercise power. This is why authorities are situated within institutions (professional organizations, sets of social norms, or informal traditions) that, ideally, counterbalance the tendency for authority to slip into domination.

When political theology is approached from above, from elite, abstract discourse, God is understood as the one authority who is incapable of domination. From the human perspective, it may appear that God dominates, but that is because of the epistemic limitations of our humanity; from the God's eye perspective, there is no arbitrariness involved in God's actions. When political theology proceeds from the top down, it authorizes humans in the world (kings and priests and fathers) to act as unaccountable authorities whose ways are mysterious to those they rule, playing God. But when political theology proceeds from the bottom up, its focus is on challenging those humans who would purport to usurp the role of God, acting as unaccountable authorities and enjoying their arbitrary rule. This is precisely what is at issue in the slave owner or prison guard: mastery, setting oneself up as a god.[55] Abolitionism, when it becomes an ethical stance, names the rejection of all such mastery—but not the rejection of all authority. Abolitionism calls for imagining a world where there is no domination, a world impossibly distant from the present.

Abolitionism, then, means imagining a future world that is not accessible from the present, not accessible by making the right series of tweaks or reforms in the present world. It means imagining a new world, after the end of this world. As Stefano Harney and Fred Moten put it, "What is, so to speak, the object of abolition? Not so much the abolition of prisons but the abolition of a society that could have prisons, that could have slavery, that could have the wage, and therefore not abolition as the elimination of anything but abolition as the founding of a new society."[56]

Put bluntly, abolitionism involves imagining the impossible. In the world of slavery, where slavery was woven into the fabric of social and economic life, the end of slavery seemed impossible, with myriad reasons weighing against it—yet it was what abolitionists demanded. In a world of prisons, like the contemporary United States, the end of the prison and the end of the police seem impossible, with reasonable people raising objection after objection—and abolitionists demand the impossible.[57] In abolitionism's new incarnation, as an ethical-religious stance, it also demands the impossible, now across the board: a new world, with no domination at all.

The pathos of necessity is a product of domination. Arbitrary rule involves not only issuing commands but also naturalizing those commands, making it feel as if they are not arbitrary at all—as if they are reasonable, even if that reason remains mysterious, as if it is impossible for things to have been otherwise. Here again we have the theological imagination at work: It is as if the master is a god, as if the words of the master must be right, must be reasonable, even if the subordinate cannot make out how that could be.

To abolish practices of domination, and domination as such, involves believing in the impossible. It requires making the necessary appear contingent. One familiar technique is to historicize: If things have not always been like this, it is not necessary that they remain this way in the future. If the economy was not always dependent on slavery, it means a future without slavery is possible. If the prison was not always necessary to prevent harm, it means a future without the prison is possible. To move from targeted abolition to general abolition requires moving to the register of the theological, or at least mythical, if we are to historicize. There once was a time without domination; we can imagine it, we can tell stories about it. Domination today is pervasive, but it is not necessary.

Put another way, a primary impulse behind abolitionism is interrogating the ways in which our imagination gets boxed in. We have the capacity to imagine wildly, to conjure worlds dramatically different from our own, and yet the futures we imagine are often only marginally different from the world we have. That affective life of domination that burdens us with the feeling of necessity pins us to the current horizon of possibility, allowing us, at most, to modestly nudge its edges. The abolitionist impulse altogether refuses the horizon of possibility that is given to us.

The ethnic studies professor and abolitionist activist Dylan Rodríguez synthesizes strands of contemporary social movement discourse when he writes, "Abolition is not merely a practice of negation—a collective attempt to eliminate institutionalized dominance over targeted peoples and populations—but also a radically imaginative, generative, and socially productive communal (and community-building) practice." Here Rodríguez is developing a core principle that is implicit in, and sometimes explicit in, abolitionist discourse: Abolition involves both negation and affirmation. It involves saying no to all forms of domination and simultaneously involves saying yes to a world without domination. Because the latter is deemed impossible from the perspective of the present, dismissed as absurd by conventional wisdom, the affirmative aspect of abolitionism is necessarily speculative (a register that is at once intellectual and corporeal). In recent years science fiction has taken on an important role in the ethos of social movement spaces. So have eclectic spiritual practices, healing practices, artistic practices, and prayer. All of this happens collectively, growing out of a collective's shared interests and strengthening the collectivity.

As Rodríguez theorizes, abolitionism is "a speculative practice of immanent futurity for people who cannot presume an individual (or even collective) tomorrow."[58] Rodríguez centers the existential stakes of abolitionism, the way it responds to our moment of crisis, our age of crisis. If the stakes are life or death, if death could come at any moment, it becomes essential to imagine a world beyond domination. If domination means death, means the susceptibility to premature death, then turning to a world beyond domination is not a luxury. It is the only way to live, to exist without being shadowed by death: imagining otherwise and allowing the light of that vision to shine into the present world. Envisioning a world beyond domination animates the present world: "immanent futurity." Put another way, the future that abolitionists collectively imagine, where there is no domination, creates norms for life in the present, norms that ensure flourishing in the present.

Once again, there is ambiguity in the abolitionist discourse that political theology can help clarify. If we are imagining a world radically other than the world we inhabit, how can we tell whether that world is good or bad, just or unjust? How can we tell whether that vision is actually a version of our present world—say, inverted—instead of a new world? In short, if speculation and imagination are essential, are there also ways in which they must be normed? Such norming would not be with respect to the content of future visions, but rather in terms of the process by which they are conjured. If I, alone, am dreaming a future I desire, disconnected from my troubles in the present, what I dream is likely little more than wish fulfilment. Rodríguez insists that our speculation must be collective, but is that sufficient guidance?

Religious communities have a great deal of experience responding to precisely this set of questions. The theological imagination conjures up a world beyond domination, but not just any world. It is a *good* world. Beyond a secular horizon of possibility (the secular is, essentially, a horizon of possibility), the theological imagination is directed not merely toward the unknown. It is directed toward the good. This is because the theological imagination grows not out of any community, but out of a community engaged in discerning the good together. It grows out of a community that is self-reflective about its history and the pull that history has on the present, a community with characteristic forms of excellence in the present, and a community that reveres practices of inwardness that distill and transform the insights of the community.[59] All of these characteristics form the imagination, even as they do not point the imagination toward this or that.

Secular social movements are quick to gesture toward the importance of community, but they are often allergic to the normative force emanating from community. Abolitionist discourse embraces radical imagination but shies away from naming the prerequisites to imagination. To turn to political theology, in such a context, does not mean urging belief in God (or asserting that activists were already believers). It means filling out and adding to the coherence of commitments already expressed in social movements. The habits of thought that follow from secularism inhibit the full development of those commitments; political theology, as a set of questions and as an invitation to think with actually existing religious traditions, aids in overcoming those inhibitions.

How do the negative and affirmative aspects of abolitionism come together in practice, in the demands made by abolitionist organizing projects? If the goal is to end domination as such, where to start? What to demand? With whom to organize?

The Highlander Research and Education Center, in rural Tennessee, once seeded and nurtured the civil rights movement, informed by the theological training of its founders. Now it embraces abolitionism as its ethical and political framework—again, informed by the theological training of its leadership. One of those leaders, Ash-Lee Henderson, describes what it means for abolitionists to make demands: "We are demanding not what we will settle for but what we need to be free."[60] In other words, turning abolitionism from theory to practice does not mean trimming its ambition. The point is not to imagine a world without domination and then think about the first practical step that would take us in that direction. Rather, the point is to compare that world of freedom and our present world, to inventory the differences, and to demand that they be addressed. What we need is to be free, not freer.

In practice, this may lead to counterintuitive policy positions. Over the last few years, a number of local abolitionist groups have opposed the construction of new jails in their communities. Advocates for construction point to jail overcrowding. The conditions inside facilities are inhumane, attacking the dignity of those incarcerated. More people are being housed in jails than those jails were designed to hold. The straightforward fix is to build a new jail, to expand capacity. Then cells designed for two people would not have to house three or four people. But abolitionists have opposed such initiatives. Their opposition is based on a counterintuitive but well-proven feature of the criminal justice system: If you increase the system's capacity, that capacity will quickly be filled and exceeded. Obviously, this has nothing to do with crime. It has to do with the logic of systems of domination, which grow and grow until they reach and push against hard constraints. This is what the abolitionist realizes: If the goal is to end domination, every policy push must aim at shrinking the system. We must reject the pleas of those who would call to expand a system of domination in the name of making it more humane.

To formalize this principle, which grows out of on-the-ground organizing experience, abolitionists have adapted an older, previously marginal leftist idiom. Abolitionists want reforms, but abolitionists are not reformists: Reforms are instrumental to the goal of ending domination as such, and reforms are only licit if they directly advance that goal—if they advance "what we need," not "what we will settle for." Therefore, abolitionists must distinguish "reformist reforms" from "nonreformist reforms."[61] The latter shrink systems of domination; the former grow those systems in the interest, eventually, of shrinking them, often in the name of ameliorating suffering. The abolitionist, aware of the power and entanglement of systems of domination, has no confidence that reformist reforms will ever shrink the system. The law professor Amna Akbar and the activist Marbre Stahly-Butts set out criteria for distinguishing these two types of reforms. They argue that a nonreformist reform

> (1) shrinks the system doing harm . . .; (2) relies on modes of political, economic, and social organization that contradict prevailing arrangements and gesture at new possibilities; (3) builds and shifts power into the hands of those directly impacted, who are often Black, brown, working class, and poor; (4) acknowledges and repairs past harm; and (5) improves, or at least does not harm, the material conditions of directly impacted people.[62]

From a secular perspective, advocating against prison construction on behalf of those incarcerated seems absurd. Even for those who sympathize with the goals of the abolitionist, this seems a step too far. But scholars of religious ethics see commitments like this, and debates around such stances, all the time. Consider the Christian pacifist tradition—say, when confronted with the Second World War. Even in that context, the practice of nonviolence was non-negotiable. Pacifists argued that, from a God's eye perspective, looking across space and time, what mattered was the commitment of Christian communities to this principle, whether it was easy or hard. When it was hard, the faith of those communities in God's grace gave them reason to persist in their commitments, even when the world gave them every reason to desist.[63]

It might seem that there is no analogue to such a commitment for the abolitionist. Without faith in a world-transcending deity, what could motivate nonreformist reforms? Moreover, without such faith, aren't such reforms motivated by personal idiosyncrasy—stubbornness, bitterness, melancholy, and the like—rather than a shared vision? Even within a collective with shared political commitments, there are scant resources for adjudicating reformist versus nonreformist reforms. Each individual in the collective imagines differently the scope of the system doing harm, what modes of organization contradict prevailing arrangements, who is directly impacted by domination, what it means to repair past harms, and what counts as improving the material conditions of directly impacted individuals.

This worry about disunity grows out of an approach to political theology that starts from above rather than from below. It starts with an account of God rather than an account of the critical practices of the faithful, suspicious of idolatry and committed to the norms and history of their community. From below, what matters is the normative force of a community and its history, including its authoritative texts and exemplary figures. When the community in question has been systematically disadvantaged, that normative force includes suspicion of systems of domination and all their tentacles. That tradition of the marginalized, anchored in a commitment to an impossible world without domination, provides criteria for adjudicating the meaning of domination, and so for adjudicating the difference between reformist and nonreformist reforms. Discerning the normative force of that tradition is ongoing work, but, once again, such practices of discernment are very familiar to religious communities.

One of the problems that plagues social movements, particularly when they arise out of a sense of urgency and particularly when they are led by youth, is a belief that, if the proper principles are applied in the proper way, the result will be success. The result will be moving toward freedom. When there are setbacks, movement leaders are susceptible to disillusion and burnout. In the abolitionist frame, where domination is pervasive and deep and the orientation to a world free of domination is essential but unstable, such setbacks are not just possible; they are inevitable. This is yet another domain with which religious traditions have much experience. They attend to the limits of our humanity, and to the choices between goods that our finitude forces upon us. Once more, these are features of the theological imagination that are primary when political theology starts from below, from those for whom finitude is unavoidable, whereas these are secondary issues, at most, for political theology from above, when the focus is on sovereignty.

While youthful activists may stumble when it comes to coping with movement failure, abolitionist theorists have a deep appreciation for the tragic. Indeed, reflecting on the prison has been especially fruitful on this front. The prison justifies itself by an illusion of safety: If only we can separate the bad people from the good, our lives will be uninterrupted by the hardness of the world. The tragic nature of the world is something that can be managed, if only we build the right institutions for sorting people in the right way. Similarly, advocates of prison reform (and reformists more generally) are committed to the view that the correct series of steps will yield an end to whatever complex social problems we confront. If we just make the right reform now, and then afterword, and then again after that, eventually the problem of the prison, like any problem, will be solved. But prison abolitionists have documented how the prison system itself arose out of, and exponentially expanded because of, reform efforts that promised an end to domination—down the line.[64]

From the abolitionist's perspective, we must acknowledge that there is no safe harbor. Life in the world involves being harmed and harming others. Given that reality, we need to work toward managing harm rather than eliminating harm, and we need to manage harm in a way that grows relationships and communities rather than severs them. The Muslim abolitionist activist Mariame Kaba exhorts her comrades to remember that "we are actually not fragile beings."[65] Even those who are recovering from harm, who seem especially vulnerable, are resilient. The processes for conflict resolution being developed as alternatives to incarceration, often growing out of grassroots organizing efforts, are experimental and imperfect.[66] But, Kaba urges, that should not prevent us from turning to them instead of turning to the criminal justice system, a system we know rends relationships and harms many of those it touches.

Kaba brings a tragic sensibility to her analysis of conflict resolution, and she brings this same sensibility to the work of organizing itself. She writes, "When we set about trying to transform society, we must remember that we ourselves will also need to transform. Our imagination of what a different world can be is limited. We are deeply entangled in the very systems we are organizing to change." Later, she observes, "Organizing is mostly about defeats."[67] While it may be the case, in theory, that a vision of a world without domination, a world of freedom, animates and guides abolitionist struggles in the present, in fact our imagination is imperfect. It is shaped by systems of domination today. Our political actions in the present are imperfect because they are guided by an imperfect vision. There is no path to purity, no way to extract ourselves from the fallen world in which we are formed. The only thing to do is to extend our critical analysis, our suspicion of domination, from the world to ourselves: to continually work toward transforming ourselves away from the habits we have acquired from the racist, patriarchal, capitalist, colonialist world in which we were formed—regardless of our own identity and knowing we will fail.

Furthermore, Kaba is arguing that we must maintain the distance between the world we desire, free of domination, and the world we inhabit. Images of that future world must remain in the register of imagination and speculation, must be presented in poetry rather than prose. Otherwise, we are tempted to think there is a path from here to there. And we are certain to be disappointed. Framed in this way, the only way for abolitionism to be plausible is by means of faith. We have every reason to disbelieve that a world beyond domination is possible, and we are sure that we cannot chart a path to reach it, yet abolitionists remain committed to envisioning it and allowing it to guide their work in the present.

While Kaba is clear on these points, the broader social movement discourse is often deeply conflicted when it comes to attending to the tragic nature of the world. On one hand, activists place a great deal of emphasis on naming and responding to harms and to building spaces insulated from harm: safe spaces. This emphasis operates both as a demand on institutions, to make themselves safe spaces or to create safe spaces within them, and also as a practice within political organizing, to have the spaces within activist communities be safe.[68] On the other hand, Kaba is not alone in acknowledging that there is no protection from harm, that it will always be part of our common life—this is part of the argument against prisons. From the abolitionist's perspective, the challenge is to experiment with managing harm outside of the known violence of the state, highlighting and developing practices that respond to harm while strengthening communities rather than developing new forms of insulation from harm.

As this tension plays itself out in social movement spaces, once again the theological imagination proves useful. After all, religious traditions have been thinking through the question of human finitude and failure for a very long time. While political theology from the top down can fuel the imagination of prison-planners, seeing the state as a vehicle for ensuring safety, political theology from the bottom up offers a different perspective. It separates the pragmatic issue of managing everyday harms from the principled issue of attacking systems that authorize and encourage harms. We ought to be dreaming up ways of insulating our communities and institutions from those systems while at the same time acknowledging that they will not be safe spaces: Each individual will always, everywhere harm and be harmed. Moreover, we will always go wrong when we try to separate systems of domination from individual bad behavior; yet this is an essential activity to attempt, and to fail better at. In a Christian theological idiom, it is essential because salvation depends on it.

The scholar of religion Tyler Roberts once wrote in the journal *Political Theology*, "We will enrich our critical theories, concepts, and terminologies if we turn away from founding our critical practice on the *critique* of religion and instead explore what various religious traditions might have to teach us about modes of attention, forms of spiritual exercise and contemplation, practices of fidelity, and experiences of grace."[69] This is precisely the sort of political theology from below that is a necessary supplement to contemporary abolitionist discourses. The framework put forward by abolitionists today is not justified by secular reason. In the heat of protest, it is supported by the effervescence generated by the practice of organizing. But such effervescence fades. Instead of looking for some transcendent source of support, we can spotlight "practices of fidelity" that swirl around contemporary social movements. It is not important whether these grow out of specific theological traditions or are products of ostensibly secular traditions. That division is a product of secularism. Once secularism is set aside, political theology from below can offer a better account of the grammar of social movements, offering assurance and guidance as movements navigate troubled times.

After all, the sense of crisis that characterized the long 2010s, like the sense of crisis that was felt in Weimar Germany, was primarily a mark of instability at the level of elite discourses and institutions. Looked at upside down, those struggling against the forces of domination continue to struggle, as they have before, as they will in the future. What sustains those struggles, in the face of epistemic changes, as the elite justification for policy and rule destabilizes and shifts, are precisely those "modes of attention, forms of spiritual exercise and contemplation, practices of fidelity, and experiences of grace" to which Roberts points.[70] Uncovering and interrogating these political-theological worlds, even if they appear neither political nor theological, is at the heart of political theology's promise.[71]

3

AN ANTHROPOLOGICAL POLITICAL THEOLOGY

VALENTINA NAPOLITANO

In Memoriam, Rafael Sánchez Chacheiro 1950–2024

March 27, 2020, Rome. The wind reveals blue patches of twilight beneath grey, gloomy clouds. A soft rain makes the sixteenth-century stones of Saint Peter's Square sparkle in the half-light. Pope Francis is limping with rheumatic pain up a long ramp to reach a cantilevered roof built for the occasion. He stands alone in this normally crowded square. Here, a beloved mediator of God staggers to the center of a globally televised ritual, expressing in his very person the tragic ethos of unfolding action.[1] Canonically speaking, these are not ordinary times, and so they demand an extraordinary papal benediction. He is to give the *Urbi et Orbi*, the most powerful blessing of the pope, directed not only to Rome but also to the world at large. At the end of the sermon and before that benediction, Francis dons a humeral veil in which he wraps his hands to lift the monstrance (the holder of the consecrated Eucharist, which cannot be touched in that liturgy by human hands), thereby underscoring his mediative role. Francis points the monstrance through the main entrance of Saint Peter, toward the starkly empty square, raising it in three directions, blessing the 11 million–plus Italians who are watching from their locked-down dwellings, and the many millions more around the world—practicing, lenient, and non-Catholic alike.[2]

As the humeral veil is removed from his shoulders, Francis walks back past the entrance of Saint Peter, and the camera captures the fierceness of the clouds as if mirroring the potent fear and vulnerability experienced by this pandemic gathering in absence. Appropriately, the pope is momentarily framed on one side by the miraculous wooden Crucifix of San Marcello, protector against the 1522 Roman plague, and the Salus Populi Romani on the other, one of the oldest icons protecting the Roman polis, its current version dating from the thirteenth century. On screen, the solitary pope mobilizes a long affective history of Christological and Marian iconographic protection even while the sovereign protection of the state has failed to defend humanity from a virus that has shut down the world. In a time when the church has been "losing" its flocks in Europe, the mediatized emptiness of this *Urbi et Orbi* blessing highlights the paradoxical geographical and temporal dislocation at its own center. But it is also an affective space generated by a power of the negative—a liturgical mediatization of community in the shared absence of people because of pandemic isolation and lockdown.

Pope Francis was the first Jesuit and Latin American pope in the history of the papacy. The overlapping racial and ethnic-political dimensions of Francis's identification as a criollo pope from the Americas and as a Jesuit within the context of the contemporary Catholic Church are shown by the rhetorical, affective, and charismatic forces he embodies. Those forces have often portrayed him in contrast with his predecessor, as being a good pastor but not an excellent theologian.[3] Different modalities of

Francis's affective actualization have been described through actions such as embracing the crowd.[4] But during this wet March twilight at the beginning of the COVID-19 pandemic, the pope, mediated through computers and TV screens, embraces and blesses a crowd in absentia, cultivating a community of collective isolation by extending a communal, unspeakable force of unknowing. The mediatized moment of this *Urbi et Orbi* that the pope's liturgy sets in motion is an interconnection of apophatic, ethnographic, and theopolitical imaginations.

My thesis is that a central element of anthropological political theology is the productive intertwinement of these three registers. The COVID-19 pandemic brought to the fore the ways that apophatic spaces allow for engagement in what Michel de Certeau called a "tuning" into heterology. This is an unspeakable alterity to the symbolic order that may lay bare both conditions of vulnerability and the abiding violence of law, through making visible marginalized bodies and their socialities.[5] What political forces emerge out of spaces of "dazzling darkness" that are shared? How does a mediatization of a papal liturgical call for the protection of humanity (in absentia) become a call to justice? When Pope Francis asks, "Why are you afraid? Have you no faith?," he is also addressing faith as an heterological discourse, an attunement to a (protective) alterity through an uncharted, different sociality, a connection to others on an absent or invisible ground.[6]

Whereas political theology asks about "what" was mobilized in Francis's call to arms, anthropology queries the "how." When Francis recalls, "That they may all be one," this is not only a plea for social solidarity among humans but also a theological call for justice as a distribution of shared risk and for serenity in the storm of a global unknowing "because with God life never dies." This theological hinge is interconfessional, because Pope Francis is embedded in a movement of dialogue and encounter between different traditions and forms of knowledge. Yet anthropologists interested in the "how" remind us of another universal. The COVID-19 pandemic also laid bare intergenerational rifts, exposing the cultural disposability of older people and the agency of the young or nonelderly, as well as the racialization of primary care labor. It did so through a shared unpreparedness and systems of imperfect care.[7] Hence, an anthropological analysis of the Catholic theological premise of the papal "culture of dialogue" and an ecumenical "may all be one" is more powerfully understood through a juxtaposition of material, ethnographic, theological, and global "frictions" between different universals, whether the "global" scale of public health models, a Christian theological universal, or the Islamic Umma. When anthropology orients us to ask how claims for truth come about, then encounters and collisions of multiple universals produce gaps and interstitial moments. Those gaps and moments might be where a new possibility to counteract hegemonic formations arises and where justice might emerge as an alternative to a current order.[8]

How do these forms of justice emerge at the point of encounter and intersection? If affective and corporal intensifications that exceed their institutional frame of reference are key to populist crowds, then a crowd that is called into being in absentia may well blur sign and substance in multiple ways.[9] The force of this March 2020 pandemic crowd articulates a blurred and overlapping fear and a call for protection against viral and emotional contagion, as well as social dissolution.[10] This mediatized *Urbi et Orbi* operates through a distribution of grace as a form of justice that blurs the line between contagion and dissolution and that oscillates between the realms of the (in)visible. Hence, conveying spaces created by the pandemic though papal liturgical labor and animated by potent symbols, including the monstrance and ancient icons, highlights the intersection of apophatic, ethnographic, and theological dimensions. This intersection prompts questions about the political force emerging from withdrawal of protection and the theological implications of a call to care, faith, and justice.

So what insights can anthropology offer here? First, ethnography *activates* political theology, making a difference in the present, an incision into the body politics. By contrast, political theology invites a normative impulse into anthropology—how relations ought to be. It invites anthropological takes that do not remain circumscribed (and "stuck") by and in the complexity of the (im)possibility of description. That is to say, anthropology interrupts political theology by historicizing and locating its claims. Second, ethnography provides a study of forms of sovereignty that oscillate between life-giving and life-taking impulses, that shape and reshape promise, protection, and risk—with and beyond the case of the *Urbi et Orbi*—the triadic backbone that is also of capital finance and its economic theologies. Third, a focus on suffering and its management shows how an ethnographic thickness colors liturgies—by one definition, that which is not performed in one's name—and therefore how the impersonal activates relations and substances, as well as humanitarian suffering and related forms of humanitarian interventions' ethnographies.[11]

Yet to speak of political theology anthropologically is to work with implicit tensions of the respective disciplines rather than attempt to override them: Not all anthropological concepts are political-theological ones, even when we pluralize the field of what political theologies might be. Whereas anthropology has been concerned with the materiality and corporeality of living and forms of life and with the nature of relations, political theology is, in its original inception, conceptually exegetical (as in its

Christian form, biblical). However, together as a methodology and analytics continuum, they can help us to reapprehend conditions of the *nonsecular*.[12] We can also apprehend the meaning of living and dying in relation to humans, more than humans, the elements, and the supranatural. Here I would dare to ask, How could ethnography be performed liturgically, but not missionarily? And with what potentials and pitfalls?

Christian theology played an important role in the missionary zeal present in the birth of ethnography in sixteenth-century missionary (mainly Jesuit and Franciscan) writings in the Americas. Twentieth- and twenty-first-century social anthropology, as a discipline, has since rebuffed these original missionary aims and origins and their racialized imagination—an imagination that Willie Jennings has counterposed to a new theological hope of unveiling a Christian machinery of death and the demonic at play in the world, of the violence of a modern project of nationhood, private property, detachment, and failed intimacy.[13] However, anthropologists are also deepening our understanding of vitality, laying the groundwork for a granular politics of molecular transformation. An attention to a power of dying as rotting, cyclical vulnerability in the potent forces of geological, human, microbial, and vegetal materialities and temporalities lays bare the limits of Jennings's evocation of death and the demonic together.[14] Decaying as death is potential for political life. Moreover, an anthropological political theology can rekindle with this point of origin by engaging with the nonsecular. To expand on analyses and methodologies of the nonsecular is to wrestle anew with the intersection of the more-than-human substance and materialities of politics, conditions of unknowing, the nature of theistic indifference and obligations, and specific and located forms of life. To foreground this nonsecular domain is also to recalibrate a relationship between anthropology and theology by placing the "political" between them as a mediating term, one that opens to existing and potential forms of justice, beyond modern and liberal separations between church and state, the religious and the political. This recalibration is what an anthropological political theology is at its best.

As we collectively stated in the introduction of this book, a challenge for this project is shaping just and dialogical futures and reorientating scholarly work in a nonsecular direction. In the rest of the chapter, I take this challenge further, unraveling more of what an anthropological political theology might be through multiple ethnographic reflections: on postwar Bosnia, Afro-Atlantic cosmologies, denizenship as an alternative to citizenship, liturgical labor in migration, and apophatic hauntings of sovereignty. I want to show that ethnography is not just an "addendum" to political theology (or, for that matter, to theological studies). Rather, it is an engagement and a method of attunement to forms of "activation" of the political and the theological—in both their life-enhancing and life-curtailing extensions and orientations toward (in)justice.[15]

But what do I mean by *activation*? Activation is not agency, if we understand it as the possibility of making a difference located in and exercised by an autonomous subject. Activation is a force that traverses and animates the flesh and substance. It is immanent, and it disrupts oppositions between subject and object, Self and Other. By doing so it may point to alternate and different forms of justice. When political theology asks questions about how to go beyond a binary imagination of a top-down transcendental sovereignty and its related immanent self-mastery, it resonates with an anthropological attention to a here-elsewhere and to the nature of forms of alterity. Anthropological attunement to an alternative—an immanent presence of an elsewhere—provides a provisional grammar on sensorial formations. In other words, the activation that anthropological attunement makes possible is a different kind of listening for forms of life within a polis. And this form of activation through anthropological attunement takes place within a polis that is still informed by patriarchal, racialized, violent, and dispossessing forms of (divine) power and sovereignty. Consequently, attunement is not merely finding a voice, but is crafting a practice necessary for learning to hear.

By placing justice at the center of rethinking political theology anthropologically, we can also understand further emerging debates in the anthropology of religion. For example, we can appreciate a reconceptualization of Afro-Atlantic "religions" as more than a language of spirit possession and witchcraft and instead as a politics of potency and more capacious forms of justice. This is the case of studies on the multisensorial modes of spiritual citizenship in Trinidad and on the performance of Obeah understood not as "devil" spirits vis-à-vis rational logic, but as forms of consequential activation of the law.[16] An example is the Obeah face-down burials in Trinidad and Tobago, which were originally read anthropologically as a vestige of a "traditional" African, "witchcraft"-oriented past counterposed to the "right" of the law of a modern state. Instead these face-down burials are now understood as experiments with power, as a different and ethical engagement with the future—a different, enfleshed type of law moved by the "spirit lash" of the dead (but alive), haunting police forces' ongoing violent discrimination.[17] These types of anthropological works are challenging a binding and binaristic conceptualization of personhood and justice, religion and politics, by reclaiming a "divining" politics. This divine is not a mastery of a certain order of legitimation or justification, nor given forms of personhood or animistic qualities of certain "spirits" read as part of "religion." It is instead the realm of the just and the impersonal, how divine forces are activated and oriented in space and time, and how anthropology provides a robust critique of "religion" by foregrounding forms of life and death and activations emerging when inhabiting a rule impersonally.[18]

To be clear, I am calling for a specific reenchantment of politics through a theology that is located in a divine-immanent continuum of everyday life forms—the latter being central to anthropological work.[19] The everyday is where the practice of anthropological fieldwork takes place, but it is also where the "other" is encountered, as well as (mis)apprehended in ethnographic representation. The "field" as in fieldwork is also encountering an (im)possibility of naming the other—the constitutive failure of anthropology to ever fully know an Other (as culture, society, kinship. etc.). This impossibility sounds familiar to a Christian theological language.[20] As a working triangulation of power, divine power, and theodicy (as suffering), the "field" (as the encounter with an other or the ultimate Other) can also be studied as a threshold between the dead and the living, desires and the demonic.

ANTHROPOLOGY AND POLITICAL THEOLOGY: MAPPING THE NEXUS

"Anthropology" is not a unified field, but one that has been in crisis for a while because it is reckoning with its colonial roots. As a discipline, anthropology is grappling with its constitutive "we."[21] Yet it can still productively contribute to the denaturalization and deprovincialization of unmarked hegemonic concepts. From this enabling perspective in this section, I succinctly map existing nexi between anthropology and theology to make clear which debates an anthropological political theology builds upon, but also takes a distance from.

First, a Christian political theology is not enough. The depoliticization of theology has led to the theologizing of politics, then anthropology, which has historically placed cultural difference and otherness in the domain of what is to be human, has for a long time circumscribed God entirely out of its political equation.[22] This is a disciplinary separation—what Khaled Furani refers to as the "Anthropodom." Furani explains that "sovereign, secular reason alone is dedicated for interrogating an other it is able to recognize as mostly human and merely 'cultural.'"[23] This disabling demarcation has also extended to economic realms, as shown in an ethnographic study of *waqf* (charitable property) in Lebanon, where secularization manifests as "continuously separating religion from economy and privatizing it" and places charitable forms of sociality moved by faith and an ethics of care for the family into a "private" domain, counterposed to a Muslim "public" charity for the good of the nation.[24] If private and public demarcations are also by-products of secularization, so are disciplinary divisions between studies of cosmologies (as in the field of anthropology) and the study of theologies (as in religious studies and divinity schools). The political theology we reckon with and bring forward in this book is a rekindling of cosmology and theologies that makes us also aware of some of their respective blind spots.

The anthropologist Ryan Cecil Jobson has called for a "burning" of the discipline of anthropology to disavow its perpetuation of liberal settlements and its connection to them.[25] The discipline is at a pivotal moment, daring to engage anew with multiple forms of political vitalism and of sovereignty "from below" that challenge some of these liberal settlements—and anthropological political theologies expand on those. However, engrained in my analysis is a good amount of skepticism as to what political theology and anthropology *are*, while I remain open to ways in which they can mutually constitute each other, shape some dialogical futures, and use their differences and divergences productively. Taken together, they can offer a critique of liberal settlements and a query of the unfortunate "schism" between theology and cultural alterity, the natural and the supranatural, while decentering key disciplinary discussions beyond Euro–North American hegemonic archives. In fact, political theology cannot and should not be contained within the form of Christian theology that has been the product, at times co-opted, at times in the service of, European and American nation-state formations. For instance, there is indeed a long and rich tradition of anthropologists studying missionization and mediations in sub-Saharan Africa and Asian contexts.[26] Anthropologists have also engaged with humanitarianism in critical relation to Christian themes of suffering, witnessing, and redemption.[27] Many of these themes are informed, often implicitly, by concepts of sovereignty and human flourishing derived from a Christian political theology.

One example to consider is the current historical moment of the Roman Catholic Church, which has seen, as de Certeau argued, an increasing disconnection between the church as an institution and its credo. Many prioritize practice and performance over having "faith" and belief—people, lenient in their faith, may be more practicing than believing.[28] A *faiblesse de croire* (a weakness of believing) may well require a real overall transformation and rupture of Christianity as a religious institution, wherein its liturgy is marked increasingly by an aesthetic performative register. Such transformations have profound political implications, emphasizing the centrality of theologies of the body, its rhythms and enfleshed contradictions.[29] These (new) theologies may not all be confined and easily identifiable with religious institutions or with their dispositif, but rather emerge in response to the crisis and demise of such institutions and of the liberal settlement. As theologies travel through this perspective of "weakness of believing," they are deterritorialized and reterritorialized and currently (at least in Catholicism) revivified in the Global South. Some of these Christian-inspired theologies are a kind of spatialized craft—of being touched or affected from multiple directions of God's encounters—with various and politically contested effects. They can be a presence of God through a 360-degree experience and theologizing movements through and with the body. The body then becomes central to theological inquiries into vulnerability, which, as suggested by Wittgenstein, does not depend on knowledge (or belief) but on certain kinds of experience, such as suffering and the porous edges of hierarchical languages.[30]

Second, cosmology is not an estranged other of theology. In a 1995 anthropological work on Western cosmology and its Adamic inheritance entitled *The Sadness of Sweetness: The Native Anthropology of Western Cosmology*, Marshall Sahlins warns us that the Augustinian tensions, such as pleasure and pain, self and society, and brutish flesh and spiritual soul, have been the foundation for a long-lived collective "Western" investment.[31] Such investment, Sahlins argues, has primarily manifested in a Hobbesian, wolf-nature, political framework, where the state restrains the libidinal drives of individuals—in short, keeping in check our "antisocial" drives. In this argument, capitalism has been central to a social production of a *mana* or force lodged in the introjection of a fantasy of individualized consciousness. Such Western cosmology, and a Christian providential outlook of the unseen that promises rescue from the tribulation of matter, informs the current planetary environmental crisis, even as this cosmology is itself in crisis. This crisis of cosmological investment is evident more than ever in climate, financial, and migration configurations. A root of this cosmological crisis could be traced to the failing of a religious sovereignty and its historical hegemony, wherein promises of protection and integration into the "whole" and "sacred" body politic are offered in exchange for obedience. The pandemic dynamics have further eroded this notion of sovereign protection.

While thinking cosmologically is not new in anthropology, the unfolding debate between cosmopolitics and political ontology is a more recent development in the discipline.[32] In conversation with this literature, this project invites us to anthropologically qualify how a theological ground of politics might emerge in historical, affective, material punctuations and eruptions, violence and tribulation, and capital and environmental toxicity toward (more) just forms of life.[33] This is to say how to endow and craft a nonsecular analysis of (un)just forms of life with a force of the impersonal at play.

Third, God is cultural agency and an else-where. Another well-known set of sociocultural anthropological work has insisted on a more robust inclusion of God within an analytical anthropological framework of culture and sociality, particularly one focused on a study of what Joel Robbins calls the "suffering slot."[34] An increased attention to theology has been used to reorient an anthropological compass toward a horizon of "human flourishing"—understood as an advancement in both disciplines.[35] And this advancement has also been interrogated via key theological concepts such as atonement, eschatology, and final judgment to trace their implicit influence on anthropological theories of culture, agency, radical change, and the economy of the gift, thereby expanding anthropological theory toward theological considerations to see their mutual limits within a

Christian frame.[36] However, culture may also be a ground where anthropology and political theology diverge while sharing a departure from a secular/religious binary paradigm, which itself stems from a secularizing understanding of the world. Literary cultural lenses, for instance, can be a bulwark against political theology as it eludes and interrupts a Schmittian hierarchical relation between divine and positive law through an imaginative process.[37] This approach has further clustered around a theologically engaged anthropology that emphasizes a need for a more comprehensive account of theology in ethnographic research.[38] However, at times this perspective tends to overlook intersectional dynamics between the two disciplines. Starting instead with an intersectional rather than simply an interdisciplinary perspective (so through co-constitutive rather than derivative elements) helps to put into focus those exclusionary sovereign conditions of patriarchy and race formations that belong to specific reiterations of Christianity and Christian theology.[39]

To engage with theological frameworks (here in the plural; see Christian, Islamic, Jewish, Buddhist, and other polytheistic strands) requires also to focus on different societies' *logos* about and interaction with God as an *else-where* (or *here-else*) mediated often by saints and holy figures, the labor of dreaming, imagination, and the imaginal.[40] Ethnographic queries, in fact, have focused on hermeneutics, affective imagination, and material culture related to the presence of God or other forms of unnameable presence, exploring the nature of the "else-where," the immanent labor of godly imagination, and an importance of God, for instance, within a triadic formation of (Islamic) charity and political and economic leadership.[41] From these perspectives, theological orientations are always located within a specificity of time and space; they are forms of emplacement.[42] Spatialization is constitutive of theological foundations that shape and are shaped by everyday life. Thus political theology can be appreciated less as an epistemic universal and more as a processual, ongoing, located field.

Fourth, a focus beyond the state and its sovereignty is key. As an emerging conversation between anthropologists, theologians, and critical theorists interested in Las Americas, theopolitics is coming into being at the intersection of politics, theology, and anthropology.[43] Drawing on negative theology and on the work of Walter Benjamin and Martin Buber, theopolitics focuses on a "divine"justice and a sovereignty that is intrinsic to a never-ending provisional nature of political orders. In doing so, it diverges from a Schmittian understanding of sovereignty as the transcendental (theological) root of a secularized state, which understands the historical Christianization of the Americas as the working of a *katechon*—a forced that holds back the Antichrist in Europe but unleashes it within the so-called New World.[44] Hence, theopolitics offers a critique of anthropological works of Christianity that fail to apprehend the demonization of other ontologies and that overlook the violence characterizing the radical expansion of Christianity in the Americas since 1492 and its role in the formation and spread of racialized primitive accumulation (a predatory connotation of capitalism and its forms of labor).[45]

A failure and incompleteness of state sovereignty can be seen, for instance, through the theopolitical forces of the dead impinging on the realm of the living and through the rhythms and sensorial theatricalities of manifestation and withdrawal, of proximity and distance, which ultimately illuminate the limits of a vertical omnipotent, transcendental power of sovereignty (and sometimes its intrinsic undecidability).[46] Furthermore, a theopolitical perspective engages with theistic renderings that have emancipatory but also subjugating and terrifying effects, as seen in neopopulist manifestations, which are mediated by regimes of the senses and their theatricality, enabling incarnated rather than metaphysical forms of power. Theopolitical analysis then points to a rich ethnographic corpus to better engage with the *substance of politics*, partly moved by a justice that focuses on the provisional nature of political orders rather than a transcendental "out of time" and closed form of political legitimacy.

It is not new that anthropology has investigated sovereignty's imperial genealogies, how these shape uneven processes of state formation and globalization and their differential consequences for people making claims to autonomy and protection. In such entailments, sovereignty is both instantiated and undone and is where dynamics of crisis,[47] refusal,[48] insularity,[49] refuge and hospitality,[50] the stranger and the monster,[51] or the return[52] are embedded in imperial political theologies of the exception. Ethnography plays a critical role in documenting but also activating the ways through which religious aesthetics, economic practices, and political theologies are short-circuited into liberal/secular, national, and capitalist formations.[53] Here, it is important to mutually interrogate ethnographies of capitalist-religious, affective formation with political-theological renderings of the faith in the market and the guilt-traction of the "invisible hand" that moves it, for the ways they illuminate each other.[54] This is also a common theme in the tension between property and possession built into colonial histories of primitive accumulation. If a financialization of faith/guilt is both a horizon of imagined liberation (freedom of the market) and a substantive entanglement of differential entitlements, then sovereignty produces both emancipatory and subjugating collective formations.[55] So then anthropological political theology shows that a substance and a materiality of politics as the production of theological knowledge and its affective and enfleshed circulation are always localized, not in a metaphorical but in a tangible way.

I cannot do justice in this rough sketch to the plural and creative voices that have and are emerging in a dialogue between anthropology, theology and the political, within but also well beyond a Christian frame. As these debates are becoming stronger, a specific sparking fire between anthropology and political theology produces a methodological-analytic continuum on the nonsecular through a sense-based and affective analysis (and methodology) of forms of life, gendered body, and the flesh. This continuum focuses on an activation of cosmologies, of materialities of politics and a "divining" substance of sovereignty.

SOVEREIGNTY, BODIES, AND THE FLESH

A political theology beyond Christianity is also one beyond its Euro-American location. In this section I warn against a universalizing impulse of Christian political theology by pluralizing points of entry into sovereignty, and their resistance to theological abstraction while mobilizing an ethnographic thickness.

If a constitution of sovereignty in Schmittian political theology is framed via a state of *sovereign exception* and its politics of inclusion by exclusion, an African "modern sovereign" is marked instead by its circulation as a violent state of *transgression*. This idea has been explained by Joseph Tonda, working on and from Gabon, when he argues that magic is a currency of transgressive potency not only in Gabon, but also as an increasing condition of capital and the circulation of fetish imagery worldwide.[56] Here, the miracle is not (as it is for Schmitt) the religious correspondence to a condition of secular exception. Instead, the miraculous diverges from daily life as experienced by ordinary members of the community. This *divergence* is not a set of beliefs, but an embodied and psychic idiom that traverses Christianity, witchcraft, the *longue durée* of colonial regimes of debt-obligation, and the modern Gabonean state. Understanding the complex body of the sovereign requires zooming in on the fetish imagery and the enfleshed intersections of African spirituality, spirit possessions, Christian Pentecostal missionary, capital, and the state, not as separate fields but as co-created by the potency of transgression, wherein boundaries bleed into one another.

Moreover, sovereignty is always constituted through an enfleshed body, in a state of "being-value" or ascribed value, which is central to fetish imagery of capital, and God's work. Tonda highlights that the puissance of a Christian God is negotiated with "traditional" ways of life and with a sorcery and/or pagan horizon. A Christian God is equally magical, not antithetical to it. However, Christianity in its colonial impulse has demanded Africans, and in this specific case Gabonese, to sacrifice through forms of subjection to whiteness as a loss that has never been fully repaid. Turning the colonial debt into a powerful theological hinge in the "explosive mix of disappointed entitlement and restless material" has produced the "modern sovereign."[57] This "modern sovereign" in and from Gabon is marked by dangerous allures of commodities and miraculous-demonic money, a form of submission to the divine via *cosubstantiality rather than transubstantiation*. In short, it is a political theology of the guts that rests in the intricate relationship between fetish imagery, God's work, commodities and money, desires, and potency. That relation is affectively present through the urban capital's black cars with tinted windows, indexing a dangerous allure of dazzling and "delirious embezzlements"—"living dreams" that constitute an African (but also beyond) modern sovereign.

Beyond the specificity of an African state, what we learn here is a call (from the South) to resist collapsing exception into a global or universal take of political theology and to resist dissolving divergent worlds and their kinship or connection into a common cosmopolitan frame. Doing so requires, as Isabelle Stengers suggests that "the idea of ontological politics needs the transformative magic of tales, rituals, modes of palaver, ways of thinking-feeling with, which re-world our ruins and open them to partial connections with other worlds."[58] A political theology of consubstantiality invites us to apprehend justice and the undoing of injustice through the interstice between the symbolic order and the real, resisting an impulse to "translate" between divergent worlds. This exercise enables a focus on the psychic, distributed imagination and an imaginal of the divine—its dazzling and delirious forms as activated in the realm of the body, its parts, its multisensorial valences—in other words, through a power of the guts.

Another anthropological example of this power of the flesh is the self-crucifixions by Peruvian inmates in Ecuadorian overcrowded penitentiaries in the early 2000s.[59] These "inmate crucifixion protests" sought to draw attention to a regime that kept thousands of criminal suspects confined without trial. By crucifying themselves in a Christ-like form (in the *Penitenciaría del Litoral* on an overcrowded facility on the coast of Guayaquil), and through spectacularized and mediatized protests, the inmates sought to galvanize public opinion and reveal the horrific conditions of the Ecuadorian penal system. The sacrifice of bodily parts, their political-theological transgression, their mediatic national resonance against the invisibility of Peruvian inmates and the dire condition of living and dying in Ecuadorian penitentiaries, simultaneously highlighted and obscured the spaces of lawlessness intrinsic to penitential regimes in Latin America. A violent, mediated, performed self-sacrifice embodied through a Christian moral ground became an act of self-sovereignty. This example highlights how a focus on the body and its incarnated forms, particularly through violence and the mobilization of bodily parts, transgression, and self-sacrifice, is an important ground for anthropological political theology. It suggests ways to open an analysis beyond (or on the side of) the nation-state, informing how political theolog(ies) may emerge in stateless societies, while relinquishing the state as the only and one condition or site of political authority. Yet it is also bringing to awareness an important divergence between a political theology that builds on theological abstractions and textual exegesis and an anthropology that focuses on materiality and theological substances, as well as the different work performed by the labor of ethnographic critique.

The work of the imagination and mediation of forms of "sovereignty from below" allows us to move beyond merely performing a work of scholarly critique—here intended in Michel-Rolph Trouillot's sense of a spirit for crusades of forgiveness and reconciliation, or for an exercise of collective or global repenting identification with pastness.[60] Instead, and motivated by the pressing need for a work of doing justice and undoing injustice, critique is an intentional arousal to a transformation of the substance of politics. Configurations of justice cannot be separated from conditions of primitive accumulation, land, and empire. However, it is important not to collapse sovereignty into the empire, or to conflate the hegemonic with the normative, or to identify Euro-America as the only hegemonic location. Instead, anthropological accounts and perspectives may attune us to a political-theological justice that is grounded in a more nuanced understanding of the land. We see this justice in the case of the town of Gacko in postwar Bosnia. In *Waiting for Elijah: Time and Encounter in a Bosnian Landscape*, Safet HadžiMuhamedović explains a singularity of the land:

The landscape hid, chronic topically, keeping in reserve its fairies and songs. When surfacing, it appeared in strange situation, always to some extent affecting what can be said about it. . . . This grammar is not how people talk about the world, but how they talk the world, or rather sing the world. It erodes the projects of "ethno-religious" cleansing, making sure that *singing the world otherwise* would be difficult at least.[61]

This ethnography engages with a religious world that is *partaken in*, but also shared and unshared between, Muslims, Christians, and Roma people in Gacko in Bosnia, in the aftermath of a fractured postwar landscape. It explores the religious temporalities of a return of people to the land, its affective cosmologies, and how life, memory, and "religion" are shaped by the traces of a long-lived history of intimacy with the landscape. Through ethnographic insights, we are reminded how remnants counteract exclusive, normative identity domains promoted by ethnic-nationalistic practices and discourses that highjack a domain of identity, revealing that the counternarrative *is* the landscape. People continuously encounter these remnants through a land that "talk[s] the world, or rather sing[s] the world." Through this valley in Bosnia, we appreciate the intertwining of Christianity, Islam, and Roma people with land, its calendrical rhythms, recurring losses, and the ways in which leaving and returning home animate, in singular and irreducible ways, the landscape, the history, and the people inhabiting them. No amount of national and ethnic accounts can fully dislodge or encompass the lived affective religiosities of this land that "sing[s] the world." The land and its storytelling are also what nourishes and transforms the body in new kinds of kinship as creation and an engagement with the commons.

An ethnographic orientation to the theistic interplay between incarnation and kenosis may be too confessional, but it also holds potential for anthropological accounts aligned with a messianic imagination that reconstitutes, always provisionally, enfleshed forms of sovereignty from below. A theological reading of this theistic understanding only as Christian is too limiting. There can be *movement* informing and constituting the "divine" and sacred forms emerging in, through, and as a specific, singular land and elements that is as relevant to non-Christian ontologies studied by anthropologists.[62] Kenosis as divine movement is then singular, emplaced, never "universal"—it is beyond the subject, traverses as a force in movement; it is part of the imaginal. Hence I make here an invitation to research kenosis beyond its Christian frame, as for an attunement to a "divine" movement of justice that extends into land, memory, rhythms, flesh, and soil—in interreligious forms of temporal, spatial attachment but also violence, interruption, and death.

It is important then to analytically and methodologically become attuned to a theistic force in movement, of manifestation and withdrawal, via staying and studying "divine" incarnation and kenosis, rather than focusing on a sovereign mode unfolded through a liturgy of glory and "vertical" divine intervention and mastery. In this way the impersonal, as that which overcomes a mechanism of discontinuity and separation between who are, are not yet, are no longer, or will never be persons becomes part of a doing and an undoing of justice, beyond a sovereignty of possession and dispossession.[63] Focusing on movement and oscillation here allows for an anthropological political theology of proclamation by contact. Proclamation (a "speaking out" of divine force) is through an intimacy with the texture of life and life forms.

Beyond a politics that operates only through a subsidiary rationale of dominion and care, there is also an "otherwise politics" that emanates from a refusal that operates through the flesh and a care of nourishment. Afro-Atlantic cosmologies, often labeled as "magic" rather than theologies, have been challenging a mind/body dualism and transcend the colonial definition of belonging to a "bestial," raw, and uncivilized "other." A politics of the guts—in eating and preparing food—revolves around the concentration of substances and bodily parts and a capacity to release them at a certain given time while affecting spaces.[64] Sovereignty and potency here intertwine in new forms of kinship, of relations of care, fortitude, and protection.[65] Hence, politics of guts are always geopolitically located. They can also be explosive realms of alliances between militant forms of dietary care and purity of the body, as in QAnon and aligned forms of neonativism and conspiracy theories.

A politics of the guts unravels through ceremony and rituals, as in the "cannibalism" of the Eucharist rite. Rituals as a performativity and as a communicative practice have been a well-rehearsed anthropological focus. Yet revisiting a liturgical theological perspective through a rich array of anthropological analyses of rituals that highlight symbolism, efficaciousness, communicative practice, performativity, and repetition then allows us to shed more light on the nature of liturgical labor. Going back to the mediatization of the papal *Urbi et Orbi*, the ritual lifting of the monstrance, the theological activation of divine matter in the crowd's absentia, but for its own protection, shows also one of the powers of the liturgy as labor. It is performing an action, laboring for growth not in one's own name, and by doing so imbuing it with an immense power of an impersonal force.

By analyzing how rituals may have both religious and political qualities, a theological angle brings into focus the social situatedness and "transcendental" value of (ritual) labor, as a labor that is not done in one's own name but in the name of *mana*, the energies that anthropologists have used to describe what traverses and mobilizes a crowd for both "liberatory" action and reactionary forces.[66] As such, anthropological exegesis can shed light on the ambivalent political-theological nature of sovereignty.

Liturgical labor has been read as a public service historically mediating the surplus of immanence, involving a mediation of spectral materiality that is transferred from a sovereign king onto the sovereignty of people. Eric Santner, dwelling on the theological transformation of the divine in the flesh of Jesus, traces this surplus force in socioeconomic relations of capitalism and argues that the royal remains are co-opted into a capitalist transformation of the relationship between use and exchange value. Political theology indeed seeks its grounding in economic theology. However, while Santner's powerful analysis of the spectral nature of the flesh belongs psychoanalytically, theologically, and economically to the sovereignty of the king as a well as to an everyday of people and market relations, he leaves underexplored an important ramification in his analyses. For Santner, a dynamic of "pressure" on the "skin of modern man" is central in the formation of the modern citizen-subject.[67] Yet this dynamic pressure that serves as a barometer of the movement of a transcendental-immanent spectral materiality is not solely cultivated by a capitalist political economy but can be interrupted by a pressure "on the skin of the soul" (if I can use the language of the mystics). This pressure is singular, an affective commitment and dedication of and from specific bodies in space. This suturing of physicality and being as a location of commitment and human action can also *interrupt* capitalist relations of accumulation, abstraction, and dispossession and the forms of secular modernity and Christianity that have produced them. Then here, more than ever, anthropology does not merely supplement political theology by providing an "ethnographic," evidential ground. Rather, it offers a critical intersectional move for what is missing: namely, *the interruption and historical (dis)continuities that mark the political-theological*.

Another form of interruption of relations of abstraction and dispossession comes from the realm of the dead. The (violently) dead can interrupt the life of the living, in ways that manifest "divine," tangible disruptions of a political (i.e., state) recognition and its force of primitive accumulation. The ritual and imaginary reassemblage of the dead can be a regeneration of social life, as well as a ghostly presence of never-ending failure and the fruition or violence of political projects and ideologies.[68] Additionally, anthropologists have engaged with the annihilating violence inflicted upon Indigenous people and the resurgence of their healing spaces, as well as with forms of justice emerging out of colonial histories of predatory capitalism and an encroachment of the state and organized crime on civil and Indigenous society.[69] As in the case of the *longue durée* of histories of counterinsurgent violence in Andean Peru in the 1980s and 1990s, the reparative justice carried out by the mothers of the disappeared through their popular (in parallel to a lack of state) forensic and memorialization efforts shows that reparation is not solely about seeking state and legal recognition of atrocities. It is a cosmological and theological attempt to recompose the world through, with, and beyond an aftermath of violence—it is an anthropological political theology. The ungovernable human remains haunt present political communities and possess the power "to reclaim the past on their own terms," contributing to a wider theological and cosmological remaking of the living world.[70] This form of being in the relation between the dead and the living as friends and collaborators is where the dead (and the living) that do not share a physicality of matter show a cultivation of intimacy and care, a rhythm of proximity and distance—an enfleshed, material imagination with sovereign effects. This configuration is theopolitically potent.

On the other hand, from a non-Christian perspective and against Kant's notion of the indivisibility of modern sovereignty and subjectivity, Khaled Furani presents a compelling political-theological counterargument, delivered in an analysis of Palestine and the Israeli state. Expanding a current Islamic political imagination, he argues that the modern state is inherently transient. By foregrounding the Qur'anic imagination of the *khalifah* (caliph, a multifaceted ethically disposed political station) as an ethics of human self-fragility and the impossibility of self-oppression, he provides another example that challenges a Westphalian political understanding of modern sovereignty. He interprets the concept of *khalifah* as embedded in a horizon of human transience and fragility, to imply a service to God and to the community. This understanding of the divine (and modern) sovereign stems from a realization of human mortality as the basis for living beings flourishing on the earth. Furani explains:

> Forgetting one's mortality, considering oneself self-sufficient and one's possessions everlasting, disregarding one's finitude amounts to committing injustice toward oneself, or *dhulm an-nafs*, in decidedly Qur'anic terms. Requiring denial of self-wronging, the indivisibility principle cements state subjects' incapacity for acknowledging that they can commit wrong against themselves. Along with an attenuated sense of finitude, this false sense of righteousness eviscerates an ethics of fragility.[71]

To trust in a *khalifah*-embodied ethics means to trust that what we receive life and the earth as finite, and so they need to be handled with care. Living a fragile and transient existence on earth, in these terms, amounts to living out faith (*iman*) in God (as infinite) by finite and fragile humans on earth.[72] Both Tonda and Furani's works invite us to expand our grasp of modern sovereignty, and of what anthropological political theology entails. Rather than reifying the singularity and the indivisibility of sovereignty, we should delve into its multiple affective dimensions and explore what sovereignty and divining sovereignty do in terms of desire and agency, flesh and body, both within and beyond the state. Yet not all debates in political theology intersect with anthropological analyses, but a practice of fieldwork (as ethnography) and spatialization can be a fertile ground in common. Neither the "space" nor the "field" is a given concept. Instead, we should ask, Is political theology a spatialized terrain? How is it a phenomenon where social, theological, and material formations intersect?

VULNERABILITY AND TRIBULATION

A black and white "Polish Christ" can be seen behind a fence, situated in the corner of the private gardens within the Catholic Seminary of the Sacred Heart in Detroit. Located in an historical area of the city marked by infrastructure deterioration over the last fifty years, the seminary and its grounds encapsulate histories of urban strife. The marble statue with a black face and a white mantle, arms outstretched and welcoming, offers a gesture of peace, yet its layers of paint reveal the racial antagonisms of a city in conflict with itself. Originally white, then painted black, then repainted white, and then painted black again during the 1967 city riots, the statue indexes ways in which a holy infrastructure such as the Catholic Church is a racial battleground between the local Black population and the waves of mainly

Polish and Italian immigrant communities that constituted, earlier and then, the heart of the "flight to the suburbs" away from the center of Detroit. It is August 2019, and I am on site conducting research with a team of researchers. Standing on the corner of this beautifully maintained compound in the neighborhood of Jamison, flanked on one side by Chicago Boulevard, we perceive a paradoxical juxtaposition of exclusive cultivation and urban disarray. Outside the fence, nature is "reconquering" every inch of the urban landscape. It is an area in much need of infrastructure improvements, with its cracked pavement, overgrown tree roots, and damp grounds, particularly with respect to stormwater runoff and flooding, and at the same time very faulty streetlight infrastructure. The Sacred Heart Major Seminary stands on and is nurtured by this soil, yet in many respects it still does not "belong" to this area of urban Detroit.

We have just been consulting the archives of the seminary and have learned from the archivist of the changes in stewardship at the seminary and in the archdioceses of Detroit—which is a constituent governing body of this seminary. This seminary has long been a North American pedagogical hub for the translation and implementation of Second Vatican Council reforms and the work of the Christian anarchist and founder of the Catholic Worker Movement, Dorothy Day, while in more recent decades and configurations it has become a more traditionalist center of American Catholicism. Through the fence, the stark contrast between the presence of the Black Polish Christ and its traces of racial and economic violence is indexed to the multiple ways in which Catholic theology and pastoral care have taken form in this Detroit region.[73] This ethnographic snapshot gives a glimpse of ways in which the Catholic Church, along with other religious denominations, becomes complicit in the complex dynamics of racialization at the intersection of multiple processes of migration and urban transformation. It prompts us to consider the political ramifications of partitions that operate as a micropower of dominion, or their undoing, especially but not exclusively when it comes to the dynamics of (contested) dwelling and pastoral, theological initiatives.

A phenomenology of dwelling may well tell us what typologies of the urban are imagined and lived, and some of their related theological underpinning. According to Anna Rowlands's reading of Gillian Rose's work, there are three different typologies of the city, and it is important to settle on the one that is neither Athens nor the new Jerusalem. It is a third city that does not subscribe to, and actually refuses to be, a universal model of political community (as Athens) and its fantasy of inclusivity (as a utopian new Jerusalem). Instead, it embraces a "broken middle"—a space of vulnerability in common that accepts and reexperiences justice and injustice via a mourning that "returns the soul of the city" by challenging the inner and outer boundaries of both, to reinvent constantly a political life of the community.[74] In the same way, migration itineraries and their liturgies in some cases may reignite a mourning, a broken middle, rather than a jubilant *imago Dei* (not *Christi)*, through the thickness of an embattled civil and political representativeness of a *ius solis sanguinis* and culture within the (European) modern state.

Those broken middles are sensorially material spaces that intersect, in a Christian theological frame, theologies of vulnerabilities, spaces of immanence, corporeality, and incarnation. Or, in a theologically plural field, these broken middles exist where Islamic theologies meet hermeneutical processes of migrant representations and cultural integration, in spaces of tribulation, conceptualized by Stefania Pandolfo as a *barzakh* (a paradoxical and imaginal liminal space). We see this in the case of young

Moroccan men on their potential trans-Mediterranean journey. As Pandolfo explains, this space is "an imaginal border that joins by separating, such as an isthmus or a bridge, and that is the site of a passage for bodies and spirits; a partition, a screen, between two modalities of being, spiritual and corporeal, widening and delimiting, this world and the other; the site where the impossible can manifest itself in concrete forms."[75] In Islamic theology, a *barzakh* is also a paradoxical space of potentially "losing your mind," living a horizon of death that is both an "ungodly" annihilation as well as a godly potential death of sacrifice. But how can we write about these horizons? This is a challenge and a potentiality for an anthropological political theology, and the mishaps and strengths of the anthropological discipline have a long history.

Ethnography emerges out of an engagement with people and places, dynamics and histories, mediations and emplacements. Rooted in a colonial history, starting with early Christian missions, anthropological archives have inscribed otherness in life forms called "cultures," rituals, and livelihood reproduction, to some extent as figments of imagination. In its missionary inception in the Americas, ethnography became a methodology that contributed to the (physical and psychical) enclosure of native Indigenous people in systems of labor extraction and taxation that would provide metrics for centuries of a colonial grammar. Current abolitionist anthropology is still searching for more enabling and emancipatory practices.[76]

Nowadays ethnographic practice and its products may take many different forms: writings, a graphic novel, an artistic production, a dramaturgical affective theater performance.[77] The field has become more open and its boundaries more porous. A triangulation between histories, language, and the performativity of the body is an intersection that produces an ethnographic field. This has been central to the work of Michel de Certeau, in which the gendered body, its possession, and forms of incarnation throughout histories had become a primary site of the political-theological. This is also a triangulation that informs a query on tribulation—as an ethical, spiritual, and bodily orientation. And tribulation is at the core of an Islamic political theology. Islamic political theology arose from the historical experience of the Umma after the Prophet Muhammad's death and developed as a close articulation of jurisprudence and orthopraxis over an orthodoxy that is both experiential and utopian, conservative and revolutionary, descriptive and normative. In that sense it resonates with an anthropological political theology that is always located and mediated by specific histories, places, and material configurations as it charts movements between abstraction and concreteness. However, anthropological political theology in so doing is not a discursive practice that patrols epistemological boundaries at given historical times. Instead, and more excitingly, it can explore multiple configurations and forms of life that constitutes worlds through the supranatural, nonhuman presence, absence, and intimacy, addressing interlocking nonsecular realms of justice as horizons of possibility as well as disenabling political mechanism. Let me illustrate my reasoning with a further example.

Tribulation is an analytic for anthropological political theology as well as a complex Islamic theological realm.[78] In a condition of crisis and the fragmentation of local communities, of embodied violence and global financial inequities, ethnographies of tribulation allow us to see those tensions in a light of the noncontemporaneity of the past to a present. Echoing de Certeau's work on mysticism and the mystics, Basit Iqbal and others have shown that tribulation (with its theological resonances) requires defamiliarization from a tyranny of the present and a hegemonic linear understanding of cause and effects. Instead, it allows us to see the contemporary fragmentation of subjectivity and sociopolitical crisis as part of an Islamic articulation of transhistorical constellations (where relations cannot be explained through linear genealogical periodization, but as analogies and entanglements). Those constellations emerge through gendered bodies, their emplacement in space and time, and their unexplained potency. Similarly, as Bruno Latour pointed out, tribulation is a struggle of religious speech (as a mystic language) that has a force of setting up a desire without giving a logical path to achieve it—making the desire potentially infinite even while incarnated.[79] Ethnographic spaces capture an unfolding of divine and demonic forces in social relations that make the worlds through life and death, putting in motion endurance, resilience, catastrophes, and revival.[80] The lesson with and beyond de Certeau, Iqbal, and Latour is to let go of linear narratives, to engage with creative fabulations and a stretching of language practices, where history and its archives have been lost. Spatial, elastic, sensorial, and imaginary perspectives invite a recalibration of an anthropological political theology and a political theology's activation through a substance of politics and storytelling.

This reasoning extends to (Black) charismatic liturgical rhythms and powers of pneuma and to Christian charismatic "outstanding elasticity."[81] Both are emplaced theological orientation in movement, which does not fit into a desire for (linear) addition, sedimentation, and accretion. The hosting of and being hosted in the divine are in the movement and the elasticity of bodies and breath. Shifting beyond a symbolic and hermeneutic understanding of human-holy-divine relations requires more attention to theistic orientations, their spatiotemporalities, through which an attribution of life and nonlife takes different orchestrations of political values at local and planetary levels.[82]

As an emplaced example, the "Polish Christ" in Detroit is a spatiotemporally conflicted orientation of the Catholic Church in a historical emplacement. The Catholic seminary and the Christ on its grounds point to forms of violence and celebration of life enmeshed in histories of black-and-white tension in Detroit, and they index a Catholicism in its complex political-theological mediation of sovereignty of the Word and the body of Christ into an urbanity in transformation.

I hope my argument is clear by now that if political theology addresses a reenchantment of politics, one of its elements is the mystery of incarnation. Capitalism's battleground is now fought around life in emerging social spaces where life as immunity and life as survival rechart political terrains.[83] Here I am aware again of the weight that incarnation has in Christian theology, but I invite us to consider incarnation as forms of life that have a metonymical quality of the divine that may counter an encroachment of existing and perceived necropolitics. I say "perceived" here to underscore a wide spectrum of what understandings of necropolitics entails as, for instance, prolife and prochoice movements. Yet I still relate incarnation to the other-than-human substance of life that counterbalances in political ways an enduring silent and violent killing built into the manifestation of necropolitical forces.

Incarnation is not only a theological force of a fellowship of love and a paradoxical condition of enfleshment (divine and human at the same time), but equally a force of undoing. Incarnation and the incarnated bring forward a kinship, a set of life-enhancing relations in a theology of reconciliation—but not only.[84] A force of immanent eschatology, incarnation, and kenosis may well create a gap, a theistic movement oriented toward an attunement to the rhythms of undoing—an undoing of injustice, challenging a *longue durée* of inclusionary and exclusionary forms of (identity) possession and dominion. Here, incarnation should not privilege reparative or ecumenical moves in a universalistic spirit, but allow instead for divergent worlds to coexist and the fabulation to imagine archives of loss and worlds to come. Fabulations are also practices of storytelling and sovereignty that reimagine a present from a Global South.[85]

A battleground around "life" is key to contemporary capitalism impinging on nuanced and locally embedded forms of life, and in a Christian theological language, life is not only in what is manifested, but in what is present in the withdrawal of its manifestation. Beyond a particular Christian angle, then, we should ask what reenchantments of politics manifest in extramaterial dimensions of politics and in a capitalist market that has acquired the quasi force of a religious cult.[86] The contentious terrain of life as an infra- and extramaterial battleground is key to an anthropological political theology, with a starting point, but also well superseding, Christian theological ideas of wealth and the miraculous.

DENIZENSHIP AND THEOLOGIES OF HABITATION

Mobility and unsettlement are another important area of research for an anthropological political theology. They put into focus a key aspect of a Schmittian political-theological sovereignty, demarcating insiders from outsiders, friends from enemies.[87] In the early 1980s, anthropology began to focus on a powerful critique of "methodological nationalism" that was challenging the perspective that the nation-state is the natural and given constitutive unit of modern societies.[88] This critique led to a wealth of studies on the relationship between migration, mobility, and religions through a lens of transnationalism as well as ethnic and diasporic communities. Following the events of

9/11, the focus then shifted to studying the social and political imaginary of migrants as "others" in the national consciousness, who were addressed as "resident strangers" subjected to but also exceeding exclusionary forms of national sovereignty.[89] Those studies warned of the dangers of a political secularism that perpetuates exclusionary forms of state (mis)recognition by creating discourses of and on religious minorities.[90]

By the 2010s, anthropological studies of migration shifted toward mobility, understood as the flow of people, objects, and resources sustained by changing infrastructures that produce complex systems of immobility and unsettlement.[91] Paying attention to unsettlements involves foregrounding conditions of indefinite displacement and deferred arrival that go beyond a framing of migrancy and transition within nation-state paradigms. It calls for a move beyond universalist paradigms of integration, while asking questions about the social dynamics and the psychic investment that inform circuits of labor and resource extraction that are related to places and conditions that lack infrastructures of permanence. A political theology of impermanence has much to contribute to such a dialogue, in which concepts such as "eschatological immanence" and Jacob Taubes's occidental eschatology offer valuable insights.[92] These multiple reflections have also given ground to a critique of long-existing dynamics and underpinnings of the globalatinization of law management and immigrant governance, particularly within the European Union context.[93] This critique also exposes how globalatinization entails an ecumenical phenomenon, where the ecumene does not allow for its own outside to exist. In short, and perhaps boldly, mobility and unsettlement are what allow political theology to rethink the limits of universals.

Anthropological encounters and the clashes of divergent religious traditions are also political-theological grounds in action. For example, consider *andalucismo*, an ongoing movement that has been reimagining the aesthetic and discursive horizon of Andalusia since the time of the sixteenth-century *Reconquista* of *al-Andalus* and how it is manifested in contemporary Spain. Here, a political-theological lens gives strength to an anthropological focus on entangled affective histories, to a study of an alive theological ground of aesthetic sensibilities, multiple interconnected traditions forming a "structuring wave" of forms of life, in the "same" space through different temporalities.[94] In a context such as that of *El Andalúz*, categorical religious differentiation may well obscure aesthetic renderings and theistic forces that, at different times, may have constituted affective spaces in common. This terrain "in common" constitutes a challenge to current political languages of separation between Christian and Muslim worlds, and between Muslim migrants and Christian (Spanish) citizens.[95]

Borderland spaces are indeed prime terrains where political and religious regimes of sovereignty become entangled, and these entanglements often concern thresholds of habitation with respect to who and what is invited across. Borderlands are the singular and radical grounds of (un)connections between divinity and the unknown, and its gracelike nature.[96] In so being, these entanglements reinstate but also interrupt spaces for framing the problem of welcoming the Other beyond its capture by the nation-state or global humanity.[97] Hence anthropology lends to political theology a methodology to "excavate" forms oscillating between language and silence, mediation and the aesthetic, backgrounding and foregrounding of life. This "excavation" is of essences that are already with us, in visible/invisible, audible/inaudible, touchable/untouchable forms, and as such may open a political rearticulation of interreligious spaces. This rearticulation can be a redefinition and reorientation toward new forms of justice in living together. More systematically to the point, anthropologists have shown that the interreligious can be studied theologically as an everyday space by focusing, for instance, on how clashes and convergences around the spread of religious conversions, nationalistic fears, and covenant gifts reanimate and bitterly divide across Christian, Catholic, Sinhalese Buddhist, and Hinduist formations, as in the case of Sri Lanka.[98]

An entangled relationship between theology, migration, and unsettlements is indeed often an interreligious domain, not exclusive to Christianity. As has been shown in northern Italy and Morocco, there is a productive interface between Islamic theology and psychiatry and between migration and specific forms of state (mis)recognition.[99] Putting "God" as a moral compass into the picture enables one to focus on the psychic makeup of migrants and their gendered subjectivity. A focus on a theistic perspective, as a troubling and ethical living according to a god's presence and among demons, allows a broader understanding of the complexity of divine horizons, attachments to land, and embodied, ethical virtues in processes of (im)mobility and trans-Mediterranean migration.[100]

This political-theological lens focused on immanent eschatology can, in turn, inform anthropological understandings of migration and mobility that cannot be easily contained by liberal (and often secular) settlements but that resonate with what anthropologists such as Audra Simpson have called a refusal of state sovereignty.[101] How can "eschatological immanence" help us to study the radical resensing and repositioning of a *longue durée* of affective histories of hospitality, and their failures? It can do so by queering and desecularizing analytics that have infused studies of migration and mobility.

A focus on "human flourishing" has been central to Euro-Atlantic Christian theological and ethical reflections on migration and immigration, as well as to social teachings of the Roman

Catholic Church addressing migration in terms of structural injustice.[102] Friendship articulates a wider set of relations that are vital to society's formation but that cannot be fully captured by binaries of friend/enemy, self/other.[103] If relations are central to sociality, a focus on their analytical denaturalization and multi-scale nature helps recalibrate a Christian theological connection between friendship and human flourishing.[104] Doing so allows us to apprehend mobility and unsettlement through alternative forms of kinship and alliances that defy a universalist "church" framework, such as relations of flight, escape, and marronage, and create a stronger potential for salvation through a provisional nature of the world.[105]

Furthermore, a political-theological perspective here gives us further insights into contested fields of everyday life, sovereignty, and self-sovereignty and how they give rise to different citizenship formations. To illustrate this connection, I draw another short example from my own body of research among Catholic Latinx migrants in Rome. By focusing on the "religious in movement" rather than on religious movements, I have argued that superorganic yet immanent (Catholic) forces traverse specific migrant bodies.[106] Those bodies become invested in a particular office while performing public rituals in Rome, "the eternal city." We see this, for example, in the case of carrying the Lord of the Miracles, *El Señor de los Milagros*, through the streets of central Rome, culminating in the main Square of Saint Peter on the third Sunday of November. The act of carrying Christ's sedan, the haptic rhythm of the carriers' bodies, and the (un)touchability of that Christ by human hands constitute a liturgical labor performed by migrants who belong to the confraternity of the Lord of the Miracles. Political theology enhances an anthropological analysis here by inviting us to probe the political nature of a liturgy—what is made present and performed in the name of an Other that is traversing noncitizen and documented migrant bodies alike. Here the liturgy provides them with a form of "self-sovereignty" that translates into a form of morally upholding "spiritual citizenship," even for noncitizens, and taken as a whole, it informs an actualization, a movement of and for an (eco)theology of habitation.[107]

In these public, liturgical celebrations, noncitizens together with documented migrants acquire a spiritual sovereignty through assemblages (in the rhythm of carrying but never touching the Christ's sedan, traversed by the force of myrrh, air, fire, breath, and repeated chanting) that cannot be separated or abstracted from the *longue durée* of Atlantic affective religious histories through which they are coming into being. Exploring a theological force in movement, such a Catholic ritual blessing performed in a liturgy by a Catholic brotherhood through the lens of political theology, requires constant historical emplacement. Here a (expanded Christian[108]) political-theological and anthropological ground, together, sheds light onto a constitutive extimacy (a Lacanian intuition on being constituted by an outside) to the world that we can only partially apprehend and yet has subjective, urban, gendered, and migratory effects.

Catholicism has never been more central to these current issues of care, kinship, and salvation through mobility and unsettlement. The charismatic and affective figure of Pope Francis was a clear point of entry for discussions on a political theology of migration, mobility, and unsettlement. Pope Francis addressed migration and mobility in many of his encyclicals and interventions. For instance, in his 2014 address to the European Parliament in Strasbourg, he charted migration as a crucial opportunity to recalibrate a European culture through a lens of kinship renewal, warning of a Europe that is now a grandmother, no longer fertile and vibrant, to take responsibility for the present with its condition of marginalization and anguish, and be capable of bestowing dignity upon it.[109] In a message for the 107th World Day of Migrants and Refugees, Pope Francis reiterated that "salvation history thus has a 'we' in its beginning and a 'we' at its end, and at its centre the mystery of Christ, who died and rose so 'that they may all be one.'"[110] In other words, a struggle about the nature of a "we" actualizes society's potential through migration and forms of habitation, as it intersects a theology of salvation and Christology.

The charismatic figure of Pope Francis, the first Jesuit pope from the Americas, epitomizes an Atlantic Return—a movement of people, desires, and materialities from peripheries to the metropole of the Catholic Church and vice versa. Francis is part of this return, which to a certain extent solidifies and amplifies the Catholic social teachings of the Second Vatican Council. However, by sitting on the "throne" of the Petrine lineage as a Jesuit and a criollo pope (and the supreme liturgist of an *Urbi et Orbi*), he was also undoing and challenging the Power and Glory of that same "throne."[111] By placing salvation history at the center of the rights in migration and for migration, Pope Francis opens a tension between the "we" and the more than we. This "more than we" may well align with insights from Indigenous ontologies that challenge divisions between individual and dividual, transcending simplistic binaries, as in the classic anthropological concept that a dividual is characterized by being "more than one and less than many."[112] Hence a modern subjectivity posited in separation from the object is one of the many forms of subjectivity existing in the world. And foregrounding ontologies of the dividual, beyond the modern individual, parallels, in my view, political theological analysis of the third person—a critique of reductionist, dyadic language.[113] This current shift from a multicultural and global world into a more fragile, unknown, and multispecies planetary one, where species are clearly disposable, shows that the friend/enemy political-theological constitution of citizenship reflecting a divine authority of the nation-state, as outlined by Carl Schmitt, is losing some of its mileage. Thus there is a need for a new language to capture some of these challenging entanglements—and an anthropological political theology can contribute toward meeting this need.

So once more, *denizenship* refers to the constitutive and potential relational entanglements of inhabiting and caring for this planet—coming into being is always a relational inhabitation. A performativity of *Heimat*—a German term that in its English translation encompasses more than the home, including conditions of habitation and the geopolitical forces that shape affects toward it—foregrounds a centrality of a sovereignty-denizenship rather that citizenship connection.[114] A focus on denizens of the planet enables a possibility of imagining ecologies of belonging where both denizens and the world come into being in "mutual exchange."[115] Feminist analyses have connected denizenship, migration, and mobility to new cultural and aesthetic potentialities, as a form of ecology of practice and worldmaking through habitation. As such, denizenship can have a direct impact on the polis and its (im)mobilities beyond a disembodied universalism or essentializing identity politics. Yet, denizenship is not simply an oppositional category in relation or as an alternative to failing conditions and aspirational desires for citizenship.[116] Nor is it simply a condition emerging from a sovereign decision based upon who is a friend or an enemy, a host and a guest. It allies instead more profoundly to ways in which kins are (un)made and (new) human and multispecies alliances are formed or severed through, I argue, emerging, Gramscian cultural and political (counter) hegemonic forms. Here denizenship can help us move away from a modern sovereignty bias toward monotheistic religions, expanding political theology toward a focus on multivectorial, kin entanglements and pluriverse relations. How we humans and multispecies may be obligated by relations to God or gods, or also as god(s), may well be indifferent to humans.

Pluriverse relations query how they may be simultaneously divergent (not translatable between worlds), highlighting the limitation of a "classic" constitutive aspect and a desire of the anthropological discipline: comparison. Yet, theologies of creation can find new paths for anthropology away from an original anthropocentric lens. A "radical ontology," characterized by generative dislodging of a straightjacketing of self-sovereignty and divine and human agency, recognizes the "opaque" entanglements of human, nonhuman, and beyond-the-human relations in the making of place and forms of habitation, all of which constitute denizenship.[117] A renewed primacy of kin care is central to this denizenship, involving relations that cannot be contained by a dyadic and vertical theology of subsidiarity (constitutive since the early twentieth century of the social teachings of the Roman Catholic Church), or limited to a pathological rescue of the poor and afflicted. Instead, they are multivectorial forms of passionate and affective constitutive obligations.[118]

However, it is important to recognize that a romanticized focus on denizenship can become an exclusionary inclusiveness, where the relational formations that are put into focus may not always be emancipatory or liberatory, but may entail exploitative and predatory dimensions. An exclusionary inclusiveness was originally perpetuated by ethnography as a discipline when it played a key role in constructing metanarratives that portrayed Indigenous and First Nations people both as a "savage slot" and as a redemptive communitarian, utopic subject, echoing the Western imagination such as depicted in Voltaire's *Candide*.

To counteract this pervasive pedagogy, scholars like Michel-Rolph Trouillot have engaged with historical subjects in their un-redemptive singularity, foregrounding the complexity and uniqueness of their experience. Trouillot writes that the "historical subject is out of reach of all metanarratives, not because all metanarratives are created equal and are equally wrong . . ., but because metanarrative claims to universality necessarily imply the muting of first persons, singular or plural, deemed marginal. To say that otherness is always specific and historical is to reject this marginality."[119] His argument highlights the intertwinement of an imagination of Europe, its political economy, the anthropological discipline's original construction of an oppositional "native," "utopic," "savage slot," ultimately creating a space, a gap now slotted in more recently with the figures of migrants, noncitizens, and refugees. Hence, by making denizenship part of a political-theological analysis of crisis and mobility, we can appreciate the limitations of (Christian-infused) discursive practices that had perpetuated notions of migration as a product of a host's imagination, characterized as either savage or redemptive. Denizenship is neither savage nor redemptive, but it can be a path of shared vulnerabilities and an unlocking of social and multispecies justice.

A Euro-American Christian missiology that historically assumed a self/other, converted/unconverted, and now a host/guest distinction is challenged by current geopolitical and ecological convergences that expose the limitations of sovereign protection by the nation-state. Where is protection to be found now? And where is the protection of the nation-state, and its Leviathan, when its power of protection is crumbling? This is precisely what the *Urbi et Orbi* liturgical labor, with which I opened the chapter, is about. Moreover, to address the intersection of denizenship, justice, and migration in political-theological terms requires confronting a sort of *theological haunting*—an attachment to a power of theologies of possession and dominion that have fueled identarian politics, while promising integration through accumulation by dispossession.

Letting go of this theological haunting is no small feat, but it is one step in the right direction and involves embracing renewed practices and theologies of habitation. Pope Francis's encyclical "Laudato Si'," on the relations between humans and multiple sentient beings, has sparked extensive debates in this direction. Drawing on the tangibility of the planetary crisis and First Nations' acknowledgment and recognition, this encyclical has opened a reflection on multiple forms of habitation and the necessity to power up a rescaling of the economy though a Franciscan-inspired economic theology. This theological intervention is part of an ongoing reflection whereby Pope Francis has drawn attention to capitalism's culture of waste and our universal denizenship on the earth as our common home in order to mobilize clergy, laypeople, and people of other faiths or nonbelievers for an integral ecology of pastoral, cultural, and ecological conversion in the interests of our collective survival. Geo-theologically, Pope Francis has highlighted the need for European society—which, as already noted, he compared to aging grandparents—to rejuvenate its long-existing cultural values through the infusion of new immigrant blood.

As discussed by Schmitt, dominion not only is a renaming of the earth, a force of expansion and encapsulation of land that came with forms of Christian missionization, but it also points to related forms of self-sovereignty, scrutiny, and account to oneself—a confessional mode. Dominion is indeed both a theological and a geopolitical concept informing a rich yet also exclusionary history and manifestation of the subject as a bearer of rights. Here, there is a long theological thread that links sameness and otherness to dominion, mobility, and nativism. This is the case of Renaissance anthropology, which, through Bartolomé de las Casas's theological position, shaped a way in which native peoples' "difference" could be read as "cultural" and thus within a sameness of humanity guaranteed by potential conversion to Christianity. To anthropologically attune with (Indigenous) spaces of divergence is also to reckon with the epistemic violence of some of the early forms of missionization, as they have informed problematic, later ramifications of modern anthropological and social sciences' drives for universal, comparative methodologies.[120]

To sum up, then, in a condition of increased border controls and anti-immigrant neopopulisms, it is vital that an anthropological political theology focuses on denizens' practices in relation to an economy of the commons, a transformation of sovereign protection, and states of offence. This is particularly important for relations of (un)care beyond the current violent end of the liberal settlement. The liberal settlement, understood as the historical and imaginary division of the world emerging from the Cold War of democratic/undemocratic, Western nation-states versus "undemocratic"/Global South ones has shaped the phantasmatic imagination of a self-contained, purposefully driven liberal subject, and the economies of dispossession and attachment to phantasy of dominion and control that such subjectivity entails. We do not have a language in common for this beyond-settlement as yet, but we are fully enmeshed in it.

A METHODOLOGY OF THE NEGATIVE

To conclude, I would like to draw attention to a power of the negative for an anthropological political theology. The *power of the negative* refers to an experiential, kenotic emptying out as an openness and vulnerability to the world in constant change, but also to the powerful, political link between negativity and affirmation that prevents any form of stasis and is enmeshed in creative lived revisionism.[121] For the theologian of late antiquity, Gregory of Nyssa, the openness that takes place in a radical negating of the possibility of knowing God (or the possibility of certainty) is the conception of apophatic theology—an insistent desire to know God through recognizing what cannot be known about God.[122] In twentieth-century continental philosophy, negative theology lays bare the gap between semantic and somatic life in a theological weighting of all discourses—in a Schmittian sense—in particular as it regards the Law, as always transcendent, theological, and to come. A power of the negative, as well as its historical dialectical form as the labor of the negative, is not nihilistic, but a concrete, immanent form and a "work of discovering relations where there seemed to be none."[123] A power of the negative is constructive and associative with a capacity for threshold habitation (living on the edges) as an ethical project of self-overcoming and a movement of decentering, of thinking from an outside.[124] Indeed, a deeper understanding of a power and methodology of the negative enables generativity of all kinds. For example, it implicitly informs anthropological work on ruins, ruination, and negative methodology in conditions of mass violence.[125] It also allows affective spaces to open by being acted upon, beyond a model of religious subjectivity based on a capacity for agency and self-cultivation.[126]

Ethnographic works on apophatic spaces, a force of the negative, have also built on Michel de Certeau's notion of a "tuning" to heterology (understood as the "speaking" of the Other), which underscores an aliveness at the borders of logos—as I explained previously.[127] The power of the negative opens a space of dwelling in an enigmatic threshold between knowing and not knowing as a process (not an object). Ethnographically, this takes form through spaces of unknowing, vulnerability, and the doing and undoing of injustice, and as a power that is always theistically provisional thus is extremely powerful. So, a deepening intersectionality between political theology and anthropology should explore how enlivening the borders of the (un)knowing has powerful sustaining, as well as annihilating, political possibilities.

This intersectionality may inform an ethnographic lens, such as in the case of undocumented migrants whose bodies cannot be named as such and yet who function in a stratified labor market of essential services on which much of the world depends.[128] It is a body politic that gets redeployed in a kind of double negation of the undocumented migrant: within a placelessness of enormous production and where undocumented migration is also an aliveness of borders, a force of political undoing and unraveling. Then how does a power of the negative inform a radical and political critique of emerging labor regimes and subjectivities? And what ethnographic and anthropological political theological forms does it currently take? I see this book opening up these directions of query.

A power of the negative puts back into the picture the movement between incarnation and kenosis, foregrounding and withdrawal, and intimacy and distance. As I have already explained, these terms are complex and have a long theological history. However, I prefer the term *incarnation* as a theological mystery regarding the intransitive and unreciprocal gift of life, a way of embodiment. The category of the *gift* is a widely used term in anthropology that derives its meaning from Maussian ideas of personhood—a capacity for reciprocal exchange. By foregrounding a notion of incarnation, I propose to reckon with how life is received and studied through an attunement to a baroque-like sensorial and theatrical reproduction[129] that asks us to think of methodology and theory as a continuum, where practices of writing are intimately tuned to practices of reading as forms of attention and intensification.

I do not wish here to make a melancholy gesture toward thirteenth-century Benedictine monastic rule and life as studied by Agamben and its modus vivendi.[130] But I cannot stop thinking about what training and attunement the work of praying does to an architecture of the heart and its modes of attention.[131] Constance Furey has showed that Martin Luther's true engagement with the Psalms is a "vivification" of words, transmitting a life force of salvation. A nonsecular anthropology may teach us how a life force is at play from a specific body or form of life and its architecture of attention.[132] A political-theological mode of analysis may itself be very distant from, but also become intertwined with, modes of training attention and inhabiting thresholds of unknowing. Yet, as a methodology of an anthropological political theology, we need to engage with what Saidiya Hartman calls narrative restraint, which is, of course, in friction with an exegetical desire to give an explanation. The purposeful withholding of narratives, the refusals of closing hermeneutical circles, the habitation of spaces where no words can be found— and no words should be found—are vital to tame the incommensurability of violence to language.

Anthropological research has been drawn to the study of the political purchase of the negative and "negative methodology."[133] Conceived as extramaterial potencies of rubble, traces, and "ruins," the power of the negative has permeated the life, war, and postwar landscape as well as colonial relations—all of which have put into focus the limits of political accounts of property, as well as nominalist and mastery-based ideas of sovereignty. For that matter, it has also put into focus a politics that is limited to visibility and tangibility and has shed light on a capitalist, destructive violence traced through the aftermath and endurance of rubble. The "negative" at work in these studies is implicitly in tension with a long theological tradition that has explored a force of the unknown. It is a radical political possibility nested in the power of the negative that can be theologically indexed in an uncertainty of not-knowing *God* "that infects our knowing of anything that is *not* God."[134] More than ever, anthropological studies of the power of the negative ally with what Benjamin calls the messianic: a "weak power" *within* history that refuses self-totalizing and self-eternalizing projects of endless growth and positivity. And yet, in a theological domain, the power of the negative is also in tension with theodicy—the unthinkable conditions of suffering as a godly (un)manifestation, as within a horizon of life, not a beyond in death, but within the theologically powerful underpinning of tribulation that I have already underscored.[135] The enfleshed insight of rubble and the limits of accounts of sovereign self-mastery can also be very spectacular and hypermediatized conditions of unthinkable suffering and its seeking for protection. That is precisely what was mediatized on March 27, 2020, in Rome.

Finally, an openness between anthropology and political theology does not have to hinge on the slippery field of ontological otherness. Posthuman scholarship has highlighted the secular limitations inherent in contemporary anthropology as it has privileged studies of Amerindian ontologies and its shamanism as a kind of "benign: and "tangible" new animism—a classic area of anthropological research.[136] But by doing so, once again, it has relegated God and the gods to an "invisible" ontological otherness or bypassed sovereign dynamics of church-statedness. This Amerindian ontological accent has been criticized for staying within a secular-liberal framework that continues to privilege human agency over human subjugation (to the divine). Instead, scholars such as Mayanthi Fernando have suggested that if we perceive God or the gods in relation to humans and multiple species through bonds, obligations, and partaking rather than through a liberal, egalitarian notion of freedom, we may have more capacious analytics to navigate an ecological political theology in the triangulation of porous selves, multispecies, gods, and supernatural beings.[137] This would be a foundational move, I argue, for a nonsecular anthropological political theology.

If our shared projects of anthropological and theological research align with an emphasis on an anthropology of the otherwise (becoming and relinquishing into an otherwise) rather than ontological otherness, we can connect with projects of political ruptures and transformation. Anthropology of the otherwise is necessary for an insurgent cartography: "a spatial process of excavation and sedimentation—of being together on the ground, in time, with time and through relationship."[138] It calibrates an insurrection of knowledge, and it produces and inhabits otherwise epistemological fields of Black studies and of Black and Latinx theologies. In all these fields, being otherwise and insurrections are linked, and a theopolitical anthropology that participates, through a close attention to materialities, relationality, and commitment, in this anarchist tradition may well help us to navigate the political borderlands characterized by the "persistence of forms of the sacred in a world that no longer relies upon God."[139]

If my departing point has been that an anthropological political theology recognizes the persisting heteronomy of modern politics, despite secular claims about its immanent self-foundation, I hope I have highlighted how discontinuities, analogies, and entanglements disturb secular and religious conceptualizations of the sources of power and authority. However, paraphrasing Carl Schmitt, not all anthropological concepts are political-theological ones, even when we pluralize a field of political theologies. Yet, if changes in the nature of concepts allow for changes in the forms and intelligibility of practice, I have argued that practices and enfleshment of the field, materialities, and anthropology's storytelling are inseparable and constitutive of "abstract" political theological concepts.[140] This configuration charts a potential for a field of anthropological political theology as praxis, method, and analytics for an attunement to forms of justice. As such, it is a storytelling, a mode of listening to incarnated politics, immanent-divine legitimization and delegitimization, liturgical forms, icons' (contested) emplacements, and relational life forms of the commons. The canvas out of which this storytelling keeps emerging is gendered, racialized bodies, tribulation and decay, and human and multispecies temporalities. And of the handle of the paintbrush, we should never be sure.

Imagine: I am in one of my classes, a cold, bright winter morning. The daylight struggles to peek through the basement windows. Inside, we are sweltering as the old pipes rattle, clearly not functioning properly. We are surrounded by university buildings that served both as connectors and barriers to the "real" city. Yet, we listen attentively to one another as we read aloud some passages from Meister Eckhart's famous Sermon 52—to be empty of all creatures' love is to be full of God, and to be full of creatures' love is to be empty of God. In our attentive silence, this is cultivation of listening.

A First Nations student asks if we could share experiences in which students successfully overcome a desire of fostering "self-mastery" and "individualization." I say I do not know, but together, we focus on how, even if we do not "know one another," we are all interconnected, even if influenced by "winning" or "losing," excelling or failing perspectives—and what it may mean to try to let go of these entrapments. Connecting to this present in class—we sit in silence for a moment.

A taste of kerygma—a divine, voicing-aloud mystery—glimpses through this attentive canopy of people. This glimpse may reveal the mystery of a "sacred" commitment, a covenant of commonality, a reimaging of time and space in a transformative way, unfolding sociality through shared reading aloud beyond the usual constraints of "productive" time "in a class at university." It is a glimpse of how an activation of political theology is in the wisdom of softening more and more the need to know, folding us together into a (political) space, maybe a radical, ultimate sense of home in the here and now.

4

LOOKING TO THE FUTURE

Emerging Pathways

LUKE BRETHERTON

The works discussed here conform to the "rules" about the future of political theology set out in the first chapter. In the field of Christian moral and political theology, these rules can be summarized as follows:

1. Treat Christianity as a means of grace and disgrace, recognizing its complexity and ambiguity and being attentive to its historical variations and development.
2. Work with an open conception of politics, one that looks beyond statecraft and questions of sovereignty to how politics is the craft of forming and sustaining a common life over time with others in specific places.
3. Ground scholarship in a nonreductive, nondeterministic, and nonmaterialistic conception of the human that includes a central place for the dignity of each person and the intrinsic nature of human freedom and creativity, both individually and collectively, and that attends to the ways that human life is constituted by and enmeshed within other than human ways of being alive.
4. Reject an immanent frame and secularism as an ideology.

5. Avoid abstraction and exercise epistemic humility by beginning with and attending to the lived realities of specific places and people, particularly of the poor and marginalized.
6. Ensure that work is interdisciplinary and crosses boundaries of geography, history, and religious and philosophical tradition.

In terms of characterizing the work highlighted in this appendix, I add another set of criteria to this list. These criteria include the following: Work should resist telling a story of either decline from a Golden Age or one of inevitable ascent and progress. Instead, it should be properly historical, that is, attentive to how things getter better *and* worse, often in paradoxical ways. It should also resist telling messianic stories about how one single approach, school of thought, subject of history, or set of experiences is the answer to everything. Instead of these kinds of ideological and antipolitical narratives, the works cited here tell stories of life in the saeculum: the ambiguous, fissured, conflict-ridden time before Christ's return. They are stories that narrate how, as an arena of discourse about the meaning and purpose of human life, Christian political theology involves both continuity and change as the church draws on its intellectual inheritances to respond to different contexts while innovating new ideas and practices in the face of emerging challenges. Following from this last point, the work highlighted here also avoids setting up false dichotomies or operating with binary, either/or thinking. And while it dares to think at the site of contradiction, it refuses Manichean stories of goodies and baddies in which all the wrong is on one side. Instead, it attends to what it means to think and act in a complex world where, no matter who you are or what your subject position is, everyone is fallen and finite.

One further word of explanation is needed. The focus here is not on books directed to specific issues or policies. Rather, the focus is on works that address the nature of political life as such and that, along with describing their material and social conditions, excavates the meaning, purpose, and character of political relations. In doing so, these works question fundamental aspects of how political and economic order is constituted and imagine different, generative possibilities for life together. In addition, these texts do not simply attend to how Christian beliefs and practices can be heard playing out in political life; they also seek to write in a constructive and confessional theological register. Given this last criterion, works by, for example, Giorgio Agamben and Achille Mbembe are not cited, despite being important figures in contemporary political theology.[1] And given this focus, not cited also are classics such as Augustine's *City of God*.

I do, however, begin with two new "classic" sources that meet all the criteria just listed. Echoing the introduction, rather than situate the origins of political theology either in a Eurocentric narrative or in a story only focused on the margins, these two sources point to alternative, "Black Atlantic," and insurgent catalysts for modern political theology that center on the intersection of metropole and periphery. These two initial works also set up the following discussion by being geographically limited to the Atlantic world, a deliberate focus.

The first is *The Interesting Narrative of the Life of Olaudah Equiano, or Gustavus Vassa, the African. Written by Himself* (1789). Published just before the French Revolution, the text can be taken to mark the shift from the early modern to the modern. It became a key point of reference in the emergent abolition movement, arguably the first modern, international social movement, the social movement itself being a distinctively modern political form. The text also exemplifies Christian humanism as a modern form of political theology that is central to the alignment of Christianity with democratic, nonviolent movements for justice.

The text itself is increasingly taken up, both critically and constructively, in postcolonial streams of thought.[2]

The second, alternative classic source is the work of William Apess.[3] Apess was a Native American convert to Christianity writing in the 1830s who not only wrote the first autobiography by a Native American but also led a successful legal challenge to the white settler political authorities in Massachusetts, known as the Mashpee Revolt. The revolt resisted the enclosure and dispossession of the Indigenous people living in Mashpee while also restoring their democratic self-government. Apess can be read in dialogue with and as anticipating the development of American Indian liberation theology as articulated by George "Tink" Tinker.[4] As a Christian humanist, abolitionist, and antiracist writer who is both inside and outside the colonial and capitalist world he inhabits, Apess, like Equiano, has a complicated, hybrid identity that resists easy categorization.

An important and vibrant stream of contemporary Christian political theology engages and interprets historical themes, practices, figures, and texts in the Christian tradition like those of Equiano and Apess in a way that puts them in conversation with contemporary concerns. In doing so, this work refuses to posit the need for a complete break or rupture with existing forms of belief and practice due to their complicity in historic harms. But neither does it simply repristinate the tradition or write erudite footnotes on classic texts. Rather, this work constitutes a form of reinspiration at the point of fracture, a renaming from the site of a wound. That is, it breathes new life into what has become dust. It can also be framed as *ressourcement* from the margins: It seeks renewal by reinterrogating themes, practices, figures, and texts, both well known and marginalized, against the grain of their dominant reception by being attentive to the experience of those on the underside of history. For example,

Matthew Elia reinterrogates Augustine by drawing on Black studies and histories of slavery to think with and against Augustine about how mastery and domination determine core aspects of Christian belief and practice as well as societies shaped by both Christianity and the afterlives of slavery.[5] A good example of retrieving a marginalized figure is Emily Dumler-Winkler's rereading of Mary Wollstonecraft as a moral and political theologian over and against how she is ignored as a source by theologians and treated in a wholly secularized way in feminist thought.[6] Dumler-Winkler draws on Wollstonecraft to develop a constructive account of how to link formation in virtue and struggles for liberation.

The work just cited primarily uses historical sources for descriptive, analytic, and critical purposes. A parallel emergent stream of Christian political theology that is more explicitly normative and constructive mobilizes historical sources in dialogue with diverse theoretical and philosophical resources to advocate for distinctive positions that are creedal and confessional while also being critical and contextual.

The first example of this kind of work is Andrew Prevot's book on prayer (also highlighted in Lloyd's section, "Crossing and Deepening").[7] Through close readings of a diverse set of interlocutors, ranging from European phenomenologists and systematic theologians to Black and Latin American liberation theologians of the Americas, Prevot articulates how prayer is not only constitutive of praise but can also be a vital practice in countering the subjective conditions of domination. The work revives an important line of thought that integrates spirituality with resistance to domination and thereby refuses the ancient binary between contemplation and action.

Matthew Jantzen does something similar for the largely ignored yet crucial doctrine of providence as a way of thinking about how time and space are ordered by theologies of history. By putting Hegel, Karl Barth, Black liberation theologian James Cone, and Womanist theologians Delores Williams and M. Shawn Copeland into diachronic and synchronic dialogue, Jantzen develops a constructive political theology of how to read God's action in history as indexed to justice and against how the direction of history is read to warrant white supremacy.[8]

The next two books focus on how forms of ecclesial life can embody alternatives to and furnish means of resisting the hegemonic form of modern political economy in the Atlantic world. The first is by Keri Day, who "reimagines" the Azusa Street Revival and early Pentecostalism.[9] Pentecostalism is much derided as either so heaven-focused that it is no earthly good or so worldly that it represents a form of sacralized capitalism. Against these kinds of dismissive readings, Day interrogates how early forms of Pentecostalism, albeit in ambiguous ways, can resource a vision of democratic politics that is able to resist the gendered and racialized structures of capitalism and embody alternative forms of life centered on justice, generosity, and mutual care. Alongside the Black radical tradition (and reading Black-led forms of Pentecostalism as a contributor to that tradition), Day draws on affect theory and Black feminism to develop her constructive political theology of a nonstate-centric conception of democratic citizenship.

The second is Elizabeth O'Donnell Gandolfo's reframing of martyrdom.[10] Gandolfo builds on a shift in Catholic theology whereby martyrs can now denote those killed in pursuit of justice, love, and solidarity with the poor—what Gandolfo, following Michael Lee, calls "martyrs of solidarity." Through historical and theological analysis of the political economy of extractivism and the lives of six "ecomartyrs" who were assassinated defending the environment and the rights of Indigenous communities,

Gandolfo develops a constructive ecopolitical theology. In doing so, she develops what might be called an "environmentalism from below" that hears the cry of the earth and the poor as a single plea. As a work of ecopolitical theology, her book points to another important emergent stream of political theology: namely, work that is developing accounts of human moral and political agency as constituted through mutually entangled relations with nonhuman forms of being alive and that sees nonhuman creation as having political agency.

Gandolfo is mindful of the contradictions and ambiguities of Christianity and the Catholic Church in Latin America. This awareness is shown by how the book brings Catholic social teaching and Latin American liberation theology into dialogue with decolonial thought, Indigenous cosmologies, African heritage religious traditions, ecofeminism, and conceptions of *buen vivir* and the commons. A key reference point throughout is the papal encyclical "Laudato Si'" (2015), which represents a form of magisterial or official political theology that embodies the criteria previously outlined. However, in contrast to "Laudato Si'," Gandolfo's work articulates how to do Christian political theology at the intersection of and informed by multiple cosmologies.

Gandolfo's book draws extensively on ethnography, and as such it points to yet another emergent stream of Christian political theology: work that is either driven or informed by ethnography.[11] This kind of work is not the same as that which self-describes as "ecclesial ethnography."[12] While distinctly and explicitly a form of political theology, ethnographically *driven* political theology nevertheless stands in the tradition of Protestant and Catholic social ethics going back to the nineteenth-century Social Gospel Movement in the United States and Christian socialism in Europe. A good example of this kind of work is that by Melissa Snarr.[13] Her book is a study of interfaith community-organizing coalitions in multiple cities across the United States and their campaign for a living wage. Drawing on social movement theory and Christian social ethics, the book develops a constructive account of how religious resources enable moral and political agency in the context of democratic struggles to overcome economic and political injustice. An important focus of the book is the gendered and racialized dynamics in play in such struggles. Like Gandolfo, Snarr seeks to develop Christian political theology at the intersection of and in dialogue with other religious traditions.

The works cited here are by no means exhaustive. Rather, they indicate emergent pathways for political theology and the different forms and genres it can take.

Crossing and Deepening

VINCENT W. LLOYD

A decade or two from now, the scholarly conversation about political theology will have been shaped by the books published today that engage deeply and seriously with religious worlds in tandem with critical theory. In that future world, we will have forgotten in which discipline an author was trained and which conferences they attended. The work that will last is the work that opened new pathways for scholarship, both in terms of subject matter and in terms of approach—and, perhaps, in terms of style.

It is also the case that the books that will have lasting impact in political theology, as in any field, are not the books that received the most praise or attention upon publication. There is a strong element of faith, and hope, involved in positing which work will have lasting importance. In more secular terms, making such choices involves a normative claim: There are some books that ought to shape the field. In scholarship as in life, alas, what ought to happen does not always happen. The flavor of a field is shaped by institutional considerations, social networks, economic and political crises, and pure contingency. The passage of time wears down these factors, but it does not eliminate them.

The two most powerful recent books that speak to political theology and that grow out of the most traditional disciplinary space, Christian systematic theology, are Andrew Prevot's *The Mysticism of Ordinary Life: Theology, Philosophy, and Feminism* (Oxford University Press, 2023) and Karen Kilby's *God, Evil, and the Limits of Theology* (Bloomsbury, 2020). Both Prevot and Kilby are US-born Roman Catholic theologians; Kilby has spent much of her career in the United Kingdom, while Prevot has been based in the United States. Prevot's first book, *Thinking Prayer*, provides an account of the centrality of spiritual life to critiques of modernity, starting in Germany and France, moving to Latin America, and concluding in the United States with Black theology's analysis of the blues.[14] In *The Mysticism of Ordinary Life*, Prevot follows a similar trajectory, from Germany and France to North America, focusing on Latina and Black feminist authors and on the critical capacities of mysticism. In both books, Prevot reads theological and secular sources together, attending to secular concerns in the theological and to the theological imagination in the secular. The result is, ultimately, an account of Black theology as critical theory—not just any critical theory, but the culmination of critical theory. Prevot shows how Black Christian thought and practice respond to the antinomies of the European critical tradition.

Negative theology has played an important role in conversations about political theology. Its promise to center the critique of idolatry, linked with ideology, attracts those who are hesitant to take on substantive religious commitments but who wish to harness the critical power of religious traditions.[15] However, appeals to negative theology often license disinterest in the texture and normativity of religious traditions—quite at odds with negative theology at its best, which is always embedded in a tradition, always doing its critical work through the subtle interplay of saying and unsaying.[16] Kilby's *God, Evil, and the Limits of Theology* struggles with the imperative to challenge suffering, and the powers that are responsible for suffering, from within a Christian tradition that retains mystery at its core. A learned and careful thinker always mindful of the call of justice, Kilby, like Prevot, exemplifies the best of political theology that grows out of a serious engagement with Christian thought and practice.

Another fruitful line of research within Christian theology involves reconstructing the political-theological vision of particular individuals, whether they are usually read as secular or Christian. David Ngong's *Senghor's Eucharist: Negritude and African Political Theology* (Baylor University Press, 2023) focuses on the often-neglected use of Christian imagery in the writings of Léopold Senghor, a hugely important and inspirational figure in Black liberation struggles. In doing so, Ngong offers a version of Black liberation that welds the secular and the religious—and reminds us that so many canonical figures in Black thought were formed in Christian communities and worked with (even when they worked against) a Christian imagination. From the opposite direction, Christian theologians have started taking the martyred archbishop of San Salvador, Óscar Romero, as more than simply a figure of veneration. He was a political actor and a theological thinker; recent scholarship is demonstrating that these two vocations, for him, were inextricable. Books by Edgardo Colón-Emeric (*Óscar Romero's Theological Vision: Liberation and the Transfiguration of the Poor*, University of Notre Dame Press, 2018) and Matthew Whelan (*Blood in the Fields: Óscar Romero, Catholic Social Teaching, and Land Reform*, Catholic University of America Press, 2022) are sophisticated examples of such work.

Then there is exemplary scholarship in political theology that assumes a voice neither clearly that of the Christian theologian nor that of the secular theorist or humanist. Institutionally, there are relatively few spaces conducive to such scholarly production, but two of these spaces have an outsized influence: Princeton University (adjacent to but unaffiliated with Princeton Theological Seminary) and the University of Chicago (containing a Divinity School integrated in a secular research university). The Princeton-trained Alda Balthrop-Lewis's *Thoreau's Religion: Walden Woods, Social Justice, and the Politics of Asceticism* (Cambridge University Press, 2021) draws on a careful reading of Thoreau's texts and their contexts to challenge our understanding of Thoreau as a solitary mystic. Balthrop-Lewis traces Thoreau's entanglements with Black and Indigenous communities as well as Christianity to develop an account of ascetics that brings together work on the self, relational negotiations, and concern for place. Angie Heo, an anthropologist teaching at the University of Chicago Divinity School, crosses lines that often divide disciplines, and divide secular scholarship from theology, in her *Political Lives of Saints: Christian-Muslim Mediation in Egypt* (University of California Press, 2018). Heo attends to Marian apparitions as they are technologically mediated, and she explores ways that these apparitions both transcend and manage the religious and political boundary between Christians and Muslims in Egypt. While employing the methods of anthropology, Heo frames Marian apparitions as theological interruptions that are irreducible to secular terms, even as they are embedded in the layered relationships of power that shape the secular world.

The field of American religion has emerged as a particularly fruitful site for applying insights from the field of political theology, as well as for pushing forward conversations in political theology based on case studies. American religion has taken shape as a distinctive field within religious studies: different from the empiricist work of historians of American religion and different from theological scholarship about US Christianity.[17]

Scholarship in American religion is influenced by the theoretically sharp world of American studies, with its attention to race, gender, sexuality, class, and, especially, the transnational context in which everything "American" is located. Religious studies scholar Lucia Hulsether's *Capitalist Humanitarianism* (Duke University Press, 2023) represents the best of this thread of emerging conversations in political theology. Liberal Protestants in the United States in the latter half of the twentieth century desired to do good in the world, but they were also aware of the pathologies brought about by the missionary impulse. Hulsether tracks the development of Protestant-inspired fair trade and microfinance, and the affective knots they bring about, as North American do-gooders suspicious of capitalism end up becoming capitalists themselves, now with a sense of religious calling. Like much of the best emerging scholarship in political theology, Hulsether uses a mix of methods and theories: She weaves together ethnographic and archival research, insights from critical theory, and autobiographical reflections that interrogate the way post-Protestant affect shapes scholarly production.

Adjacent to the scholarly energy in American religion is a burst of energy around law and religion. Just as American religion used to be crudely empiricist but has recently found its own, distinctive voice, conversations about religion and law until quite recently tended to focus on legal doctrine and on the internal logic of the law. Now, scholars are drawing on critical theory and cultural studies, with the result that political theology, which was once closely tied to law, is again engaging with questions of law. Exemplary in this regard, both for her scholarship and her behind-the-scenes field-shaping work, is Winnifred Sullivan. In her book *Church State Corporation: Construing Religion in US Law* (University of Chicago Press, 2020), Sullivan talks about court decisions, but she uses them as opportunities to reflect on the broader social—really political-theological—imagination that shapes and is shaped by these decisions.

The way the secular state manages religious communities and the way that religion inspires challenges to the secular state are in some ways the bread and butter of political theology. Ludger Viefhues-Bailey and Janet Jakobsen have recently argued that such analysis, which is to say, political theology as such, goes badly wrong if questions of gender and sexuality are not taken as central issues or as constitutive of the problematics in question.[18] In *No Separation: Christians, Secular Democracy, and Sex* (Columbia University Press, 2023), Viefhues-Bailey analyzes the supposed separation of religion and the state in Germany, France, and the United States, concluding that gender and sexuality are necessary ingredients in any explanation of these dynamics. It is no coincidence that, across national contexts, the issues that attract public attention to the religious/secular divide, such as same-sex marriage and Muslim veiling, are about gender and sexuality. In *The Sex Obsession: Perversity and Possibility in American Politics* (New York University Press, 2020), Jakobsen tracks the cultural politics of the United States over recent decades. She analyzes the way conservatives mobilize religion to police sexuality and the way community organizers mobilize forms of religious practice, imagery, and thought to pursue sexual justice. In doing so, she also exemplifies one of the most exciting trends in recent scholarship in political theology: Her writing grows out of long-term collaboration with community organizers envisioning a radically new world.

Around the turn of the millennium, coinciding with the scholarly response to September 11, a surge of historians noticed that religion was a topic worth investigating. Religion went from a tertiary interest in the discipline of history to a primary interest, and the result has been a flowering of powerful scholarship that has reminded both academic and broader-than-academic audiences of religion's central role across time and place. Because of the contingencies of disciplinary convention, historians in the US academy are largely dogmatic empiricists. For that reason, while conversations in political theology have benefited from the recent work of North American historians, that work cannot be properly considered a thread within the network of political theology itself.

However, there has been important scholarship within the constellation of political theology that is grounded in history and engaged with critical theory—just not scholarship written by historians. For example, the English professor Jared Hickman's ambitious and original *Black Prometheus: Race and Radicalism in the Age of Atlantic Slavery* (Oxford University Press, 2016) retells the narrative of the Black Atlantic as a theological story: a story about the contest between certain strands of European Christianity entangled with the interests of the powerful and the variety of alternative theologies in the Caribbean, Latin America, Africa, North America, and Europe that contested but also co-constituted European Christian modernity. Hickman links these many threads through the figure of Prometheus, a man aspiring to thwart the will of the gods, and he asks what it would mean to start political theology upside down, as it were: from the perspective of Prometheus.

Medieval Europe is particularly fruitful for engagements in political theology, as religion (and not just Christianities) is so clearly a necessary part of any narrative of that place and time. Once again, those within the guild of history in the anglophone world have stood at a distance from conversations in political theology, but scholars trained in other disciplines who are interested in medieval Europe have become important voices in these conversations. Niklaus Largier is a scholar of literature, and he reads medieval mystical texts with attention to the ways religious thought, affect, and critique are entangled. His book *Figures of Possibility: Aesthetic Experience, Mysticism, and the Play of the Senses* (Stanford University Press, 2022) uses theological categories to open a comparison between medieval and modern experiments in thinking and living otherwise. From a quite different direction, working closely with Christian theology, Mark D. Jordan has demonstrated how productive it can be not only to engage with medieval texts but also to reflect on how they are "policed"—and on how they "police" us in the present.[19] In *Transforming Fire: Imagining Christian Teaching* (Eerdmans, 2021), Jordan reflects on the politics of pedagogy and on how Christian as well as secular texts, medieval as well as modern, attune our critical capacities in ways that are, essentially, political-theological.

Some of the most exciting work in political theology that engages with history is animated by questions of empire and colonialism. The religious studies scholar Azfar Moin's finely textured scholarship on the way Muslim sovereigns positioned themselves as synthesizing the sacred and secular in order to advance claims to imperial legitimacy demonstrates the fruitfulness of this approach.[20] Moin has recently extended this research agenda in a comparative direction without losing its theoretical or theological sophistication in the book he coedited with Alan Strathern, *Sacred Kingship in World History: Between Immanence and Transcendence* (Columbia University Press, 2022). With similar care and theoretical sophistication, Milinda Banerjee traces the theological imagination of elites and the disenfranchised in colonial Bengal in *The Mortal God: Imagining the Sovereign in Colonial India* (Cambridge University Press, 2017).

While comparative scholarship can put important pressure on assumptions that have long shaped conversations in political theology, writing that crosses ideas from different traditions, that plays with their resonances and dissonances, that swirls their affect and experiments with their practices—such writing opens new vistas, in the academy and beyond. The French activist Houria Bouteldja's *Whites, Jews, and Us: Toward a Politics of Revolutionary Love* (Semiotext[e], 2017) is such a work, moving between elements of the Islam found in communities of immigrants in France and elements of the Christianity found in the Black radical tradition. All this crossing is done in the wake of rejecting a political horizon in France, where the Christian, the secular, and the colonial interlock and advance the interests of the powers that be—and it is done in the interest of imagining what a new, decolonial horizon might make possible. The religion scholar Gil Anidjar represents another crossing between traditions. His scholarship tries out new starting points for political theology, in the crevices between Judaism and Islam and between Judaism and Christianity. In his most recent book, *On the Sovereignty of Mothers: The Political as Maternal* (Columbia University Press, 2024), Anidjar uses a close reading of texts that span religious and secular traditions to ask what it would mean to recenter political theology not on the axis of God-sovereign-father but in the paradoxes of motherhood.

A Celebratory Roadmap

VALENTINA NAPOLITANO

Roadmaps may lead somewhere and nowhere; they guide as they omit, are capacious yet partial. This section is a roadmap with a twist—it wishes to stay put. It wants to give a sense of directions but also a celebration of a here and now: an ethnographic and analytical richness produced in the last two decades of what I see as a coalescing field of sociocultural anthropology and political theology.[21] Connecting works that have been recognized to have made a mark together with more recent works, I think of them as a whole. In the palpable suffering of current conditions of living, and as critiques have moved toward the limitations of what academic practice is and can be in and for the world at large, it is important to offer this coalescing body of work for the uprising of a *courageous* and *curious* political theology—a reflective political theology that does not shy away from work to be done yet also celebrates the force it has.

Take the recent work of Mareike Winchell, *After Servitude: Elusive Property and the Ethics of Kinship in Bolivia* (University of California Press, 2023). Using ethnographic engagement with sovereignty in the Bolivian highlands and the entanglement of land, property, and people while also advocating for broader approaches to justice beyond individual self-interest and property ownership, Winchell shows that sovereignty is deeply rooted in a recognition that land and property are economic forms imbued with the language and performativity of kinship and history. To address colonial and capitalist frameworks that have historically prioritized individual ownership and self-possession is to show how, locally and historically, kinship has been a source of the material, community resilience of Indigenous ways of life against the backdrop of mestizo sovereignty based on patriarchal and colonial ideas of consanguinity and inheritance. Instead, focusing on Indigenous forms of unpaid labor, systems of aid, and alternative exchange relations tells us how all of this connects to other and more just forms of political sovereignty. The political theology that we champion in this book is the craft of documenting and sustaining a common life and pays attention to a finer granular, emplaced study of the co-creation of sovereignty, kinship, land, and the gods, beyond the Schmittian conceptions of the division between friends and enemies or the intimate connection between dominion as possession and Christian manifested destiny. If political theology in its earlier debates has been charted as a study of the relations between religion, politics, and the public sphere, for us (me) it is also adamantly intimate.

Political theology is made of the stuff of kinship. It is rooted in, and a discursive practice on, the intimate ways in which we relate and are made as persons through relations with God, gods, and the more-than-human. It is how we may understand the divine as a force that traverses and disrupts life, manifested in its waxing and waning and in participating in a logic of divinization. This insight is brought to bear in Bhrigupati Singh's *Poverty and the Quest for Life: Spiritual and Material Striving in Rural India* (University of Chicago Press, 2015). In a theopolitical outlook that follows up on how gods' charismatic potency affects both the living and the dead, this work questions the limits of Agamben's concept of sovereignty and goes beyond the scope of the nation-state or the maintenance of bare life. Suggesting instead that sovereignty can be considered a threshold where life is intensified or reduced and where practices of agonistic encounter, martyrdom, and violence become central, this work opens up political theology to exploring concepts of sovereignty, neighboring, and the transcendent through agonistic intimacy with multiple gods. These gods wax and wane, coming into being and dying. Forms of asceticism, a warrior ethos, and an agonistic intimacy with the gods all disrupt traditional ideas of fraternity and equality (in a context like India, which is deeply stratified by caste differences). And more than ever, storytelling is what connects theological thinking with lived experience—the two are not separate.

Storytelling, ethnographic, and political-theological work on the granular nature of sovereignty builds upon a now-classic work in the field that has introduced the potency of "refusal" as a performative act against a modern nation-state and its politics of recognition. This is the work of Audra Simpson in *Mohawk Interruptus: Political Life Across the Borders of Settler States* (Duke University Press, 2014), which is centered on a politics of failed multicultural recognition and the Kahnawà:ke Mohawk people. Reflecting on how the invasive Canadian regulation of the 1876 Indian Act forcibly transferred traditional matrilineal descent to the patrilineal line and introduced a bioregulatory 50 percent blood quantum for membership status, we realize how women's membership within an Indigenous collective and vis-à-vis the state has been doubly disenfranchised. The form of sovereignty that this book puts in motion is also about the reflective sovereignty of Simpson as a Kahnawà:ke Mohawk anthropologist.

Hence writers of political theology (and anthropologists, for that matter) may have a political force in life and in the entextualization they are exemplifying. Political theologians are coproducing a reality that they may be ethnographically engaging with. There are no "abstract" viewers, but always entangled writers.

This entanglement of epistemic practices and language has been central to the reflections of Talal Asad and his discussions of secularism. For instance, in his *Secular Translations: Nation-State, Modern Self, and Calculative Reason* (Columbia University Press, 2018), he explores language as a fundamental aspect of life, akin to Wittgenstein's concept of language as forms of life. Hence, translation as a form of life has the potential to break down language's boundaries: as in an aporia, an impossibility of translations expands and extends the language translated into. Emphasizing the centrality of the body, translation, for Asad, is centered on how religious language impacts us rather than being merely about us. Hence ritual and religious language are integral to a communal life, not confined to individual will or a justice-oriented God. Political theology is involved in a translation of forms of life across different geopolitical contexts. Movements like Black Lives Matter are pivotal in political theology because they demand justice rather than mere recognition, but they also put the untranslatable of the body, as a presence, experience, and form of life, in a language that is not theirs, and by doing so, they implode the language of recognition that fails them in the first place.

Many of Asad's original students have been very influential in the debates on secularism and political theology and the engaged experience of the limits of translation of (secular) language. Needless to mention is the last work of the late Saba Mahmood, *Religious Difference in a Secular Age: A Minority Report* (Princeton University Press, 2015), which is a very refined take—anthropological, legal, and literary—on the making of political secularism as a troubling political category (with, but well beyond the case of, Copts in Egypt). This is a category that nation-state secularist discourse brackets while compounding religious difference and discrimination, especially as it allows for individual practices of religious-based family law while at the same time promoting public majority's religious values and sensibilities as a language of political, public egalitarianism. Political-theological work must constantly think "outside its box"—its own condition of thinkability—while critiquing and transcending limiting binary and Manichean views such as reason and faith, religion and politics, and virtues and vices.

A further central theme in our proposition for "what political theology is" rests on the centrality, or the "node," of the body. The body and the historical attunement to architectural and sonic formations are the theme of Charles Hirschkind's *The Feeling of History: Islam, Romanticism, and Andalusia* (University of Chicago Press, 2020). It is an archival and ethnographic rendering of *El Andalúz* as a processual space of engagement, a revivification of the past, and a political force for a present and a future to come through the racialization and intimacy of suffering that have crafted not only the multiple religious, architectural, and aesthetic inceptions of this region but also, Hirschkind argues, the ground for a robust critique of a straightjacketing and reductive fabulation of a European "West." "Europe," then, from this "corner" of Andalusia and the work of *Andalucistas*, becomes a past-present-future that is sedimented in traces and in sensorial modes and affective archives that are craftily renewed with and beyond language. Moving us away from a "salvation mode" to rescue repressed histories, instead it addresses our research to attune an ethnographic sensibility to the entangled copresence of aesthetic formations, mixed-race protagonists, and the epistemic value of a *fondo sonoro*—musical of ground—to reapprehend the entanglement of Christian, Muslim, and Jewish affective histories in the present. Here, as in other works, political theology seeks the religious in movement and the *longue durée* of affective histories. This is also the case of the Atlantic and trans-Mediterranean histories that undo political-theological illiberal democratic ideas that short-circuit Europe and the Atlantic into a political narrative of "authentic" Christian heritage.[22]

Political theology needs a richer analysis of the intersections between religion, politics, and aesthetic forms. Carl Schmitt's key idea in studying the Catholic Church, that all political concepts are theological secularized ones, is about the capacity of a church's aesthetics to contain very antithetical positions and narratives. This is the case of the insightful work of Elayne Oliphant, *The Privilege of Being Banal: Art, Secularism, and Catholicism in Paris* (University of Chicago Press, 2021). Powerful political aesthetics and devotional habitations of inclusion and exclusion unveil how "universal" and national sensibilities of a French *läicité* are strictly connected to Catholic multiple sensorial and class imaginations of a (medieval) past. To study museums, aesthetic forms, and urban architectures as granular spaces of the political-theological is to open and implode "secularism" and interreligious spaces.

To continue questioning secularism as an ideology and an immanent frame, we need a shift in perspectives. Rather that an interreligious space, what is an intertheological space? How does it manifest within and beyond political secularism as the managing of religious difference? Here, the work of Neena Mahadev, *Karma and Grace: Religious Difference in Millennial Sri Lanka* (Columbia University Press, 2023) is illuminating. Theopolitics in Sri Lanka, involving Catholicism, Pentecostal Christianity, Sinhala Buddhism, and Hinduism, illustrates an intertheological space as a lived contestation of sovereignty. Following Theravada traditions, Sinhala Buddhism emphasizes the significance of the Buddha's sacred relics and the miracles that exceptionally manifest through them, while (Sri Lanka) Pentecostal Christians view the miraculous in pneumatic transmissions of the Holy Ghost as ordinary. Against a Sinhala Buddhism perception of "mushrooming," new, and "cacophonic exuberant" Christian converted churches, this emplaced strand of Buddhism is nonetheless contested by Pentecostals to be theologically vulnerable to idols and semigods and to practice a silence susceptible to demonic predation. The intertheological space here is not about the continuum or clash of different ritual practices, or an ideational content of theology, but about how the theological imagination is constantly made and remade through the soil, the land, and the different ways in which questions of "ontological states and materialization of various kinds of spirits can pass in and out of the human sensorium."[23]

Theology, like any other discourse, possesses historicity, and as a language it has a mediatic capacity akin to anthropological discourse. As Alireza Doostdar aptly analyzes in the case of the Iranian Islamic Republic in *The Iranian Metaphysicals: Explorations in Science, Islam, and the Uncanny* (Princeton University Press, 2018), the theological imagination is public and intimate, and it constantly forges (or tries to) a "collective will" of the people, in a form of give and take with god, different yet not so entirely distant from Pentecostal Christianity.[24] (I am aware I am being provocative here.) In Iranian Sufism, demonic forces are conceptualized as entities with distinct personhood and ethical contours, similar to forms of jinn. While the Sufi and Pentecostal Christian theological imaginations may diverge, both engage in an everyday life presence of the unseen, the miraculous, and the demonic.

In post-1979 revolutionary Sufi Iran, the miraculous was contoured as a divine sign that shaped the revolutionary will of the people while simultaneously transforming human souls. Within this Ayatollah revolutionary framework, people engaged with a metaphysical presence and the unseen on an ordinary basis, constantly inquiring into the relationship between the material and the spiritual. Extending but also distancing from Foucault's reading of the Iranian Revolution, Doostdar wonders if the Iranian 1979 revolutionary impulse might also be interpreted as a political spirituality centered around an infinite creativity of God, where revolutionary sovereignty cannot be confined to a secular analysis because it may be well nurtured by a wellspring of human and God's creativity.

But sovereignty is also a problem of excess and void. Claude Lefort rightly pointed out the actual persistence of a religious sensibility in the space of "secular" modernity. The modern state has an issue with the visibility/invisibility of the body of the sovereign, which is the problem of the "dis-incarnation" of the modern state.[25] Hence it becomes central to look at how excess of being is manifested and how a void resides at the center of the modern state—a presence by absence that requires a constant mise-en-scène. This dynamic opens studies of the "crowd" in modernity, a central theme of political theology.[26] Here, it is essential to refer to *mana* as a key anthropological theme on the indivisibility of aesthetic and power authority. As William Mazzarella's *The Mana of Mass Society* (University of Chicago Press, 2017) tells us, *mana* is a force of traditional exchange practices in "primitive" societies that is shared in the "magical seductive character" of contemporary mass publicity. To be effective, power always has to be affectively transmitted. A curious and vital political theology is one that engages with how the force of *mana*, in its secrecy and magic, sits as a gap between the potency of crowds, mass mediation, and the exhaustion of traditional institutions.

Building on Lefort, the late Rafael Sánchez made a magisterial contribution to political-theological studies of populism and the crowd in *Dancing Jacobins: A Venezuelan Genealogy of Latin American Populism* (Fordham University Press, 2016). Analyzing Venezuelan populism and the legacy of Simón Bolívar, he demonstrates how collective memory and a national body are constructed through monumentalization and public performances. By examining the cyclical dynamics of governance, the desire for a unified national identity, and the performative nature of political leadership, Sánchez's work provides seminal insights into the complexities of nation-building and the challenges of (not) achieving social cohesion in a postcolonial context.

If populism and the formation of the crowd are not a pathology but a political movement (in the sense of *to move*), then we need to focus on managing and governing the movements of excess and on monumental governmentality. A Foucauldian biopolitical lens is not enough to understand a political theology of excesses, the movement of a sovereignty that is rebounding in excess. This is the case, for instance, across multiple billboards of body-eyes in 2000s Caracas (an indistinguishable blurring of the ones of Chavez and Bolívar), as a constant mise-en-scène of a totalitarianism that sees and never sees while it arises in a "frontier" colony (as Venezuela is, and the land of Simón Bolívar). And so we learn a great deal from a rendering of the flesh and its excesses, spirit possession, and a living iconicity of a nation-state.[27]

For this and more, I have no doubt this roadmap's celebration shall continue.

NOTES

INTRODUCTION: TRAJECTORIES IN POLITICAL THEOLOGY

1. While the 2010s iteration of this phenomenon is new and distinctive, political theology has long produced unexpected bedfellows. Consider, for example, the way secularism was attacked by the Religious Right in the United States and abroad in the 1990s, with public intellectuals like Richard John Neuhaus in the lead, while a critique of secularism was being developed from the Left in the work of figures like Talal Asad. Vincent Lloyd, "Secularism's Two Ends," The Immanent Frame, November 10, 2017, accessed April 5, 2024, https://tif.ssrc.org/2017/11/10/secularisms-two-ends.
2. See, for example, Rod Dreher, *The Benedict Option: A Strategy for Christians in a Post-Christian Society* (Sentinel, 2018).
3. In this way, we are offering a response to ethnoreligious nationalism, but we worry about an overly simplistic framing of "good" political theology as the apt response to the complex social formation that is ethnoreligious nationalism. For some of the pitfalls of an overly simplistic framing, see Lucia Hulsether, "Tabitha's Trauma: Christian Nationalism, Centrist Jeremiad, and the Reconstruction of the American Family," in *Political Theology Reimagined*, ed. Alex Dubilet and Vincent Lloyd (Duke University Press, 2025).
4. Here we find it generative to think with the incisive analysis of doppelgangers as a tool for understanding left-right resonances in Naomi

Klein, *Doppelganger: A Trip into the Mirror World* (Farrar, Straus and Giroux, 2023).

5. Édouard Glissant, *Caribbean Discourse: Selected Essays*, trans. J. Michael Dash (University Press of Virginia, 1989).

6. Paul Gilroy, *The Black Atlantic: Modernity and Double Consciousness* (Harvard University Press, 1993).

7. Luke Bretherton, *Christ and the Common Life: Political Theology and the Case for Democracy* (Eerdmans, 2019), 51–198.

8. Elizabeth Foster, *African Catholic: Decolonization and the Transformation of the Church* (Harvard University Press, 2019); David Ngong, *Senghor's Eucharist: Negritude and African Political Theology* (Baylor University Press, 2023); Bretherton, *Christ and the Common Life*, 119–59.

9. Kwok Pui-lan, *Postcolonial Politics and Theology: Unraveling Empire for a Global World* (Westminster John Knox Press, 2021), 1–38. See also Kwok Pui-lan, ed., *Transpacific Political Theology: Perspectives, Paradigms, Proposals* (Baylor University Press, 2024). Sarah Azaransky's account of the exchanges between foundational figures in the American civil rights movement and the nonviolent liberation movement led by Mahatma Gandhi is a microcosm of this interaction. Sarah Azaransky, *This Worldwide Struggle: Religion and the International Roots of the Civil Rights Movement* (Oxford University Press, 2017).

10. Leaving aside the welter of Prosperity and other preachers who assume the compatibility between Christianity and capitalism, among those who develop formal political theologies there are very few who explicitly support a bourgeois liberal capitalist order. Michael Novak could be construed as one. However, he, along with a figure like Max Stackhouse, who also writes in favor of a liberal bourgeois capitalist form of life, is more accurately deemed a public theologian.

11. Sarah Shortall, *Soldiers of God in a Secular World: Catholic Theology and Twentieth-Century French Politics* (Harvard University Press, 2021).

12. Foster, *African Catholic*.

13. Gary Dorrien is the assiduous chronicler of this history, on both sides of the Atlantic, through monumental works such as *Social Ethics in the Making: Interpreting an American Tradition* (Wiley-Blackwell, 2008); *The New Abolition: W. E. B. Du Bois and the Black Social Gospel* (Yale University Press, 2015); *Social Democracy in the Making: Political and Religious Roots of European Socialism* (Yale University Press, 2019); and

American Democratic Socialism: History, Politics, Religion, and Theory (Yale University Press, 2021).

14. Bretherton, *Christ and the Common Life*, 359–99.
15. See, for example, María Pilar Aquino, "Theological Method in U.S. Latino/a Theology: Toward an Intercultural Theology for the Third Millennium," in *From the Heart of Our People: Latino/a Explorations in Catholic Systematic Theology*, ed. Orlando O. Espín and Miguel H. Díaz (Orbis, 1999), 6–48; and Ada María Isasi-Díaz, *Mujerista Theology* (Orbis, 1996), 66–72.
16. Katie Cannon, *Black Womanist Ethics* (Scholars Press, 1988).
17. Juan Carlos Scannone, "Pope Francis and the Theology of the People," *Theological Studies* 77, no. 1 (2016): 118–35; Rafael Luciani, *Pope Francis and the Theology of the People* (Orbis, 2017).
18. Isasi-Díaz, *Mujerista Theology*, 64; 69–70; 69–70; 72. See also Ada María Isasi-Díaz, *La Lucha Continues: Mujerista Theology* (Orbis, 2004), 92–106.
19. See Michel de Certeau, *The Practice of Everyday Life* (University of California Press, 1984); Silvia Federici, *Caliban and the Witch* (Autonomedia, 2004); and Verónica Gago, "Dangerous Liaisons: Latin American Feminists and the Left," *NACLA Report on the Americas* 40, no. 2 (2007): 17–19.
20. Charles Villa-Vicencio, *A Theology of Reconstruction: Nation-Building and Human Rights* (Cambridge University Press, 1992). A cohort of younger, Black South African theologians have pushed against this trend. See R. S. Tshaka and M. K. Makofane, "The Continued Relevance of Black Liberation Theology for Democratic South Africa Today," *Scriptura* 105 (2010): 532–46; and Rothney Tshaka, "Karl Barth and Public Theologies! Why Black Theology of Liberation Is Still Relevant in the Wake of a Public Theology Euphoria," *Revista Pistis & Praxis* 14, no. 1 (2022): 62–87.
21. For an account of the different origin stories of public theology and its emergence into a set of intersecting but contextually orientated theological paradigms, see Dirk Smit, "The Paradigm of Public Theology—Origins and Development," in *Contextuality and Intercontextuality in Public Theology*, ed. Heinrich Bedford-Strohm, Florian Höhne, and Tobias Reitmeier (LIT Verlag, 2013), 11–23.
22. See, for example, William Cavanaugh, *Theopolitical Imagination* (T&T Clark, 2003).

23. More recently, the term *public* in *public theology* has come to mean theological reflection on what is shared or common. This shift redefines public theology as what Charles Mathewes calls a "theology of public life"; see Charles Mathewes, *A Theology of Public Life* (Cambridge University Press, 2007). In this new, predominantly Roman Catholic iteration, public theology seeks to identify and name a realm of common life amid difference and plurality that may or may not involve the state. Such a shift reframes public theology as another form of political theology. For an account of public theology along these lines, see Nicholas Hayes-Mota, "Public Theology in North America: Commonality amid Plurality," in *T&T Clark Handbook of Public Theology*, ed. Christoph Hübenthal and Christiane Alpers (Bloomsbury, 2022), chap. 29.
24. See Catherine Keller and Mayra Rivera, "The Coloniality of Apocalypse," The Immanent Frame, March 31, 2021, accessed December 7, 2024, https://tif.ssrc.org/2021/03/31/the-coloniality-of-apocalypse. This contrast between public theology and political theology could also be approached by tracking their respective journals: *International Journal of Public Theology* and *Political Theology*. The latter was originally subtitled a "Journal of Christian Socialism." While it evolved away from a particularly Christian focus, the left-of-liberal political orientation remains, tied to its embrace of the nexus of critical theory and religious traditions.
25. For an extensive discussion of what is meant by the "technocratic paradigm," see Pope Francis, "Laudato Si'," The Holy See, May 24, 2015, accessed December 7, 2024, https://www.vatican.va/content/francesco/en/encyclicals/documents/papa-francesco_20150524_enciclica-laudato-si.html.
26. Michael Gillespie, *The Theological Origins of Modernity* (University of Chicago Press, 2008); Paul Avis, *Theology and the Enlightenment: A Critical Enquiry into Enlightenment Theology and Its Reception* (Bloomsbury, 2022); Charles Taylor, *A Secular Age* (Belknap, 2007).
27. Jeremy Waldron, *God, Locke, and Equality: Christian Foundations of John Locke's Political Thought* (Cambridge University Press, 2002); Diego Lucci, *John Locke's Christianity* (Cambridge University Press, 2021); Eric Gregory, "Before the Original Position: The Neo-Orthodox Theology of the Young John Rawls," *Journal of Religious Ethics* 35, no. 2 (2007): 179–206.

28. Teresa Bejan, *Mere Civility: Disagreement and the Limits of Toleration* (Harvard University Press, 2017); Eric Nelson, *The Hebrew Republic: Jewish Sources and the Transformation of European Political Thought* (Harvard University Press, 2010).
29. Shortall, *Soldiers of God*; Foster, *African Catholic*.
30. Samuel Moyn, *Christian Human Rights* (University of Pennsylvania Press, 2015).
31. Alison McQueen, *Political Realism in Apocalyptic Times* (Cambridge University Press, 2018).
32. See, for example, Eric Voegelin, *The New Science of Politics: An Introduction* (University of Chicago Press, 1952); and Ernest Tuveson, *Millennium and Utopia: A Study in the Background of the Idea of Progress* (University of California Press, 1949).
33. James Chappel, *Catholic Modern: The Challenge of Totalitarianism and the Remaking of the Church* (Harvard University Press, 2018); Carlo Invernizzi-Accetti, *What Is Christian Democracy? Politics, Religion and Ideology* (Cambridge University Press, 2019).
34. The tension between a political theology of climate change inspired by an orthodox, trinitarian conception of God and one derived from the African Caribbean Spiritual Baptist tradition, which apprehends God as the earth, is discussed in J. Brent Crosson, "'The Earth Is the Lord' or 'God Is a Trini'? The Political Theology of Climate Change, Environmental Stewardship, and Petroleum Extraction," in *Climate Politics and the Power of Religion*, ed. Evan Berry (Indiana University Press, 2022). See also Ely Orrego Torres and Diego Rossello, "Imagining Ecopolis: Visions of Ecofeminist Political Theology and Ecocriticism in Latin America." *Social Compass* 71, no. 3 (2024): 442–64.
35. See, for example, Anthony Waterman, *Political Economy and Christian Theology Since the Enlightenment: Essays in Intellectual History* (Palgrave Macmillan, 2004); Odd Langholm, *The Legacy of Scholasticism in Economic Thought: Antecedents of Choice and Power* (Cambridge University Press, 1998); Giacomo Todeschini, *Franciscan Wealth: From Voluntary Poverty to Market Society* (Franciscan Institute, 2004); Philip Goodchild, *Economic Theology: Credit and Faith, II* (Rowman and Littlefield, 2020); Robert Nelson, *Economics as Religion: From Samuelson to Chicago and Beyond* (Penn State University Press, 2002); and Stefan Schwarzkopf, ed., *The Routledge Handbook of Economic Theology* (Routledge, 2020).

36. Claude Lefort, "The Permanence of the Theologico-political?," in *Political Theologies: Public Religions in a Post-Secular World*, ed. Hent de Vries and Lawrence E. Sullivan (Fordham University Press, 2006); Marcel Gauchet, *The Disenchantment of the World* (Princeton University Press, 1997); Warren Breckman, "Democracy Between Disenchantment and Political Theology: French Post-Marxism and the Return to Religion," *New German Critique* 94 (2005): 72–105.
37. Giorgio Agamben, *Homo Sacer: Sovereign Power and Bare Life* (Stanford University Press, 1995); Achille Mbembe, *Necropolitics* (Duke University Press, 2019).
38. See Elettra Stimilli, *Debt and Guilt: A Political Philosophy* (Bloomsbury Academic, 2019).
39. Amaryah Shaye Armstrong, "Losing Salvation: Notes Toward a Wayward Black Theology," *Critical Times* 6, no. 2 (2023): 324–44; Alex Dubilet, "A Political Theology of Interpellation: On Subjection, Individuation, and Becoming Nothing," *Cultural Critique* 122 (2024): 132–61; Kirill Chepurin, *Bliss Against the World: Schelling, Theodicy, and the Crisis of Modernity* (Oxford University Press, 2025).
40. A proposed political theology program unit of the American Academy of Religion, the primary North American guild for religious studies, was rejected by that organization's program committee before being accepted with a provisional status after a concerted lobbying effort. This was one of the reasons behind the formation of the Political Theology Network, an interdisciplinary scholarly association.
41. Some corners of religious studies have welcomed, to some extent, scholarship in or adjacent to political theology: most notably, religious ethics and the nebulous field of religion and modernity. The contingencies of institutional configuration mean that certain universities have programs in "religion, ethics, and politics" that have been particularly welcoming to political theology. (The most important of these programs has been at Princeton University.)
42. See, for example, Miguel Vatter, *Living Law: Jewish Political Theology from Hermann Cohen to Hannah Arendt* (Oxford University Press, 2021); and Hamid Dabashi, *Islamic Liberation Theology: Resisting the Empire* (Routledge, 2008). Bretherton's chapter examines a turn in the Latin American context to explore multiple cosmologies, often referred to as

the pluriverse. Here the interaction is not with a world religion but with Indigenous and animist cosmologies and divergent ontologies.
43. See Azaransky, *This Worldwide Struggle*.
44. Shadaab Rahemtulla, *Qur'an of the Oppressed: Liberation Theology and Gender Justice in Islam* (Oxford University Press, 2017), 10–52. For an example of reading Christian political theology in the context of developing constructive Islamic political thought from someone shaped by the anti-apartheid struggle, see Ebrahim Moosa, "The Idea of Progress and Its Discontents in Islamic Thought," Contending Modernities, January 10, 2023, https://contendingmodernities.nd.edu/theorizing-modernities/moosa-inaugural-lecture.
45. George Shulman, *American Prophecy: Race and Redemption in American Political Culture* (University of Minnesota Press, 2008).
46. A second example is how mysticism informs pathways that integrate action and contemplation. When mysticism and the political intersect, they can open up critical theory and shed new light on how we live together beyond the secular. Eleanor Craig and Amy Hollywood, "Mysticism and the Politics of Theory," *English Language Notes* 56, no. 1 (2018): 7–20.
47. Gil Anidjar, "Secularism," *Critical Inquiry* 33, no. 1 (2006): 52–77. For a broader discussion of conceptions of secularism and secularity, see Bretherton, *Christ and the Common Life*, 227–257.
48. Talal Asad, "The Construction of Religion as an Anthropological Category," in *Genealogies of Religion: Discipline and Reasons of Power in Christianity and Islam* (Johns Hopkins University Press, 1993), 27–54; Peter van der Veer, *Imperial Encounters: Religion and Modernity in India and Britain* (Princeton University Press, 2001); Brent Nongbri, *Before Religion: A History of a Modern Concept* (Yale University Press, 2013); Tisa Wenger, *We Have a Religion: The 1920s Pueblo Indian Dance Controversy and American Religious Freedom* (University of North Carolina Press, 2009). On modernization as a mode of Protestantization, see Hans Joas, *Faith as an Option: Possible Futures for Christianity*, trans. Alex Skinner (Stanford University Press, 2014), 50–62.
49. For an especially pointed analysis of this dynamic, see Saba Mahmood, "Secularism, Hermeneutics, and Empire: The Politics of Islamic Reformation," *Public Culture* 18, no. 2 (2006): 323–47.

50. Robert Bellah, *Religion in Human Evolution: From the Paleolithic to the Axial Age* (Belknap, 2011), 1.
51. Failure to evaluate different traditions in terms of their own frames of reference leads to misinterpretation and misunderstanding, which in turn generate ill-judged action on the part of "outsiders." Examples include government officials confusing Sikhs with Muslims and Reformed Jews not being distinguished from ultra-Orthodox ones.
52. Thanks to participants in a manuscript workshop at Villanova University for their helpful feedback on an earlier version of this manuscript: Molly Farneth, Paulina Ochoa-Espejo, Hanna Reichel, Jesse Couenhoven, Kristyn Sessions, and Wonchul Shin. Thanks also to Laura Simpson for support during that workshop.

1. POLITICAL THEOLOGY AS TESTIMONY

1. This distinction is drawn from Gustavo Gutiérrez, for whom the task of the church is to *denounce* every dehumanizing situation that is contrary to fellowship, justice, and liberation. At the same time, it *announces* the Gospel that the love of the Father calls all persons in Christ and through the action of the Spirit to union among themselves and communion with him. Gustavo Gutiérrez, *A Theology of Liberation: History, Politics, and Salvation*, rev. ed. (Orbis, 1988), 150–56.
2. See Augustine, *City of God*, 11–22, trans. William Babcock (New City, 2013), 385–86 (19.24).
3. As the seventeenth-century Anglican divine Jeremy Taylor puts it: "Death is not an action, but a whole state and condition." *Holy Living and Holy Dying*, 2 vols, ed. P. G. Stanwood (Clarendon, 1989), 2:69.
4. Sergei Bulgakov, *Philosophy of Economy: The World as Household*, trans. Catherine Evtubov (Yale University Press, 2000), 69–73.
5. For a meditation on this theme and the centrality of the life-death relation to Christian belief and practice, see Dietrich Bonhoeffer, *Ethics*, trans. Reinhard Krauss et al., ed. Clifford Green, vol. 6 of *Dietrich Bonhoeffer Works* (Fortress, 2005), 90–102.
6. On this topic, see Sarah Jobe, *No Godforsaken Place: Prison Chaplaincy, Karl Barth, and Practicing Life in Prison* (Bloomsbury, 2025).

1. POLITICAL THEOLOGY AS TESTIMONY • 241

7. Paul Gilroy, "The Black Atlantic and the Re-enchantment of Humanism: Suffering and Infrahumanity," in *The Tanner Lectures on Human Values*, ed. Mark Matheson (University of Utah Press, 2016), vol. 34.
8. For a variation on this theme of insurgent life in the face of death, see Lloyd's discussion of Aimé Césaire's *Notebook* poem in chapter 2.
9. James Cone, *The Spirituals and the Blues: An Interpretation* (Seabury, 1972), 32–33.
10. Desmond Tutu, *God Has a Dream: A Vision of Hope for Our Time* (Rider, 2005), 4. See also Bonhoeffer, *Ethics*, 90–102.
11. See, for example, Marx's discussion of the "mystical character of the commodity" in Karl Marx, *Capital*, vol. 1, trans. Ben Fowkes (Penguin, 1990), 164–65.
12. Gillian Rose, *The Broken Middle: Out of Our Ancient Society* (Blackwell, 1992).
13. Lloyd's essay reads contemporary abolitionism as navigating this tension constructively. His account of how political theology is born out of existential struggles represents a nontheological but also nonsecularizing account of the life-death relation as foundational for political theology that is parallel to the one set out here.
14. Mikhail Bakunin, "The Political Theology of Mazzini," in *Mikhail Bakunin: Selected Writings*, ed. Arthur Lehning (Jonathan Cape, 1973), 221.
15. Rufinus of Sorrento, *De Bono Pacis* (Hahn, 1997).
16. Stanley Marrow, "κόσμος in John," *Catholic Biblical Quarterly* 64 (2002): 90–102.
17. See, for example, Bonhoeffer, *Ethics*, 47–102, 219–45.
18. See, for example, Oliver O'Donovan's account of the political existence of the church as constituted through recapitulating the Christ event in *The Desire of the Nations: Rediscovering the Roots of Political Theology* (Cambridge University Press, 1996), 174–92.
19. It is worth noting the tension here between my arguing for the possibilities of conversion as against the more apophatic position set out in chapter 2 by Lloyd.
20. It should be noted that social contract theorists such as Hobbes and Locke who posit a "prepolitical" state of nature in which the individual rather than some form of community is the basic unit of being in the world stand in stark and deliberate contrast to Aristotle.

21. See Sara Brill, *Aristotle on the Concept of Shared Life* (Oxford University Press, 2020), 86–127.
22. See, for example, Charles Mathewes, *A Theology of Public Life* (Cambridge University Press, 2007); and Michael Lamb, *A Commonwealth of Hope: Augustine's Political Thought* (Princeton University Press, 2022).
23. See Luke Bretherton, *Christ and the Common Life: Political Theology and the Case for Democracy* (Eerdmans, 2019), 238–88.
24. Hannah Arendt, *The Human Condition* (University of Chicago Press, 1958; repr. University of Chicago Press, 1998), 198.
25. Milinda Banerjee and Jelle J. P. Wouters, *Subaltern Studies 2.0: Being Against the Capitalocene* (Prickly Paradigm, 2022), 62.
26. Gerrard Winstanley, "A Declaration to the Powers of England (The True Levellers Standard Advanced)," in *The Complete Works of Gerrard Winstanley*, ed. Thomas N. Corns, Ann Hughes, and David Loewenstein (Oxford University Press, 2010), 2:1–30.
27. John Gurney, *Brave Community: The Digger Movement in the English Revolution* (Manchester University Press, 2007), 177.
28. As the tradition of just war theory contends, war is still an arena of moral concern. My contention is that rather than being either constitutive of politics or on a spectrum with politics, war represents a disjunctive arena of moral concern and human endeavor, even as the line between war and politics is often blurred in practice. Conversely, at some point, if life is to go on, there must be a shift from war to politics, such that politics sets the limits of war: If we are killing each other, we are not forming a common life; and if we are in dialogue together trying to address shared problems (i.e., doing politics), then we are not killing each other.
29. Against skeptical approaches, I am advocating an understanding of politics as an intrinsically moral activity. My view contests "realist" views that suspend ethics in the name of politics, collapse politics into statecraft, and reduce power to violence, thereby denying the reality of relational power. The division here is *not* one between ideal and nonideal theories. The account I give is more pragmatic and attuned to the reality of politics and its possibilities than the truncated account of politics advocated by realists.
30. On the contrast between political relationships and violence, see Hannah Arendt, "On Violence," in *Crises of the Republic* (Harcourt Brace, 1972), 103–84.

1. POLITICAL THEOLOGY AS TESTIMONY • 243

31. Soul power or the power from within is shorthand for the subjective, internal element that enables individual action over, with, or for others. It includes drive, motivations, gifts (including spiritual gifts), will, dispositions (whether toward virtue or vice), sense of vocation, and personality, charisma, or spirit. Relational power, or power with, is shorthand for ends-oriented and conscious action in concert. In contrast to command and obedience forms of top-down, unilateral power, relational power is distributed and shared. Generated as it is through forms of cooperation and solidarity, the more people involved, the more there is. The early labor and civil rights movements are paradigmatic examples of such relational power in action, and both depended on traditions of popular piety such as those found in Black-led churches, Methodism, and Roman Catholicism. Hannah Arendt sketches a conception of relational power in "On Violence," 105–98, and *On Revolution* (Viking, 1963; repr., Penguin, 2006), 166–67. The distinction between "power with" and "power over" originates with Mary Parker Follett, *Creative Experience* (Longmans, Green, 1924; repr., Longmans, Green, 1930).

32. See Ada María Isasi-Díaz, "Afterwords: Strangers No Longer," in *Hispanic/Latino Theology: Challenge and Promise*, ed. Ada María Isasi-Díaz and Fernando F. Segovia (Fortress, 1996), 367–74; Rubén Rosario-Rodríguez, *Racism and God-Talk: A Latino/a Perspective* (New York University Press, 2008); and Lara Medina, "Nepantla," in *Hispanic American Religious Cultures*, ed. Miguel de la Torre (ABC-CLIO, 2009), 403–8. It is important to note that notions of *mestizaje* have also been taken up within nationalist and racist projects that seek to homogenize and stabilize populations. On this topic, see Néstor Medina, *Mestizaje: (Re)Mapping Race, Culture, and Faith in Latino/a Catholicism* (Orbis, 2009).

33. Bernard Crick, *In Defence of Politics* (Weidenfeld & Nicolson, 1962; repr., University of Chicago Press, 1993), 4.

34. As the Reformed theologian Karl Barth puts it in his articulation of Christian personalism: "The Christian message is interested in the particular individual as well as in the fellowship of individuals, but it puts the emphasis always on the individual being *together* with other individuals. As far as fellowship is concerned, it is always meant to be constituted by the mutually free responsibility of different individuals." Karl Barth, "The New Humanism and the Humanism of God," *Theology Today* 8 (1951): 162.

35. Carl Schmitt, *The Concept of the Political*, trans. George Schwab (Duncker & Humblot, 1932; repr., University of Chicago Press, 2007), 27, 65.
36. For Schmitt, words like *state, republic, class,* and *sovereignty* only make sense when one knows "who is to be affected, combated, refuted, or negated by such a term" (Schmitt, *The Concept of the Political*, 31). Or, as Schmitt puts it most sharply later: "The enemy is he who defines me." *Theory of the Partisan: Intermediate Commentary on the Concept of the Political*, trans. G. L. Ulmen (Telos, 2007), 85n89.
37. Walter Benjamin, "Theses on the Philosophy of History" (1940), in *Illuminations: Essays and Reflections*, ed. Hannah Arendt, trans. Harry Zohn (Schocken, 2007), 256.
38. Frantz Fanon, *The Wretched of the Earth*, trans. Richard Philcox (Grove, 2004), 236.
39. Sylvia Wynter, "The Re-Enchantment of Humanism," interview by David Scott, *Small Axe* 8 (September 2000): 176–82; Sylvia Wynter, "Unsettling the Coloniality of Being/Power/Truth/Freedom: Towards the Human, After Man, Its Overrepresentation—An Argument," *CR: The New Centennial Review* 3, no. 3 (2003): 257–337.
40. Wynter, "Unsettling the Coloniality," 321.
41. Wynter, "The Re-Enchantment of Humanism," 121. For the argument that Frantz Fanon has a parallel agonistic conception of humanism, see An Yountae, "Decolonizing the Cosmo-Polis: Cosmopolitanism as a Rehumanizing Project," in *Decolonial Christianities: Latinx and Latin American Perspectives*, ed. Raimundo Barreto and Roberto Sirvent (Palgrave Macmillan, 2019), 167–82.
42. Jonathan Tran, *Asian Americans and the Spirit of Racial Capitalism* (Oxford University Press, 2021), 18–19. A more prevalent version of this same dynamic today is the consent form used in medical and other forms of research on human subjects. Consent is a social technique for simultaneously recognizing a human as human (understood in liberal terms as an autonomous, self-reflexive, willing subject) and, through a process of consent, converting that human into a source of data. The research needs the humanity of the human subject but also needs a way to render that human an object that is open to extraction and exploitation. Consent is the means to fulfill these two purposes.

1. POLITICAL THEOLOGY AS TESTIMONY • 245

43. Schmitt insists in *The Concept of the Political* that while the other or enemy represents a threat, they should not be demonized, treated as evil, or rendered as subhuman and so outside the human community. However, given Schmitt's Nazism, there is a hollow ring to this claim. In his later work, Schmitt distinguishes between the "real enemy" and the "absolute enemy." The latter is one who is declared to be totally criminal and inhuman, "to be a total non-value" (*Theory of the Partisan*, 94). The notion of the absolute enemy is identified as a distinctly modern phenomenon that arises with the advent of absolute or total war conducted by revolutionary and regular forces.
44. Of note here is that the standard justification for slavery is that the slave is a captive in war whose enslavement is a commuted death sentence. To be cast outside the realm of political life is to be cast as one existing in a state of death.
45. See, for example, the argument running through Bretherton, *Christ and the Common Life*.
46. Bretherton, *Christ and the Common Life*, 41–45; Luke Bretherton, *A Primer in Christian Ethics: Christ and the Struggle to Live Well* (Cambridge University Press, 2023), 330–37.
47. Jennifer Awes Freeman, *The Good Shepherd: Image, Meaning, and Power* (Baylor University Press, 2021); Timothy Laniak, *Shepherds After My Own Heart: Pastoral Traditions and Leadership in the Bible* (Intervarsity, 2006).
48. Michel Foucault, "The Subject and Power," in *Power: Essential Works*, vol. 3, ed. James D. Faubion (New Press, 2001), 334.
49. Louis Althusser, *On the Reproduction of Capitalism: Ideology and Ideological State Apparatuses*, trans. G. M. Goshgarian (Verso, 2014), 201–3. Simon Critchley, *Infinitely Demanding: Ethics of Commitment, Politics of Resistance* (Verso, 2007), 93, notes "the silence or hostility to ethics that one finds in Marx and in many Marxist or post-Marxist thinkers."
50. Schmitt, *The Concept of the Political*, 27–28.
51. Gary Dorrien, *Social Democracy in the Making: Political and Religious Roots of European Socialism* (Yale University Press, 2019), 27–113.
52. Arguably, all tragedy is a form of political theology. However, while the tragedies of Sophocles, Euripides, and Shakespeare focus on the fate of the powerful and prosperous, in the modern, democratic age, the tragic

figure is ordinary, quotidian, and lowly. Arthur Miller's *The Death of a Salesman* is a case in point.

53. Quoted in Saul Alinsky, *Rules for Radicals: A Pragmatic Primer for Realistic Radicals* (Random House, 1971; repr., Vintage, 1989), 14. James here echoes Augustine's somber picture of life in the earthly city, which must be held in tension with his account of the reality and beauty of earthly goods (cf. *City of God* 22.24).

54. See Luke Bretherton, *Resurrecting Democracy: Faith, Citizenship, and the Politics of a Common Life* (Cambridge University Press, 2015).

55. Other examples include Donald M. MacKinnon, "Tragedy and Ethics," in *Explorations in Theology 5* (SCM, 1979), 182–95; and Cornel West, "Subversive Joy and Revolutionary Patience in Black Christianity," in *The Cornel West Reader*, ed. Cornel West (Basic Books, 1999), 435–39.

56. Norman Cohn, *The Pursuit of the Millennium: Revolutionary Millenarians and Mystical Anarchists of the Middle Ages* (Oxford University Press, 1970).

57. Martin Buber, *Paths in Utopia* (Macmillan, 1950).

58. Jürgen Moltmann, *The Coming of God: Christian Eschatology*, trans. Margaret Kohl (Fortress, 1996; repr., Fortress, 2004), 184–92.

59. For a discussion of Joachim of Fiore's theology of history, see Bernard McGinn, *The Calabrian Abbot: Joachim of Fiore in the History of Western Thought* (Macmillan, 1985).

60. Stanley Hauerwas, "The Reality of the Church: Even a Democratic State Is Not the Kingdom," in *Against the Nations: War and Survival in a Liberal Society* (Winston, 1985), 122–31.

61. Stanley Hauerwas, "Seeing Peace: L'Arche as a Peace Movement," in Stanley Hauerwas and Romand Coles, *Christianity, Democracy, and the Radical Ordinary* (Cascade, 2008), 309–21.

62. Moltmann, *The Coming of God*, 187–89.

63. Eric Voegelin, *The New Science of Politics: An Introduction* (University of Chicago Press, 1952). For a more detailed and nuanced study of how various modern political ideologies echo or draw on Joachimite impulses, see Marjorie Reeves, *Joachim of Fiore and the Prophetic Future* (SPCK, 1976); and Matthias Riedl, "Longing for the Third Age: Revolutionary Joachism, Communism, and National Socialism," in *A Companion to Joachim of Fiore*, ed. Matthias Riedl (Brill, 2017).

1. POLITICAL THEOLOGY AS TESTIMONY • 247

64. Herman Pleij, *Dreaming of Cockaigne: Medieval Fantasies of the Perfect Life*, trans. Diane Webb (Columbia University Press, 2001).
65. Strains of these myths can be seen in "transhumanism," "accelerationism," "fully automated luxury communism," and the work of Michael Hardt and Antonio Negri. See F. H. Pitts and A. C. Dinerstein, "Corbynism's Conveyor Belt of Ideas: Postcapitalism and the Politics of Social Reproduction," *Capital and Class* 41, no. 3 (2017): 423–34.
66. J. C. Davies, "Utopianism," in *The Cambridge History of Political Thought: 1450–1700*, ed. J. H. Burns and Mark Goldie (Cambridge University Press, 1991), 341–42.
67. James H. Cone, *Black Theology and Black Power* (Seabury, 1969; repr., Orbis, 1997), 27, 67.
68. James H. Cone, *God of the Oppressed*, rev. ed. (Orbis, 1997), 65.
69. Cone, *God of the Oppressed*, 60.
70. See J. Deotis Roberts, *A Black Political Theology* (Westminster John Knox Press, 1974); and J. Deotis Roberts, *Liberation and Reconciliation: A Black Theology* (Orbis, 2005). One way to understand the difference between Cone and Roberts is to see that Roberts centers a conception of politics as the formation of a common life, whereas Cone prioritizes politics as determined by the friend/enemy antithesis.
71. Cone, *God of the Oppressed*, 224.
72. On Proudhon as a figure whom theology must learn from, see Henri de Lubac, *The Un-Marxian Socialist: A Study of Proudhon* (Sheed & Ward, 1948).
73. Carl Schmitt, *Political Theology: Four Chapters on the Concept of Sovereignty*, trans. George Schwab (University of Chicago Press, 2005), 36.
74. It should also be noted that he concludes his antitheological political theology with a racist diatribe against the "Asiatic hordes" who threaten European liberty, envisaging "Asia" as the seedbed of all religions.
75. Another version of this analogy is Walter Benjamin's parable of the puppet and the dwarf. See Benjamin, "Theses on the Philosophy of History," 253.
76. The question of whether modern political concepts are secularized theological ones or are in actuality new concepts was a formative debate in political theology between Karl Löwith and Hans Blumenberg. For Löwith (himself an ardent critic of Schmitt), modernity and the idea of

progress are secularized forms of Christian eschatology. In this account, historical consciousness, when indexed to a sense of linear development within and through history, is a Judeo-Christian formation. Marxism is a case in point. For all its historical materialism, it is still determined by a messianic eschatology that has a theological shape and form. For Löwith, secularism both fulfills Christianity and dissolves it. See Karl Löwith, *The Meaning of History* (University of Chicago Press, 1949), 18, 202. Blumenberg rejects Löwith's (and Schmitt's) arguments, contending that modernity is a new and distinct set of phenomena with its own consciousness rather than a secularized and immanentized version of Christianity. Modernity thereby supersedes and replaces Christianity. See Hans Blumenberg, *The Legitimacy of the Modern Age*, trans. R. M. Wallace (MIT Press, 1985). Schmitt answers Blumenberg in *Political Theology II*, wholly rejecting Blumenberg's rejection of secularization as a notion. See especially Carl Schmitt, "Postscript," in *Political Theology II: The Myth of the Closure of Any Political Theology*, trans. Michael Hoetzl and Graham Ward (Polity, 2008), 116–30.

77. One example in practice is that, as the likes of Talal Asad and Charles Taylor argue, notions of the secular and secularization are themselves produced by and reproduce theological discourse even as they generate its transvaluation.

78. Michel Foucault, *The History of Sexuality*, vol. 1 (Random House, 1990), 59.

79. Lynn White, "The Historical Roots of Our Ecological Crisis," *Science* (1967) 155: 1203–7.

80. Pope Francis, "Laudato Si'," The Holy See, May 24, 2015, §101–21, accessed December 7, 2024, https://www.vatican.va/content/francesco/en/encyclicals/documents/papa-francesco_20150524_enciclica-laudato-si.html.

81. Schmitt, *Political Theology*, 41.

82. Saba Mahmood's study of secularism and secularity as a mode of governmentality in Egypt, along with Didier Fassin's analysis of how humanitarianism, far from being nonreligious, is a form of political theology, exemplifies this kind of focus. Saba Mahmood, *Religious Difference in a Secular Age: A Minority Report* (Princeton University Press, 2016); Didier Fassin, *Humanitarian Reason: A Moral History of the Present Times* (University of California Press, 2012).

83. See Banerjee and Wouters, *Subaltern Studies 2.0*; and Raj Bharat Patta, *Subaltern Public Theology: Dalits and the Indian Public Sphere* (Palgrave Macmillan, 2023).
84. Achille Mbembe, *Necropolitics* (Duke University Press, 2019).
85. Marisol de la Cadena, "Indigenous Cosmopolitics in the Andes: Conceptual Reflections Beyond 'Politics,'" *Cultural Anthropology* 25, no. 2 (2010): 345.
86. Quoted in Catherine E. Walsh, "The Decolonial For," in Walter D. Mignolo and Catherine E. Walsh, *On Decoloniality: Concepts, Analytics, Praxis* (Duke University Press, 2018), 18.
87. Alex Callinicos, *The Resources of Critique* (Polity, 2006); Gayatri Chakravorty Spivak, "Religion, Politics, Theology: A Conversation with Achille Mbembe," *boundary 2* 34, no. 2 (2007): 149–70.
88. Marisol de la Cadena, *Earth Beings: Ecologies of Practice Across Andean Worlds* (Duke University Press, 2015).
89. Walter D. Mignolo, "Foreword: On Pluriversality and Multipolarity," in *Constructing the Pluriverse: The Geopolitics of Knowledge*, ed. Bernd Reiter (Duke University Press, 2018), x.
90. For a summary of its multiple iterations and genealogy, see Antonio Luis Hidalgo-Capitán and Ana Patricia Cubillo-Guevara, "Deconstruction and Genealogy of Latin American Good Living (*Buen Vivir*): The (Triune) Good Living and Its Diverse Intellectual Wellsprings," *International Development Policy/Revue Internationale de Politique de Développement* 9, no. 9 (2017): 23–50.
91. Pope Francis, "Querida Amazonia," The Holy See, February 2, 2020, §71, accessed December 7, 2024, https://www.vatican.va/content/francesco/en/apost_exhortations/documents/papa-francesco_esortazione-ap_20200202_querida-amazonia.html.
92. Catherine Walsh, "Development as *Buen Vivir*: Institutional Arrangements and (de)Colonial Entanglements," *Development* 53, no. 1 (2010): 188.
93. Roger Merino, "An Alternative to 'Alternative Development'? *Buen Vivir* and Human Development in Andean Countries," *Oxford Development Studies* 44, no. 3 (2016): 276; Joe Quick and James T. Spartz, "On the Pursuit of Good Living in Highland Ecuador: Critical Indigenous Discourses of Sumak Kawsay," *Latin American Research Review* 53, no. 4 (2018): 757–69; and de la Cadena, "Indigenous Cosmopolitics in the Andes," 354.

94. Walter D. Mignolo, "What Does It Mean to Decolonize?," in Mignolo and Walsh, *On Decoloniality*, 124–28.
95. See, for example, Arturo Escobar, *Pluriversal Politics: The Real and the Possible*, trans. David Frye (Duke University Press, 2020).
96. Pope Francis, "Querida Amazonia," §§8, 26, 34, 71 Hidalgo-Capitán and Cubillo-Guevara, "Deconstruction and Genealogy," 34–35.
97. Merino, "An Alternative," 273; Julien Vanhulst and Adrian E. Beling, "*Buen Vivir*: Emergent Discourse Within or Beyond Sustainable Development?," *Ecological Economics* 101 (2014): 61.
98. A book that exemplifies this kind of work is Elizabeth O'Donnell Gandolfo, *Ecomartydom in the Americas: Living and Dying for Our Common Home* (Orbis, 2023).
99. Foucault, *The History of Sexuality*, 58–59.

2. POLITICAL THEOLOGY FROM BELOW

1. Reinhard Mehring, *Carl Schmitt: A Biography*, trans. Daniel Steuer (Polity, 2014).
2. Though they displaced their origin story from student and decolonial revolt to the Jewish Holocaust. See Vincent Lloyd, "Christian Responses to the Holocaust: Political Theology in Europe," in *T&T Clark Handbook of Political Theology*, ed. Rubén Rosario Rodríguez (T&T Clark, 2020).
3. Warren Breckman, "Democracy Between Disenchantment and Political Theology: French Post-Marxism and the Return to Religion," *New German Critique* 94 (2005): 72–105.
4. Yannik Thiem [as Annika Thiem], "Schmittian Shadows and Contemporary Theological-Political Constellations," *Social Research* 80, no. 1 (2013): 1–32.
5. When I refer to social movements in the pages that follow, I am referring to justice-oriented social movements, that is, grassroots movements that challenge domination. I recognize that determining what counts as such a movement is not trivial, but I do not think it is impossible.
6. Morgan Bassichis, Alexander Lee, and Dean Spade, "Building an Abolitionist Trans and Queer Movement with Everything We've Got," in *Captive Genders: Trans Embodiment and the Prison Industrial Complex*, ed. Eric A. Stanley and Nat Smith (AK Press, 2011), 36. Italics removed.

2. POLITICAL THEOLOGY FROM BELOW • 251

7. I develop this social movement grammar in *Black Dignity: The Struggle Against Domination* (Yale University Press, 2022), chap. 5.
8. Ruth Wilson Gilmore, *Golden Gulag: Prisons, Surplus, Crisis, and Opposition in Globalizing California* (University of California Press, 2007), 247.
9. "Herstory," Black Lives Matter, July 7, 2017, accessed April 5, 2024, https://blacklivesmatter.com/herstory.
10. Keeanga-Yamahtta Taylor, ed., *How We Get Free: Black Feminism and the Combahee River Collective* (Haymarket, 2017), 15, 16, 17.
11. Raymond Geuss, *Philosophy and Real Politics* (Princeton University Press, 2008).
12. For an overview, see Oliver Marchart, *Post-Foundational Political Thought: Political Difference in Nancy, Lefort, Badiou and Laclau* (Edinburgh University Press, 2007). Compare to Luke Bretherton's account of politics and the political in his contribution to this book.
13. Andrew Arato, "Political Theology and Populism," *Social Research* 80, no. 1 (2013): 143–72.
14. Carl Schmitt, *The Concept of the Political* (University of Chicago Press, 2007 [1932]).
15. Chantal Mouffe, ed., *The Challenge of Carl Schmitt* (Verso, 1999); Chantal Mouffe, *The Return of the Political* (Verso, 1993); Jodi Dean, *The Communist Horizon* (Verso, 2018); Banu Bargu, "The Predicaments of Left-Schmittianism," *South Atlantic Quarterly* 113, no. 4 (2014): 713–27.
16. Richard Wolin, "Carl Schmitt, Political Existentialism, and the Total State," *Theory and Society* 19, no. 4 (1990): 389–416.
17. Carl Schmitt, *Political Theology: Four Chapters on the Concept of Sovereignty* (University of Chicago Press, 2005 [1934]), 15.
18. Schmitt, *The Concept of the Political*, 35.
19. Quoted in Wolin, "Carl Schmitt," 406.
20. This is starting to change as figures such as Alain Badiou weave an existential dimension into their work and figures such as Simone de Beauvoir receive renewed attention.
21. Academic conversations in political theology are often dominated by mainline Protestants and Catholics, who have less patience for the existential than do their evangelical cousins. Luke Bretherton dissents on this point, suggesting that evangelicals are embracing "public theology," which is a refusal of existential questions, whereas in a document such

as Pope Francis's "Laudato Si'" one finds existential concern. I agree that the landscape is nuanced, but my point has to do with the sociology of the academy.

22. Although this is beginning to change as a generation of academics who were trained during the long 2010s enters the professoriate.
23. See, for example, Alex Dubilet and Vincent Lloyd, eds., *Political Theology Reimagined* (Duke University Press, 2025).
24. For accounts of this period and its global context, see Anton Jäger and Arthur Borriello, *The Populist Moment: The Left After the Great Recession* (Verso, 2023); Vincent Bevins, *If We Burn: The Mass Protest Decade and the Missing Revolution* (PublicAffairs, 2023); and Joshua Green, *The Rebels: Elizabeth Warren, Bernie Sanders, Alexandria Ocasio-Cortez, and the Struggle for a New American Politics* (Penguin, 2024).
25. An important exception was the massive mobilizations around global justice, occasioned by the meetings of the World Bank, International Monetary Fund, and World Trade Organization, in the few years before September 11, 2001, an event that brought an abrupt end to emerging left energy.
26. Robyn Marasco, "The Real Possibility of Physical Killing: A Critique of Carl Schmitt," *American Journal of Political Science* 67, no. 3 (2023): 1067–79. I have greatly appreciated Marasco's analysis, which parallels in some ways my own.
27. Joshua Cherniss, *Liberalism in Dark Times: The Liberal Ethos in the Twentieth Century* (Princeton University Press, 2021).
28. From a Christian perspective, the distinctiveness of the Christian story is that, in Jesus, the sensuousness of living is essentially linked with God beyond the world.
29. Bonnie Honig, *Emergency Politics: Paradox, Law, Democracy* (Princeton University Press, 2011); George Shulman, *American Prophecy: Race and Redemption in American Political Culture* (University of Minnesota Press, 2008).
30. See Christian Smith, *The Emergence of Liberation Theology: Radical Religion and Social Movement Theory* (University of Chicago Press, 1991). The connection between Black liberation theology and Black Christian communities has been decidedly more tenuous. See, for example, Raphael G. Warnock, *The Divided Mind of the Black Church: Theology,*

Piety, and Public Witness (New York University Press, 2014). Luke Bretherton argues that this distance between academia and church is greater for Cone than for currents of Black theology represented by J. Deotis Roberts or Albert Cleage. I disagree. While Roberts and Cleage may be more engaged with Black churches, they are not widely influential figures. Indeed, even the activism of Martin Luther King Jr. was opposed by a majority of Black churches.

31. For a useful reflection on the relationship between German Christian political theology and liberation theology by an exponent of the former, see Jürgen Moltmann, "Political Theology and Liberation Theology," *Union Seminary Quarterly Review* 45 (1991): 205–17.

32. See also Arne Rasmusson, *The Church as Polis: From Political Theology to Theological Politics as Exemplified by Jürgen Moltmann and Stanley Hauerwas* (University of Notre Dame Press, 1995), chap. 8.

33. For particularly sophisticated scholarship in liberation theology along these lines, see the work of Marcella Althaus-Reid, for example, *Indecent Theology: Theological Perversions in Sex, Gender and Politics* (Routledge, 2000).

34. See, for example, Linell Elizabeth Cady and Tracy Fessenden, eds., *Religion, the Secular, and the Politics of Sexual Difference* (Columbia University Press, 2013); and Jonathon Kahn and Vincent W. Lloyd, eds., *Race and Secularism in America* (Columbia University Press, 2016).

35. For a particularly powerful example of political theology in popular political discourse, see Houria Bouteldja, *Whites, Jews, and Us: Toward a Politics of Revolutionary Love* (Semiotext[e], 2017). Bouteldja was a keynote speaker at the first Political Theology Network conference, held at Emory University in 2018.

36. Aimé Césaire, *Discourse on Colonialism* (Monthly Review Press, 2000), 48; Aimé Césaire, *The Complete Poetry of Aimé Césaire* (Wesleyan University Press, 2017), 57. Parenthetical references refer to this work. I discuss the passage from Césaire's *Discourse* in the introduction to Vincent Lloyd, ed., *Race and Political Theology* (Stanford University Press, 2012). J. Kameron Carter uses this passage to read Césaire's *Notebook* as offering "what amounts to an abyssal theory of Blackness, if not of Black religion, staged as an alternative ritual of celebration"; see "The Excremental Sacred: A Paraliturgy," in *Beyond Man: Race, Coloniality, and the Philosophy of*

Religion, ed. An Yountae and Eleanor Craig (Duke University Press, 2021). In contrast, I read Césaire as a fundamentally dialectical thinker and writer, engaging within and across his poetry with the changing conditions of the world around him and his deepening understanding of the physical and conceptual space he occupies. And I read negotiating the Christian grammar he inherits as essential to Césaire's dialectical orientation. In this, I find inspiration in Carter's earlier, more dialectical work, especially "Race, Religion, and the Contradictions of Identity: A Theological Engagement with Douglass's 1845 *Narrative*," *Modern Theology* 21, no. 1 (2005): 37–65. My reading of Césaire is *political* and *theological*, whereas Carter's reading of Césaire aspires to be *ontological* and *mystical*.

37. For the best political-theoretic analysis of Césaire, see Gary Wilder, *Freedom Time: Negritude, Decolonization, and the Future of the World* (Duke University Press, 2015). For Césaire's own reflections on his political trajectory and thought, see Césaire, *Resolutely Black: Conversations with Françoise Vergès* (Polity, 2020).

38. Elizabeth A. Foster, *African Catholic: Decolonization and the Transformation of the Church* (Harvard University Press, 2019), 59.

39. For another exception to the prevalent secularizing reading of Césaire, one that focuses on the way African religious cosmology and practice shapes his poetics, see Jason Allen-Paisant, *Engagements with Aimé Césaire: Thinking with Spirits* (Oxford University Press, 2024).

40. I develop these themes in Vincent Lloyd, "What Life Is Not: Aimé Césaire as Phenomenologist of Domination," *Symposium: Canadian Journal of Continental Philosophy* 26, nos. 1–2 (2022): 224–41. Some of the paragraphs here draw on that article.

41. On the theological resonances of such imagery in negritude, see David Ngong, *Senghor's Eucharist: Negritude and African Political Theology* (Baylor University Press, 2023).

42. Valentina Napolitano helpfully drew my attention to the equivocal nature of prostration, as both the fact of submission and as ritual, as participation in a political order.

43. For a rather different reading, with emphasis on the apocalyptic rather than the eschatological and prayerful, see John Drabinski, "Césaire's Apocalyptic Word," *South Atlantic Quarterly* 115, no. 3 (2016): 567–84.

44. Michel Henry, *I Am the Truth: Toward a Philosophy of Christianity* (Stanford University Press, 2003); Donna V. Jones, *The Racial Discourses*

of Life Philosophy: Negritude, Vitalism, and Modernity (Columbia University Press, 2010).

45. I take Michel Henry's work to be centrally concerned with demonstrating how this line of thought does not lead to wallowing in the ordinary—in the obvious—but instead entails a critical, dialectical engagement with the world. See Henry, *I Am the Truth*; and Michel Henry, *Marx: A Philosophy for Human Reality*, trans. Kathleen McLaughlin (Indiana University Press, 1983).

46. Compare the related questions that Abdul R. JanMohamed, in a largely secular register but with attention to the multiplicity of "resurrections," finds Richard Wright exploring in JanMohamed's *The Death-Bound-Subject: Richard Wright's Archaeology of Death* (Duke University Press, 2005).

47. Wilder, *Freedom Time*.

48. Or at least the North American social movements.

49. On this New Age vice, see Vincent Lloyd, "Love, Judgment, and Antisemitism: The Case of Alice Walker," in *The King Is in the Field: Essays in Modern Jewish Political Thought*, ed. Julie E. Cooper and Samuel Hayim Brody (University of Pennsylvania Press, 2023).

50. Luke Bretherton helpfully and provocatively suggests that overcompliance with covid restrictions is an example of this dynamic. The foundational conceptual work on the theme of carcerality is Michel Foucault, *Discipline and Punish: The Birth of the Prison* (Vintage, 1995), but "carcerality" has taken on a life of its own as it has circulated in social movement spaces and been theorized anew in those spaces.

51. Elizabeth Bernstein, "The Sexual Politics of the 'New Abolitionism,'" *differences* 18, no. 3 (2007): 128–51. See also Aya Gruber, *The Feminist War on Crime: The Unexpected Role of Women's Liberation in Mass Incarceration* (University of California Press, 2021).

52. See Derecka Purnell, *Becoming Abolitionists: Police, Protests, and the Pursuit of Freedom* (Astra, 2021).

53. Allegra McLeod, "Prison Abolition and Grounded Justice," *UCLA Law Review* 62 (2015): 1167–68.

54. Jo Freeman's work is the locus classicus on this point, and it has recently been picked up again in US discussions of "left toxicity." Jo Freeman, "The Tyranny of Structurelessness," Jo Freeman.com, accessed December 8, 2024, https://www.jofreeman.com/joreen/tyranny.htm.

55. For a consideration of these issues that constructs a critical dialogue between Augustine's thought and Black studies, see Matthew Elia, *The Problem of the Christian Master: Augustine in the Afterlife of Slavery* (Yale University Press, 2024).
56. Stefano Harney and Fred Moten, *The Undercommons: Fugitive Planning and Black Study* (Minor Compositions, 2013), 42.
57. For an exploration of the shared grammar of nineteenth- and twenty-first-century abolition movements that tracks the key role of religion, see Joshua Dubler and Vincent W. Lloyd, *Break Every Yoke: Religion, Justice, and the Abolition of Prisons* (Oxford University Press, 2019).
58. Dylan Rodríguez, "Abolition as Praxis of Human Being," *Harvard Law Review* 132 (2019): 1576, 1579.
59. On practices of inwardness, I have found Andrew Prevot's work especially helpful: *Thinking Prayer: Theology and Spirituality amid the Crises of Modernity* (University of Notre Dame Press, 2015); *The Mysticism of Ordinary Life: Theology, Philosophy, and Feminism* (Oxford University Press, 2023). See also Kevin Quashie, *The Sovereignty of Quiet: Beyond Resistance in Black Culture* (Rutgers University Press, 2012).
60. Quoted in Marbre Stahly-Butts and Amna A. Akbar, "Reforms for Radicals? An Abolitionist Framework," *UCLA Law Review* 68 (2022): 1553. Henderson's leadership partner, Highlander Center co-executive director Allyn Maxfield-Steele, has a Master of Divinity degree from Vanderbilt, previously worked as a pastor, and attended the Political Theology Network's inaugural conference.
61. André Gorz, *Strategy for Labor: A Radical Proposal* (Beacon, 1962); Amna A. Akbar, "Non-Reformist Reforms and Struggles over Life, Death, and Democracy," *Yale Law Journal* 132 (2023): 2497–577.
62. Stahly-Butts and Akbar, "Reforms for Radicals?," 1552.
63. H. Richard Niebuhr, "The Grace of Doing Nothing," *Christian Century* 49 (1932): 378–80.
64. See, for example, Naomi Murakawa, *The First Civil Right: How Liberals Built Prison America* (Princeton University Press, 2014).
65. Mariame Kaba, *We Do This 'Til We Free Us: Abolitionist Organizing and Transforming Justice* (Haymarket, 2021), 142.
66. For an account of the complexity involved in developing restorative justice practices from the perspective of religious studies, see Jason

Springs, *Restorative Justice and Lived Religion: Transforming Mass Incarceration in Chicago* (New York University Pres, 2024).
67. Kaba, *We Do This*, 4, 127.
68. This language of safety closely echoes mainstream discourse around the pandemic, strengthening its hold.
69. Tyler Roberts, "From Secular Criticism to Critical Fidelity," *Political Theology* 18, no. 8 (2017): 706–707.
70. For a thoughtful study of the ethical ambivalence of such practices, and an appreciation of the way they scramble secular-religious divides, see Caleb Smith, *Thoreau's Axe: Disciplines of Attention in a Secular Age* (Princeton University Press, 2023).
71. Thanks to Luke Bretherton and Valentina Napolitano for their very helpful feedback on multiple iterations of this essay, as well as to audiences at the University of Copenhagen; the École normale supérieure; the Council for World Mission's Discernment and Radical Engagement Global Forum in Bangkok; St. Patrick's Pontifical University, Maynooth; Lancaster University; Grinnell College; United Lutheran Seminary; and Villanova University.

3. AN ANTHROPOLOGICAL POLITICAL THEOLOGY

1. Ato Quayson, *Tragedy and Postcolonial Literature* (Cambridge University Press, 2021).
2. Maya Mayblin, "The Lapsed and the Laity: Discipline and Lenience in the Study of Religion," *Journal of the Royal Anthropological Institute* 23, no. 3 (2017): 503–22.
3. Valentina Napolitano, "Francis, a Criollo Pope," *Religion and Society* 10, no. 1 (2019): 63–80.
4. John C. Cavadini and Donald Wallenfang, eds., *Pope Francis and the Event of Encounter: Global Perspectives on the New Evangelization* (Pickwick, 2018).
5. Michel de Certeau, *Heterologies: Discourse on the Other*, trans. Brian Massumi (University of Minnesota Press, 1986).
6. Pope Francis, "Extraordinary Moment of Prayer Presided over by Pope Francis," The Holy See, March 27, 2020, accessed December 7, 2024,

https://www.vatican.va/content/francesco/en/homilies/2020/documents/papa-francesco_20200327_omelia-epidemia.html.

7. Lawrence Cohen, "The Culling: Pandemic, Gerocide, Generational Affect," *Medical Anthropology Quarterly* 34, no. 4 (2020): 542–60; Ellen Badone, "From Cruddiness to Catastrophe: COVID-19 and Long-Term Care in Ontario," *Medical Anthropology* 40, no. 5 (2021): 389–403.
8. Anna Lowenhaupt Tsing, *Friction: An Ethnography of Global Connection* (Princeton University Press, 2005).
9. William Mazzarella, *The Mana of Mass Society* (University of Chicago Press, 2017); Francis Cody, "Wave Theory: Cash, Crowds, and Caste in Indian Elections," *American Ethnologist* 47, no. 4 (2020): 402–16.
10. Cori Hayden, "From Connection to Contagion," *Journal of the Royal Anthropological Institute* 27, no. S1 (2021): 95–107.
11. Didier Fassin and Paula Vasquez, "Humanitarian Exception as the Rule: The Political Theology of the 1999 Tragedia in Venezuela," *American Ethnologist* 32, no. 3 (2005): 389–405.
12. I use the term *nonsecular* not in opposition to what the secular is, but as what exceed, expand beyond, and can also contain secular categorizations.
13. Willie James Jennings, *The Christian Imagination: Theology and the Origins of Race* (Yale University Press, 2010).
14. By "vegetal materialities and temporalities," I am referring to the work on Colombian Amazonia on the vital relations between peasants and soil and their multiple coexisting temporalities. Kristina M. Lyons, *Vital Decomposition: Soil Practitioners and Life Politics* (Duke University Press, 2020), 174–76.
15. Anthropologists and historians have begun to productively engage with God or the gods in relation to humans and multiple species through bonds, obligations, and partaking, rather than through a liberal, egalitarian notion of freedom. A shared effort is emerging on a more capacious analytics on ecological political theology through a triangulation of porous selves, multispecies, and gods and supernatural beings; see Milinda Banerjee and Jelle J. P. Wouters, *Subaltern Studies 2.0: Being Against the Capitalocene* (Prickly Paradigm, 2022). There is also a need to focus on a more "supple and nuanced, fleshed out and embodied, account of how vernacular theologies and other-than-human entanglements are transforming the scope of the political"; see Mareike

Winchell, "Afterword: Theos | Cosmos | Ontos: Rethinking Religion's Politics from Latin America," *American Religion* 5, no. 2 (2024): 201–2.

16. N. Fadeke Castor, *Spiritual Citizenship: Transnational Pathways from Black Power to Ifá in Trinidad* (Duke University Press, 2017).
17. J. Brent Crosson, *Experiments with Power: Obeah and the Remaking of Religion in Trinidad* (University of Chicago Press, 2020), 84–85.
18. Setrag Manoukian, "Thinking with the Impersonal: An Ethnographic View from Iran," *Antropologia* 6, no. 1 (2019): 199–215. And on the "just" of justice, see Alex Dubilet, "The Just Without Justification: On Meister Eckhart and Political Theology," *postmedieval* 13, no. 1 (2022): 5–28.
19. I take as a starting point a definition of theology by Johann Baptist Metz, who was influential in post–Vatican II debates. It is a form of "talking to God" that emerges from an open-ended vulnerability, an attention to suffering, and a deep concern for a "passion for compassion," and of political theology as an actualization of God's biblical presence in history. See Johann Baptist Metz, *Remembering and Resisting: The New Political Theology* (Wipf and Stock, 2022), 13.
20. I am indebted on this thinking to Aaron Eldridge and Candace Lukasik.
21. Liana Chua and Nayanika Mathur, "Introduction," in *Who Are We? Reimagining Alterity and Affinity in Anthropology* (Berghahn, 2018).
22. Paul W. Kahn, *Political Theology: Four New Chapters on the Concept of Sovereignty* (Columbia University Press, 2011).
23. Khaled Furani, *Redeeming Anthropology: A Theological Critique of a Modern Science* (Oxford University Press, 2019), 22.
24. Nada Moumtaz, *God's Property: Islam, Charity, and the Modern State* (University of California Press, 2020).
25. Ryan C. Jobson, "The Case for Letting Anthropology Burn: Sociocultural Anthropology in 2019," *American Anthropologist* 122, no. 2 (2020): 259–71.
26. Ruth Marshall, *Political Spiritualities: The Pentecostal Revolution in Nigeria* (University of Chicago Press, 2009); Brian Larkin, *Signal and Noise: Media, Infrastructure, and Urban Culture in Nigeria* (Duke University Press, 2008); David Mosse, *The Saint in the Banyan Tree: Christianity and Caste Society in India* (University of California Press, 2012).
27. Didier Fassin, "The Predicament of Humanitarianism," *Qui Parle: Critical Humanities and Social Sciences* 22, no. 1 (2013): 33–48.

28. Mayblin, "The Lapsed and the Laity."
29. Michel de Certeau and Luce Giard, *La faiblesse de croire* (Seuil, 1987).
30. Charles Hirschkind, "On the Virtues of Holding Your Tongue," *Critical Times* 3, no. 3 (2020): 471–77.
31. Marshall Sahlins et al., "The Sadness of Sweetness: The Native Anthropology of Western Cosmology," *Current Anthropology* 37, no. 3 (1996): 395–428.
32. Mario Blaser, "Is Another Cosmopolitics Possible?," *Cultural Anthropology* 31, no. 4 (2016): 545–70; Marisol de la Cadena, "Indigenous Cosmopolitics in the Andes: Conceptual Reflections Beyond 'Politics,'" *Cultural Anthropology* 25, no. 2 (2010): 334–70; Arturo Escobar, "Territorios de Diferencia: La Ontología Política de los 'Derechos al Territorio,'" *Cuadernos de Antropología Social* 41 (2015): 25–38.
33. Valentina Napolitano, "Immanent Singularity," Political Theology Network, May 5, 2022, accessed December 7, 2024, https://politicaltheology.com/immanent-singularity.
34. Joel Robbins, "Beyond the Suffering Subject: Toward an Anthropology of the Good," *Journal of the Royal Anthropological Institute* 19, no. 3 (2013), 448.
35. James S. Bielo, "Anthropology, Theology, Critique," *Critical Research on Religion* 6, no. 1 (2018): 28–34.
36. Joel Robbins, *Theology and the Anthropology of Christian Life* (Oxford University Press, 2020).
37. Victoria Kahn, "Political Theology and Liberal Culture: Strauss, Schmitt, Spinoza, and Arendt," in *Political Theology and Early Modernity*, ed. Graham Hammill and Julia Reinhard Lupton (University of Chicago Press, 2012).
38. Derrick J. Lemons, "An Introduction to Theologically Engaged Anthropology," *Ethnos* 86, no. 3 (2021): 401–7.
39. Elayne Oliphant, "The Secular and the Global: Rethinking the Anthropology of Christianity in the Wake of 1492," *Religion* 51, no. 4 (2021): 577–92.
40. Amira Mittermaier, "Dreams from Elsewhere: Muslim Subjectivities Beyond the Trope of Self-Cultivation," *Journal of the Royal Anthropological Institute* 18, no. 2 (2012): 247–65; Robert A. Orsi, *Between Heaven and Earth* (Princeton University Press, 2013); Chiara Bottici,

"Imagination, Imaginary, Imaginal: Towards a New Social Ontology?," *Social Epistemology* 33, no. 5 (2019): 433–41.

41. Annalisa Butticci and Amira Mittermaier, "Afterword: The Elsewhere Beyond Religious Concerns," *Religion and Society* 11, no. 1 (2020): 176–85; Amira Mittermaier, *Giving to God: Islamic Charity in Revolutionary Times* (University of California Press, 2019); Marshall, *Political Spiritualities*.

42. A classic anthropological case is the study by Julian Pitt-Rivers of "grace" in Andalusia as an "extra" to social and gender relations: "The Place of Grace in Anthropology," *HAU: Journal of Ethnographic Theory* 1, no. 1 (2011): 423–50.

43. Carlota McAllister and Valentina Napolitano, "Introduction: Incarnate Politics Beyond the Cross and the Sword," *Social Analysis* 64, no. 4 (2020): 1–20.

44. Carlota McAllister and Valentina Napolitano, "Political Theology/Theopolitics: The Thresholds and Vulnerabilities of Sovereignty," *Annual Review of Anthropology* 50 (2021): 109–27.

45. Adam Kotsko, *The Prince of This World* (Stanford University Press, 2020); Oliphant, "The Secular and the Global."

46. Walter Benjamin, *The Origin of the German Tragic Drama* (Verso, 2009); Bruno Reinhardt, "The Katechon and the Messias: Time, history, and threat in Brazil's aspirational fascism," *Current Anthropology* 66, no. 3 (2025): 332–61.

47. Janet Roitman, *The Anti-Crisis* (Duke University Press, 2014).

48. Jessica R. Cattelino, *High Stakes: Florida Seminole Gaming and Sovereignty* (Duke University Press, 2008); Audra Simpson, *Mohawk Interruptus: Political Life Across the Borders of Settler States* (Duke University Press, 2014).

49. Yarimar Bonilla, *Non-Sovereign Futures: French Caribbean Politics in the Wake of Disenchantment* (University of Chicago Press, 2015); Paul Nadasdy, *Sovereignty's Entailments: First Nation State Formation in the Yukon* (University of Toronto Press, 2017).

50. Julian Pitt-Rivers, "The Law of Hospitality," in *The Fate of Shechem, or the Politics of Sex*, ed. J. Pitt-Rivers (Cambridge University Press, 1977), 94–112.

51. Dominic Boyer, "Time of Monsters," Society for Cultural Anthropology, October 31, 2018, https://culanth.org/fieldsights/series/time-of-monsters.

52. Jean Comaroff and John Comaroff, "Occult Economies and the Violence of Abstraction: Notes from the South African Postcolony," *American Ethnologist* 26, no. 3 (1999): 279–30; Valentina Napolitano, *Migrant Hearts and the Atlantic Return: Transnationalism and the Roman Catholic Church* (Fordham University Press, 2016).
53. See, for instance, Elayne Oliphant, "Beyond Blasphemy or Devotion: Art, the Secular, and Catholicism in Paris," *Journal of the Royal Anthropological Institute* 21, no. 2 (2015): 352–73.
54. Daromir Rudnyckyj and Filippo Osella, *Religion and the Morality of the Market* (Cambridge University Press, 2017).
55. Elettra Stimilli, *Debt and Guilt: A Political Philosophy* (Bloomsbury Academic, 2019).
56. Joseph Tonda, *The Modern Sovereign: The Body of Power in Central Africa (Congo and Gabon)*, trans. Chris Turner (Seagull, 2021).
57. Tonda, *The Modern Sovereign*, 154.
58. Isabelle Stengers, "The Challenge of Ontological Politics," in *A World of Many Worlds*, ed. Marisol de la Cadena and Mario Blaser (Duke University Press, 2018), 109.
59. Chris Garces, "The Cross Politics of Ecuador's Penal State," *Cultural Anthropology* 25, no. 3 (2010): 459–96.
60. Michel-Rolph Trouillot, "The Otherwise Modern," in *Critically Modern: Alternatives, Alterities, Anthropologies*, ed. Bruce M. Knauft (Indiana University Press, 2002).
61. Safet Hadžimuhamedović, *Waiting for Elijah: Time and Encounter in a Bosnian Landscape* (Berghahn, 2022), 163.
62. Franca Tamisari, *Enacted Relations: Performing Knowledge in an Australian Indigenous Community* (Berghahn, 2024).
63. See Roberto Esposito's rethinking of Simon Weil's understanding of impersonal justice: Roberto Esposito, "For a Philosophy of the Impersonal," trans. Timothy Campbell, *CR: The New Centennial Review* 10, no. 2 (2010): 121–34.
64. Annemarie Mol, *Eating in Theory* (Duke University Press, 2021).
65. Elizabeth Pérez, *The Gut: A Black Atlantic Alimentary Tract* (Cambridge University Press, 2022).
66. Mazzarella, *The Mana of Mass Society*; William Mazzarella, "The Anthropology of Populism: Beyond the Liberal Settlement," *Annual Review of Anthropology* 48 (2019): 45–60.

3. AN ANTHROPOLOGICAL POLITICAL THEOLOGY • 263

67. Eric L. Santner, *The Weight of All Flesh: On the Subject-Matter of Political Economy*, ed. Kevis Goodman (Oxford University Press, 2016).
68. Maurice Bloch and Jonathan Parry, eds., *Death and the Regeneration of Life* (Cambridge University Press, 1982); Emily Ng, *A Time of Lost Gods: Mediumship, Madness, and the Ghost After Mao* (University of California Press, 2020).
69. Michael Taussig, *Shamanism, Colonialism, and the Wild Man: A Study in Terror and Healing* (University of Chicago Press, 2008).
70. Isaias Rojas-Perez, *Mourning Remains: State Atrocity, Exhumations, and Governing the Disappeared in Peru's Postwar Andes* (Stanford University Press, 2017), 26, 259.
71. Khaled Furani, "Khalifah and the Modern Sovereign: Revisiting a Qur'anic Ideal from Within the Palestinian Condition," *Journal of Religion* 102, no. 4 (2022): 497.
72. Furani, "Khalifah and the Modern Sovereign," 503.
73. For more on this ethnographic work, see Stephen Berquist, Valentina Napolitano, and Elizabeth Rigotti, "Holy Infrastructures: Catholicism, Detroit Borderlands, and the Elements," *Comparative Studies of Society and History* 65, no. 4 (2024): 786–813.
74. Anna Rowlands, "The Politics of Mourning: Reading Gillian Rose in COVID Times," ABC Religion & Ethics, May 24, 2020, accessed December 7, 2024, https://www.abc.net.au/religion/anna-rowlands-gillian-rose-the-politics-of-mourning/12281170.
75. Stefania Pandolfo, *Knot of the Soul: Madness, Psychoanalysis, Islam* (University of Chicago Press, 2018), 156.
76. Savannah Shange, "Abolition in the Clutch: Shifting Through the Gears with Anthropology," *Feminist Anthropology* 3, no. 2 (2022): 187–97.
77. Cristiana Giordano and Greg Pierotti, "Getting Caught: A Collaboration On- and Offstage Between Theatre and Anthropology," *TDR/The Drama Review* 64, no. 1 (2020): 88–106.
78. Basit Kareem Iqbal, "Reprising Islamic Political Theology: Genre and the Time of Tribulation," *Political Theology* 23, no. 6 (2022): 525–42.
79. Bruno Latour, *Rejoicing: Or the Torments of Religious Speech* (Wiley, 2018).
80. Basit Kareem Iqbal, "Economy of Tribulation: Translating Humanitarianism for an Islamic Counterpublic," *The Muslim World* 112, no. 1 (2022): 33–56.

81. For "pneuma," see Ashon T. Crawley, *Blackpentecostal Breath: The Aesthetics of Possibility* (Fordham University Press, 2016).
82. Elizabeth A. Povinelli, *Geontologies: A Requiem to Late Liberalism* (Duke University Press, 2016).
83. Roberto Esposito, "Community, Immunity, Biopolitics," in Roberto Esposito, *Community, Immunity and the Proper* (Routledge, 2017).
84. Bielo, "Anthropology, Theology, Critique."
85. For a centrality of storytelling and a sophisticated path of decolonization from the African continent, see Felwine Sarr, *Afrotopia* (University of Minnesota Press, 2020). For a championing of storytelling to decolonial First Nation philosophy, see Brian Burkhart, *Indigenizing Philosophy Through the Land: A Trickster Methodology for Decolonizing Environmental Ethics and Indigenous Futures* (Michigan State University Press, 2019); and Dana Lloyd, *Land Is Kin: Sovereignty, Religious Freedom, and Indigenous Sacred Sites* (University Press of Kansas, 2023).
86. Walter Benjamin, "Capitalism as Religion," in Walter Benjamin, *Toward the Critique of Violence* (Stanford University Press, 2021).
87. Kahn, "Political Theology and Liberal Culture," 3.
88. Linda Basch, Nina Glick Schiller, and Cristina Szanton Blanc, *Nations Unbound: Transnational Projects, Postcolonial Predicaments, and Deterritorialized Nation-States* (Routledge, 1992).
89. Alessandro Dal Lago, *Non-Persone: L'esclusione dei Migranti in Una Società Globale* (Feltrinelli Editore, 2006); Donatella Di Cesare, *Resident Foreigners: A Philosophy of Migration*, trans. David Broder (Polity, 2020).
90. Saba Mahmood, *Religious Difference in a Secular Age: A Minority Report* (Princeton University Press, 2015).
91. Weiqiang Lin, Johan Lindquist, Biao Xiang, and Brenda S. A. Yeoh, "Migration Infrastructures and the Production of Migrant Mobilities," *Mobilities* 12, no. 2 (2017): 167–74.
92. Alastair Roberts, "The Politics of Eschatological Imminence—1 Corinthians 7:29–31," Political Theology Network, January 19, 2015, accessed December 7, 2024, https://politicaltheology.com/the-politics-of-eschatological-imminence-1-corinthians-729-31; Thomas Lynch, *Apocalyptic Political Theology: Hegel, Taubes and Malabou* (Bloomsbury, 2019); Elettra Stimilli, "Jacob Taubes e il Senso Antistorico

dell'Escatologia," in *Escatologia Occidentale* (Quodlibet, 2019); Kyle B. T. Lambelet, "The Lure of the Apocalypse: Ecology, Ethics, and the End of the World," *Studies in Christian Ethics*, 34, no. 4 (2021): 482–97.

93. *Globalatinization* refers to the process by which secularization, influenced by Christian and Latin roots, has become a global phenomenon. See Jacques Derrida, "Above All, No Journalists!," in *Religion and Media*, ed. Samuel Weber and Hent de Vries (Fordham University Press, 2001); and Gil Anidjar, "Of Globalatinology," *Derrida Today* 6, no. 1 (2013): 11–22.

94. Charles Hirschkind, *The Feeling of History: Islam, Romanticism, and Andalusia* (University of Chicago Press, 2020); Aaron Frederick Eldridge, "A Cartographic Exercise," *Political Theology* 24, no. 1 (2023): 128–33.

95. Mikaela H. Rogozen-Soltar, *Spain Unmoored: Migration, Conversion, and the Politics of Islam* (Indiana University Press, 2017).

96. See Pitt-Rivers, "The Place of Grace in Anthropology."

97. McAllister and Napolitano, "Political Theology/Theopolitics."

98. Neena Mahadev, *Karma and Grace: Religious Difference in Millennial Sri Lanka* (Columbia University Press, 2023).

99. Pandolfo, *Knot of the Soul*; Cristiana Giordano, *Migrants in Translation: Caring and the Logics of Difference in Contemporary Italy* (University of California Press, 2014).

100. Pandolfo, *Knot of the Soul*.

101. Simpson, *Mohawk Interruptus*.

102. Luke Bretherton, *Christ and the Common Life: Political Theology and the Case for Democracy* (William B. Eerdmans, 2019); Kristin E. Heyer, "Migration and Structural Injustice," in *Christian Theology in the Age of Migration: Implications for World Christianity*, ed. Peter Phan (Lexington, 2020).

103. Marilyn Strathern, *Relations: An Anthropological Account* (Duke University Press, 2020).

104. Dipesh Chakrabarty, "The Planet: An Emergent Humanist Category," *Critical Inquiry* 46, no. 1 (2019): 1–31.

105. Sylvia Wynter, "Unsettling the Coloniality of Being/Power/Truth/Freedom: Towards the Human, After Man, Its Overrepresentation—An Argument," *CR: The New Centennial Review* 3, no. 3 (2003): 257–337;

Katie Walker Grimes, *Fugitive Saints: Catholicism and the Politics of Slavery* (Fortress, 2017).

106. Valentina Napolitano, "On a Political Economy of Political Theology: El Señor de los Milagros," in *The Anthropology of Catholicism: A Reader*, ed. Kristin Norget, Maya Mayblin, and Valentina Napolitano (University of California Press, 2017).

107. Napolitano, "On a Political Economy," 254.

108. I use the word *expanding* here to gesture that this chapter's focus on Euro-American Christianity should not be conflating the composite and enriching dimensions of Eastern Christianity. This chapter can only be a point of departure for future, more encompassing analyses.

109. Pope Francis, "Address of Pope Francis to the European Parliament," The Holy See, November 25, 2014, accessed December 8, 2024, https://www.vatican.va/content/francesco/en/speeches/2014/november/documents/papa-francesco_20141125_strasburgo-parlamento-europeo.html.

110. Pope Francis, "Message of His Holiness Pope Francis for the 107th World Day of Migrants and Refugees 2021," The Holy See, September 26, 2021, accessed December 8, 2024, https://www.vatican.va/content/francesco/en/messages/migration/documents/papa-francesco_20210503_world-migrants-day-2021.html. The pope was quoting John 17:21.

111. Criollos are those born in the New World from European parentage; see Napolitano, "Francis, a Criollo Pope."

112. Eduardo Kohn, *How Forests Think* (University of California Press, 2013); Marilyn Strathern, *Partial Connections* (Rowman & Littlefield, 1991), 35.

113. Roberto Esposito, *The Third Person* (Polity, 2012).

114. Regina Römhild, "Global Heimat: (Post)Migrant Productions of Transnational Space," *Anthropological Journal of European Cultures* 27, no. 1 (2018): 27.

115. Marsha Meskimmon, "From the Cosmos to the Polis: On Denizens, Art and Postmigration Worldmaking," *Journal of Aesthetics and Culture* 9, no. 2 (2017): 25, 33.

116. Nicholas De Genova, "Denizens All: The Otherness of Citizenship," in *Citizenship and Its Others*, ed. Bridget Anderson and Vanessa Hughes (Palgrave Macmillan UK, 2015).

117. Arturo Escobar, *Pluriversal Politics: The Real and the Possible* (Duke University Press, 2020), xvii.

118. Elena Pulcini, *Tra Cura e Giustizia: Le Passioni Come Risorsa Sociale* (Bollati Boringhieri, 2020).
119. Michel-Rolph Trouillot, "Anthropology and the Savage Slot: The Poetics and Politics of Otherness," in *Recapturing Anthropology: Working in the Present*, ed. Richard G. Fox (School of American Research, 1991), 27.
120. I am thinking in particular of Jesuit José de Acosta (1540–1600) and his *Natural and Moral History of the Indies* (1590).
121. See David Newheiser, "Why the World Needs Negative Political Theology," *Modern Theology* 36, no. 1 (2020): 5–12.
122. Thomas A. Carlson, *Indiscretion: Finitude and the Naming of God* (University of Chicago Press, 1999), 9.
123. Judith Butler, *Subjects of Desire: Hegelian Reflections in Twentieth-Century France* (Columbia University Press, 2012), 41.
124. Arthur Bradley, *Unbearable Life: A Genealogy of Political Erasure* (Columbia University Press, 2019).
125. Yael Navaro et al., eds., *Reverberations: Violence Across Time and Space* (University of Pennsylvania Press, 2021).
126. Mittermaier, "Dreams from Elsewhere."
127. de Certeau, *Heterologies*.
128. The question of how the present may be unrepresentable is central here, as well as the conditions under which a particular configuration of a concept or event is unrepresentable, or even unthinkable. Jacques Rancière, "Are Some Things Unrepresentable?," in *The Future of the Image* (Verso, 2019).
129. Benjamin, *The Origin of German Tragic Drama*.
130. Giorgio Agamben, *The Highest Poverty: Monastic Rules and Form-of-Life* (Stanford University Press, 2013).
131. I am indebted to Aaron Eldridge's work on Christian monastic renunciatory withdrawal in Lebanon for this rendering. Aaron Frederick Eldridge, "From the Margins of the Colophon: Arab Orthodox Monasticism in Ruins," *Exchange* 49, nos. 3–4 (2020): 379–400. For "modes of attention," see Niklaus Largier, "The Plasticity of the Soul: Mystical Darkness, Touch, and Aesthetic Experience," *MLN* 125, no. 3 (2010): 536–51.
132. Constance M. Furey, "Vivifying Poetry: Sidney, Luther, and the Psalms," in Constance M. Furey, Sarah Hammerschlag, and Amy Hollywood, *Devotion: Three Inquiries in Religion, Literature, and Political Imagination* (University of Chicago Press, 2021).

133. Yael Navaro, "The Aftermath of Mass Violence: A Negative Methodology," *Annual Review of Anthropology* 49 (2020): 162.
134. Catherine Keller, *Cloud of the Impossible: Negative Theology and Planetary Entanglement* (Columbia University Press, 2014), 5.
135. Simona Forti, *The New Demons: Rethinking Power and Evil Today* (Stanford University Press, 2014).
136. Banerjee and Wouters, *Subaltern Studies 2.0*.
137. Mayanthi Fernando, "Uncanny Ecologies: More-than-Natural, More-than-Human, More-than-Secular," *Comparative Studies of South Asia, Africa and the Middle East* 42, no. 3 (2022): 568–83.
138. Laura McTighe, "Insurgent Cartography," Society for Cultural Anthropology, July 31, 2019, https://culanth.org/fieldsights/insurgent-cartography.
139. Kahn, *Political Theology*, 26.
140. Talal Asad, *Formations of the Secular: Christianity, Islam, Modernity* (Stanford University Press, 2003).

4. LOOKING TO THE FUTURE
Emerging Pathways

1. A good example of a work that meets all the criteria outlined here and is attentive to how theology plays out politically but does not seek to do constructive theological work is Stefan Skrimshire, *Politics of Fear, Practices of Hope: Depoliticisation and Resistance in a Time of Terror* (Continuum, 2008). Skrimshire's book combines continental philosophy, systematic theology, media analysis, sociology, and graffiti art to examine the nature of fear and hope in contemporary apocalyptic protest and utopian politics.
2. See, for example, Willie Jennings's critical evaluation of Equiano, which contrasts sharply with Paul Gilroy's use of Equiano as exemplifying what Gilroy calls "reparative humanism." William James Jennings, *The Christian Imagination: Theology and the Origins of Race* (Yale University Press, 2010), chap. 4; Vincent L. Wimbush, *White Men's Magic: Scripturalization as Slavery* (Oxford University Press, 2012); Paul Gilroy, "The Black Atlantic and the Re-enchantment of Humanism," in *The Tanner Lectures on Human Values*, vol. 34, ed. M. Matheson (University of Utah

Press, 2016); Paul Gilroy, "Never Again: Refusing Race and Salvaging the Human," 2019 Holberg Lecture, University of Bergen, Norway, June 4, 2019, https://holbergprize.org/events-and-productions/holberguken-2019/holbergforelesningen-never-again-refusing-race-and-salvaging-the-human/.

3. William Apess, *On Our Own Ground: The Complete Writings of William Apess, A Pequot*, ed. Barry O'Connell (University of Massachusetts Press, 1992).

4. See, for example, George E. "Tink" Tinker, *American Indian Liberation: A Theology of Sovereignty* (Orbis, 2008).

5. Matthew Elia, *The Problem of the Christian Master: Augustine in the Afterlife of Slavery* (Yale University Press, 2024). In an epilogue to this book, Elia gives an account of how tradition might be fashioned anew that parallels the account given here.

6. Emily Dumler-Winkler, *Modern Virtue: Mary Wollstonecraft and a Tradition of Dissent* (Oxford University Press, 2022).

7. Andrew Prevot, *Thinking Prayer: Theology and Spirituality amid the Crisis of Modernity* (University of Notre Dame Press, 2015).

8. Matt R. Jantzen, *God, Race, and History: Liberating Providence* (Lexington, 2021).

9. Keri Day, *Azusa Reimagined: A Radical Vision of Religious and Democratic Belonging* (Stanford University Press, 2022). In parallel to Day, Jonathan Tran also turns to forms of ecclesial practices to resource alternatives to racial capitalism. Jonathan Tran, *Asian Americans and the Spirit of Racial Capitalism* (Oxford University Press, 2022).

10. Elizabeth O'Donnell Gandolfo, *Ecomartydom in the Americas: Living and Dying for Our Common Home* (Orbis, 2023).

11. For the distinction between theology that is either ethnographically driven, informed, or haunted, see Luke Bretherton, "Theology and Social Science," in *Ford's The Modern Theologians*, ed. Rachel Muers and Ashley Cocksworth, 4th ed. (Wiley-Blackwell, 2024).

12. For a broader account of the relationship between political theology and ethnography, see Luke Bretherton, "Political Theology and Qualitative Research," in *The Wiley Blackwell Companion to Theology and Qualitative Research*, ed. Pete Ward and Knut Tveitereid (Wiley-Blackwell, 2022).

13. Melissa Snarr, *All You That Labor: Religion and Ethics in the Living Wage Movement* (New York University Press, 2011). Other examples include Kyle Lambelet, *¡Presente! Nonviolent Politics and the Resurrection of the Dead* (Georgetown University Press, 2019); and Luke Bretherton, *Resurrecting Democracy: Faith, Citizenship and the Politics of a Common Life* (Cambridge University Press, 2015).

Crossing and Deepening

14. Andrew Prevot, *Thinking Prayer: Theology and Spirituality amid the Crises of Modernity* (University of Notre Dame Press, 2015).
15. For a particularly helpful work exploring idolatry as a political-theological category, see William T. Cavanaugh, *The Uses of Idolatry* (Oxford University Press, 2024).
16. Denys Turner's work is an important point of reference on these issues; see *The Darkness of God: Negativity in Christian Mysticism* (Cambridge University Press, 1995).
17. See the journals *Religion and American Culture* and *American Religion*.
18. See also Karma Ben-Johanan and Brandy Daniels, "(How to Do) Political Theology Without Men," *Political Theology* 25, no. 6 (2024): 510–518.
19. Mark D. Jordan, "St. Thomas and the Police," in Mark D. Jordan, *Rewritten Theology: Aquinas After His Readers* (Blackwell, 2006).
20. A. Azfar Moin, *The Millennial Sovereign: Kingship and Sainthood in Islam* (Columbia University Press, 2014).

A Celebratory Roadmap

21. For the sake of space, I am only referring to work in this arc-period and in book monograph form. I wish to give the reader a canvas for further readings that consolidates and expands some of the strands of thought that I engage with in my chapter and that we collectively address in the introduction.
22. See Valentina Napolitano, *Migrant Hearts and the Atlantic Return: Transnationalism and the Roman Catholic Church* (Fordham University Press, 2016). And on the religious in movement, see Valentina

Napolitano, "On a Political Economy of Political Theology: El Señor de los Milagros," in *The Anthropology of Catholicism: A Reader*, ed. Kristin Norget, Maya Mayblin, and Valentina Napolitano (University of California Press, 2017).

23. Neena Mahadev, *Karma and Grace: Religious Difference in Millennial Sri Lanka* (Columbia University Press, 2023), 118.
24. See also Alireza Doostdar, "God and Revolution in Iran," *Comparative Studies of South Asia, Africa and the Middle East* 45, no. 1 (2025): 91–104.
25. Claude Lefort, "The Permanence of the Theologico-Political?," in *Political Theologies: Public Religions in a Post-Secular World*, ed. Hent de Vries and Lawrence E. Sullivan (Fordham University Press, 2006).
26. I discuss this topic at length in the analysis of the 2020 Pope Francis *Urbi et Orbi* in my chapter in this book.
27. Another seminal work that inspired Sánchez on the magic of the state is Michael Taussig, *The Magic of the State* (Routledge, 2013). For a more recent work on governing through an iconicity of monumentalization and an "infrastructure of the sensible" in India, see Kajri Jain, *Gods in the Time of Democracy* (Duke University Press, 2021).

BIBLIOGRAPHY

Agamben, Giorgio. *The Highest Poverty: Monastic Rules and Form-of-Life.* Stanford University Press, 2013.

Agamben, Giorgio. *Homo Sacer: Sovereign Power and Bare Life.* Stanford University Press, 1995.

Akbar, Amna A. "Non-Reformist Reforms and Struggles over Life, Death, and Democracy." *Yale Law Journal* 132 (2023): 2497–577.

Alinsky, Saul. *Rules for Radicals: A Pragmatic Primer for Realistic Radicals.* Vintage, 1989.

Allen-Paisant, Jason. *Engagements with Aimé Césaire: Thinking with Spirits.* Oxford University Press, 2024.

Althaus-Reid, Marcella. *Indecent Theology: Theological Perversions in Sex, Gender and Politics.* Routledge, 2000.

Althusser, Louis. *On the Reproduction of Capitalism: Ideology and Ideological State Apparatuses.* Trans. G. M. Goshgarian. Verso, 2014.

An Yountae. "Decolonizing the Cosmo-Polis: Cosmopolitanism as a Rehumanizing Project." In *Decolonial Christianities: Latinx and Latin American Perspectives*, ed. Raimundo Barreto and Roberto Sirvent. Palgrave Macmillan, 2019.

Anidjar, Gil. "Of Globalatinology." *Derrida Today* 6, no. 1 (2013): 11–22.

Anidjar, Gil. *On the Sovereignty of Mothers: The Political as Maternal.* Columbia University Press, 2024.

Anidjar, Gil. "Secularism." *Critical Inquiry* 33, no. 1 (2006): 52–77.

Apess, William. *On Our Own Ground: The Complete Writings of William Apess, A Pequot.* Ed. Barry O'Connell. University of Massachusetts Press, 1992.

Aquino, María Pilar. "Theological Method in U.S. Latino/a Theology: Toward an Intercultural Theology for the Third Millennium." In *From the Heart of Our People: Latino/a Explorations in Catholic Systematic Theology*, ed. Orlando O. Espín and Miguel H. Díaz. Orbis, 1999.

Arato, Andrew. "Political Theology and Populism." *Social Research* 80, no. 1 (2013): 143–72.

Arendt, Hannah. *The Human Condition*. University of Chicago Press, 1998.

Arendt, Hannah. *On Revolution*. Viking, 1963. Reprint, Penguin, 2006.

Arendt, Hannah. "On Violence." In Hannah Arendt, *Crises of the Republic*. Harcourt Brace, 1972.

Armstrong, Amaryah Shaye. "Losing Salvation: Notes Toward a Wayward Black Theology." *Critical Times* 6, no. 2 (2023): 324–44.

Asad, Talal. "The Construction of Religion as an Anthropological Category." In Talal Asad, *Genealogies of Religion: Discipline and Reasons of Power in Christianity and Islam*. Johns Hopkins University Press, 1993.

Asad, Talal. *Formations of the Secular: Christianity, Islam, Modernity*. Stanford University Press, 2003.

Asad, Talal. *Secular Translations: Nation-State, Modern Self, and Calculative Reason*. Columbia University Press, 2018.

Augustine. *City of God*, 11–22. Trans. William Babcock. New City, 2013.

Avis, Paul. *Theology and the Enlightenment: A Critical Enquiry into Enlightenment Theology and Its Reception*. Bloomsbury, 2022.

Azaransky, Sarah. *This Worldwide Struggle: Religion and the International Roots of the Civil Rights Movement*. Oxford University Press, 2017.

Badone, Ellen. "From Cruddiness to Catastrophe: COVID-19 and Long-Term Care in Ontario." *Medical Anthropology* 40, no. 5 (2021): 389–403.

Bakunin, Mikhail. "The Political Theology of Mazzini." In *Mikhail Bakunin: Selected Writings*, ed. Arthur Lehning. Jonathan Cape, 1973.

Balthrop-Lewis, Alda. *Thoreau's Religion: Walden Woods, Social Justice, and the Politics of Asceticism*. Cambridge University Press, 2021.

Banerjee, Milinda. *The Mortal God: Imagining the Sovereign in Colonial India*. Cambridge University Press, 2017.

Banerjee, Milinda, and Jelle J. P. Wouters. *Subaltern Studies 2.0: Being Against the Capitalocene*. Prickly Paradigm, 2022.

Bargu, Banu. "The Predicaments of Left-Schmittianism." *South Atlantic Quarterly* 113, no. 4 (2014): 713–27.

Barth, Karl. "The New Humanism and the Humanism of God." *Theology Today* 8 (1951): 157–66.
Basch, Linda, Nina Glick Schiller, and Cristina Szanton Blanc. *Nations Unbound: Transnational Projects, Postcolonial Predicaments, and Deterritorialized Nation-States*. Routledge, 1992.
Bassichis, Morgan, Alexander Lee, and Dean Spade. "Building an Abolitionist Trans and Queer Movement with Everything We've Got." In *Captive Genders: Trans Embodiment and the Prison Industrial Complex*, ed. Eric A. Stanley and Nat Smith. AK Press, 2011.
Bejan, Teresa. *Mere Civility: Disagreement and the Limits of Toleration*. Harvard University Press, 2017.
Bellah, Robert. *Religion in Human Evolution: From the Paleolithic to the Axial Age*. Belknap, 2011.
Benjamin, Walter. "Capitalism as Religion." In Walter Benjamin, *Toward the Critique of Violence: A Critical Edition*. Stanford University Press, 2021.
Benjamin, Walter. *The Origin of German Tragic Drama*. Verso, 2009.
Benjamin, Walter. "Theses on the Philosophy of History." In *Illuminations: Essays and Reflections*, ed. Hannah Arendt, trans. Harry Zohn. Schocken, 2007.
Bernstein, Elizabeth. "The Sexual Politics of the 'New Abolitionism.'" *differences* 18, no. 3 (2007): 128–51.
Berquist, Stephen, Valentina Napolitano, and Elizabeth Rigotti. "Holy Infrastructures: Catholicism, Detroit Borderlands, and the Elements." *Comparative Studies of Society and History* 66, no. 4 (2024): 786–813.
Bevins, Vincent. *If We Burn: The Mass Protest Decade and the Missing Revolution*. PublicAffairs, 2023.
Bielo, James S. "Anthropology, Theology, Critique." *Critical Research on Religion* 6, no. 1 (2018): 28–34.
Blaser, Mario. "Is Another Cosmopolitics Possible?" *Cultural Anthropology* 31, no. 4 (2016): 545–70.
Bloch, Maurice, and Jonathan Parry, eds. *Death and the Regeneration of Life*. Cambridge University Press, 1982.
Blumenberg, Hans. *The Legitimacy of the Modern Age*. Trans. R. M. Wallace. MIT Press, 1985.
Bonhoeffer, Dietrich. *Ethics*. Trans. Reinhard Krauss et al. Ed. Clifford Green. Vol. 6, *Dietrich Bonhoeffer Works*. Fortress, 2005.

Bonilla, Yarimar. *Non-Sovereign Futures: French Caribbean Politics in the Wake of Disenchantment*. University of Chicago Press, 2015.

Bottici, Chiara. "Imagination, Imaginary, Imaginal: Towards a New Social Ontology?" *Social Epistemology* 33, no. 5 (2019): 433–41.

Bouteldja, Houria. *Whites, Jews, and Us: Toward a Politics of Revolutionary Love*. Semiotext(e), 2017.

Boyer, Dominic. "Time of Monsters." Society for Cultural Anthropology, October 31, 2018. https://culanth.org/fieldsights/series/time-of-monsters.

Bradley, Arthur. *Unbearable Life: A Genealogy of Political Erasure*. Columbia University Press, 2019.

Breckman, Warren. "Democracy Between Disenchantment and Political Theology: French Post-Marxism and the Return to Religion." *New German Critique* 94 (2005): 72–105.

Bretherton, Luke. *Christ and the Common Life: Political Theology and the Case for Democracy*. Eerdmans, 2019.

Bretherton, Luke. "Political Theology and Qualitative Research." In *The Wiley Blackwell Companion to Theology and Qualitative Research*, ed. Pete Ward and Knut Tveitereid. Wiley Blackwell, 2022.

Bretherton, Luke. *A Primer in Christian Ethics: Christ and the Struggle to Live Well*. Cambridge University Press, 2023.

Bretherton, Luke. *Resurrecting Democracy: Faith, Citizenship, and the Politics of a Common Life*. Cambridge University Press, 2015.

Bretherton, Luke. "Theology and Social Science." In *Ford's The Modern Theologians*, ed. Rachel Muers and Ashley Cocksworth. 4th ed. Wiley-Blackwell, 2024.

Brill, Sara. *Aristotle on the Concept of Shared Life*. Oxford University Press, 2020.

Buber, Martin. *Paths in Utopia*. Macmillan, 1950.

Bulgakov, Sergei. *Philosophy of Economy: The World as Household*. Trans. Catherine Evtuhov. Yale University Press, 2000.

Burkhart, Brian. *Indigenizing Philosophy Through the Land: A Trickster Methodology for Decolonizing Environmental Ethics and Indigenous Futures*. Michigan State University Press, 2019.

Butler, Judith. *Subjects of Desire: Hegelian Reflections in Twentieth-Century France*. Columbia University Press, 2012.

Butticci, Annalisa, and Amira Mittermaier. "Afterword: The Elsewhere Beyond Religious Concerns." *Religion and Society* 11, no. 1 (2020): 176–85.

Cady, Linell Elizabeth, and Tracy Fessenden, eds. *Religion, the Secular, and the Politics of Sexual Difference.* Columbia University Press, 2013.
Callinicos, Alex. *The Resources of Critique.* Polity, 2006.
Cannon, Katie. *Black Womanist Ethics.* Scholars, 1988.
Carlson, Thomas A. *Indiscretion: Finitude and the Naming of God.* University of Chicago Press, 1999.
Carter, J. Kameron. "The Excremental Sacred: A Paraliturgy." In *Beyond Man: Race, Coloniality, and the Philosophy of Religion*, ed. An Yountae and Eleanor Craig. Duke University Press, 2021.
Carter, J. Kameron. "Race, Religion, and the Contradictions of Identity: A Theological Engagement with Douglass's 1845 Narrative." *Modern Theology* 21, no. 1 (2005): 37–65.
Castor, N. Fadeke. *Spiritual Citizenship: Transnational Pathways from Black Power to Ifá in Trinidad.* Duke University Press, 2017.
Cattelino, Jessica R. *High Stakes: Florida Seminole Gaming and Sovereignty.* Duke University Press, 2008.
Cavadini, John C., and Donald Wallenfang, eds. *Pope Francis and the Event of Encounter: Global Perspectives on the New Evangelization.* Pickwick, 2018.
Cavanaugh, William T. *Theopolitical Imagination.* T & T Clark, 2003.
Cavanaugh, William T. *The Uses of Idolatry.* Oxford University Press, 2024.
Césaire, Aimé. *The Complete Poetry of Aimé Césaire.* Wesleyan University Press, 2017.
Césaire, Aimé. *Resolutely Black: Conversations with Françoise Vergès.* Polity, 2020.
Chakrabarty, Dipesh. "The Planet: An Emergent Humanist Category." *Critical Inquiry* 46, no. 1 (2019): 1–31.
Chappel, James. *Catholic Modern: The Challenge of Totalitarianism and the Remaking of the Church.* Harvard University Press, 2018.
Chepurin, Kirill. *Bliss Against the World: Schelling, Theodicy, and the Crisis of Modernity.* Oxford University Press, 2025.
Cherniss, Joshua. *Liberalism in Dark Times: The Liberal Ethos in the Twentieth Century.* Princeton University Press, 2021.
Chua, Liana, and Nayanika Mathur. Introduction to *Who Are We? Reimagining Alterity and Affinity in Anthropology.* Berghahn, 2018.
Cody, Francis. "Wave Theory: Cash, Crowds, and Caste in Indian Elections." *American Ethnologist* 47, no. 4 (2020): 402–16.

Cohen, Lawrence. "The Culling: Pandemic, Gerocide, Generational Affect." *Medical Anthropology Quarterly*. 34, no. 4 (2020): 542–60.

Cohn, Norman. *The Pursuit of the Millennium: Revolutionary Millenarians and Mystical Anarchists of the Middle Ages*. Oxford University Press, 1970.

Colón-Emeric, Edgardo. *Óscar Romero's Theological Vision: Liberation and the Transfiguration of the Poor*. University of Notre Dame Press, 2018.

Comaroff, Jean, and John Comaroff. "Occult Economies and the Violence of Abstraction: Notes from the South African Postcolony." *American Ethnologist* 26, no. 3 (1999): 279–303.

Cone, James H. *Black Theology and Black Power*. Orbis, 1997.

Cone, James H. *God of the Oppressed*. Rev. ed. Orbis, 1997.

Cone, James H. *The Spirituals and the Blues: An Interpretation*. Seabury, 1972.

Craig, Eleanor, and Amy Hollywood. "Mysticism and the Politics of Theory." *English Language Notes* 56, no. 1 (2018): 7–20.

Crawley, Ashon T. *Blackpentecostal Breath: The Aesthetics of Possibility*. Fordham University Press, 2016.

Crick, Bernard. *In Defence of Politics*. 4th ed. University of Chicago Press, 1993.

Critchley, Simon. *Infinitely Demanding: Ethics of Commitment, Politics of Resistance*. Verso, 2007.

Crosson, J. Brent. "'The Earth Is the Lord' or 'God Is a Trini'? The Political Theology of Climate Change, Environmental Stewardship, and Petroleum Extraction." In *Climate Politics and the Power of Religion*, ed. Evan Berry. Indiana University Press, 2022.

Crosson, J. Brent. *Experiments with Power: Obeah and the Remaking of Religion in Trinidad*. University of Chicago Press, 2020.

Dabashi, Hamid. *Islamic Liberation Theology: Resisting the Empire*. Routledge, 2008.

Dal Lago, Alessandro. *Non-Persone: L'esclusione dei Migranti in Una Società Globale*. Feltrinelli Editore, 2006.

Davies, J. C. "Utopianism." In *The Cambridge History of Political Thought: 1450–1700*, ed. J. H. Burns and Mark Goldie. Cambridge University Press, 1991.

Day, Keri. *Azusa Reimagined: A Radical Vision of Religious and Democratic Belonging*. Stanford University Press, 2022.

de Certeau, Michel. *Heterologies: Discourse on the Other*. Trans. Brian Massumi. University of Minnesota Press, 1986.

de Certeau, Michel. *The Practice of Everyday Life*. University of California Press, 1984.
de Certeau, Michel, and Luce Giard. *La faiblesse de croire*. Seuil, 1987.
De Genova, Nicholas. "Denizens All: The Otherness of Citizenship." In *Citizenship and Its Others*, ed. Bridget Anderson and Vanessa Hughes. Palgrave Macmillan UK, 2015.
de la Cadena, Marisol. *Earth Beings: Ecologies of Practice Across Andean Worlds*. Duke University Press, 2015.
de la Cadena, Marisol. "Indigenous Cosmopolitics in the Andes: Conceptual Reflections Beyond 'Politics.'" *Cultural Anthropology* 25, no. 2 (2010): 334–70.
de Lubac, Henri. *The Un-Marxian Socialist: A Study of Proudhon*. Sheed & Ward, 1948.
Dean, Jodi. *The Communist Horizon*. Verso, 2018.
Derrida, Jacques. "Above All, No Journalists!" In *Religion and Media*, ed. Hent de Vries and Samuel Weber. Fordham, 2001.
Di Cesare, Donatella. *Resident Foreigners: A Philosophy of Migration*. Trans. David Broder. Polity, 2020.
Doostdar, Alireza. "God and Revolution in Iran." *Comparative Studies of South Asia, Africa and the Middle East* 45, no. 1 (2025): 91–104.
Doostdar, Alireza. *The Iranian Metaphysicals: Explorations in Science, Islam, and the Uncanny*. Princeton University Press, 2018.
Dorrien, Gary. *American Democratic Socialism: History, Politics, Religion, and Theory*. Yale University Press, 2021.
Dorrien, Gary. *The New Abolition: W. E. B. Du Bois and the Black Social Gospel*. Yale University Press, 2015.
Dorrien, Gary. *Social Democracy in the Making: Political and Religious Roots of European Socialism*. Yale University Press, 2019.
Dorrien, Gary. *Social Ethics in the Making: Interpreting an American Tradition*. Wiley-Blackwell, 2008.
Drabinski, John. "Césaire's Apocalyptic Word." *South Atlantic Quarterly* 115, no. 3 (2016): 567–84.
Dreher, Rod. *The Benedict Option: A Strategy for Christians in a Post-Christian Society*. Sentinel, 2018.
Dubilet, Alex. "The Just Without Justification: On Meister Eckhart and Political Theology." *postmedieval* 13, no. 1 (2022): 5–28.

Dubilet, Alex. "A Political Theology of Interpellation: On Subjection, Individuation, and Becoming Nothing." *Cultural Critique* 122 (2024): 132–61.

Dubilet, Alex, and Vincent Lloyd, eds. *Political Theology Reimagined*. Duke University Press, 2025.

Dubler, Joshua, and Vincent W. Lloyd. *Break Every Yoke: Religion, Justice, and the Abolition of Prisons*. Oxford University Press, 2019.

Dumler-Winkler, Emily. *Modern Virtue: Mary Wollstonecraft and a Tradition of Dissent*. Oxford University Press, 2022.

Gandolfo, Elizabeth O'Donnell. *Ecomartydom in the Americas: Living and Dying for Our Common Home*. Orbis, 2023.

Gregory, Eric. "Before the Original Position: The Neo-Orthodox Theology of the Young John Rawls." *Journal of Religious Ethics* 35, no. 2 (2007): 179–206.

Eldridge, Aaron Frederick. "A Cartographic Exercise." *Political Theology* 24, no. 1 (2023): 128–33.

Eldridge, Aaron Frederick. "From the Margins of the Colophon: Arab Orthodox Monasticism in Ruins." *Exchange* 49, nos. 3–4 (2020): 379–400.

Elia, Matthew. *The Problem of the Christian Master: Augustine in the Afterlife of Slavery*. Yale University Press, 2024.

Escobar, Arturo. *Pluriversal Politics: The Real and the Possible*. Trans. David Frye. Duke University Press, 2020.

Escobar, Arturo. "Territorios de Diferencia: La Ontología Política de los 'Derechos al Territorio.'" *Cuadernos de Antropología Social*, no. 41 (2015): 25–38.

Esposito, Roberto. "Community, Immunity, Biopolitics." In *Community, Immunity and the Proper*, ed. Greg Bird and Jon Short. Routledge, 2017.

Esposito, Roberto. "For a Philosophy of the Impersonal." Trans. Timothy Campbell. *CR: The New Centennial Review* 10, no. 2 (2010): 121–34.

Esposito, Roberto. *The Third Person*. Polity, 2012.

Fanon, Frantz. *The Wretched of the Earth*. Trans. Richard Philcox. Grove, 2004.

Fassin, Didier. *Humanitarian Reason: A Moral History of the Present Times*. University of California Press, 2012.

Fassin, Didier. "The Predicament of Humanitarianism." *Qui Parle: Critical Humanities and Social Sciences* 22, no. 1 (2013): 33–48.

Fassin, Didier, and Paula Vasquez. "Humanitarian Exception as the Rule: The Political Theology of the 1999 Tragedia in Venezuela." *American Ethnologist* 32, no. 3 (2005): 389–405.

Federici, Silvia. *Caliban and the Witch*. Autonomedia, 2004.

Fernando, Mayanthi. "Uncanny Ecologies: More-than-Natural, More-than-Human, More-than-Secular." *Comparative Studies of South Asia, Africa and the Middle East* 42, no. 3 (2022): 568–83.

Follett, Mary Parker. *Creative Experience*. Longmans, Green, 1924. Reprint, Longmans, Green, 1930.

Forti, Simona. *The New Demons: Rethinking Power and Evil Today*. Stanford University Press, 2014.

Foster, Elizabeth A. *African Catholic: Decolonization and the Transformation of the Church*. Harvard University Press, 2019.

Foucault, Michel. *Discipline and Punish: The Birth of the Prison*. Vintage, 1995.

Foucault, Michel. *The History of Sexuality*. Vol. 1. Random House, 1990.

Foucault, Michel. "The Subject and Power." In *Power: Essential Works*, vol. 3, ed. James D. Faubion. New Press, 2001.

Francis, Pope. "Address of Pope Francis to the European Parliament." The Holy See, November 25, 2014. https://www.vatican.va/content/francesco/en/speeches/2014/november/documents/papa-francesco_20141125_strasburgo-parlamento-europeo.html.

Francis, Pope. "Extraordinary Moment of Prayer Presided over by Pope Francis." The Holy See, March 27, 2020. https://www.vatican.va/content/francesco/en/homilies/2020/documents/papa-francesco_20200327_omelia-epidemia.html.

Francis, Pope. "Laudato Si'." The Holy See, May 24, 2015. Accessed December 7, 2024. https://www.vatican.va/content/francesco/en/encyclicals/documents/papa-francesco_20150524_enciclica-laudato-si.html.

Francis, Pope. "Message of His Holiness Pope Francis for the 107th World Day of Migrants and Refugees 2021." The Holy See, September 26, 2021. Accessed December 8, 2024. https://www.vatican.va/content/francesco/en/messages/migration/documents/papa-francesco_20210503_world-migrants-day-2021.html.

Francis, Pope. "Querida Amazonia." The Holy See, February 2, 2020. Accessed December 7, 2024. https://www.vatican.va/content/francesco/en/apost_exhortations/documents/papa-francesco_esortazione-ap_20200202_querida-amazonia.html.

Freeman, Jennifer Awes. *The Good Shepherd: Image, Meaning, and Power*. Baylor University Press, 2021.

Freeman, Jo. "The Tyranny of Structurelessness." Jo Freeman.com. Accessed December 8, 2024. https://www.jofreeman.com/joreen/tyranny.htm.

Furani, Khaled. "Khalifah and the Modern Sovereign: Revisiting a Qur'anic Ideal from Within the Palestinian Condition." *Journal of Religion* 102, no. 4 (2022): 482–506.

Furani, Khaled. *Redeeming Anthropology: A Theological Critique of a Modern Science*. Oxford University Press, 2019.

Furey, Constance M. "Vivifying Poetry: Sidney, Luther, and the Psalms." In Constance M. Furey, Sarah Hammerschlag, and Amy Hollywood, *Devotion: Three Inquiries in Religion, Literature, and Political Imagination*. University of Chicago Press, 2021.

Gago, Verónica. "Dangerous Liaisons: Latin American Feminists and the Left." *NACLA Report on the Americas* 40, no. 2 (2007): 17–19.

Garces, Chris. "The Cross Politics of Ecuador's Penal State." *Cultural Anthropology* 25, no. 3 (2010): 459–96.

Gauchet, Marcel. *The Disenchantment of the World*. Princeton University Press, 1997.

Geuss, Raymond. *Philosophy and Real Politics*. Princeton University Press, 2008.

Gillespie, Michael. *The Theological Origins of Modernity*. University of Chicago Press, 2008.

Gilmore, Ruth Wilson. *Golden Gulag: Prisons, Surplus, Crisis, and Opposition in Globalizing California*. University of California Press, 2007.

Gilroy, Paul. "The Black Atlantic and the Re-enchantment of Humanism: Suffering and Infrahumanity." In *The Tanner Lectures on Human Values*, vol. 34, ed. Mark Matheson. University of Utah Press, 2016.

Gilroy, Paul. *The Black Atlantic: Modernity and Double Consciousness*. Harvard University Press, 1993.

Gilroy, Paul. "Never Again: Refusing Race and Salvaging the Human." 2019 Holberg Lecture, University of Bergen, Norway, June 4, 2019. https://holbergprize.org/events-and-productions/holberguken-2019/holberg-forelesningen-never-again-refusing-race-and-salvaging-the-human/.

Giordano, Cristiana. *Migrants in Translation: Caring and the Logics of Difference in Contemporary Italy*. University of California Press, 2014.

Giordano, Cristiana, and Greg Pierotti. "Getting Caught: A Collaboration On- and Offstage Between Theatre and Anthropology." *TDR/The Drama Review* 64, no. 1 (2020): 88–106.

Glissant, Édouard. *Caribbean Discourse: Selected Essays.* Trans. J. Michael Dash. University Press of Virginia, 1989.

Goodchild. Philip. *Economic Theology: Credit and Faith, II.* Rowman and Littlefield, 2020.

Gorz, André. *Strategy for Labor: A Radical Proposal.* Beacon, 1962.

Green, Joshua. *The Rebels: Elizabeth Warren, Bernie Sanders, Alexandria Ocasio-Cortez, and the Struggle for a New American Politics.* Penguin, 2024.

Grimes, Katie Walker. *Fugitive Saints: Catholicism and the Politics of Slavery.* Fortress, 2017.

Gruber, Aya. *The Feminist War on Crime: The Unexpected Role of Women's Liberation in Mass Incarceration.* University of California Press, 2021.

Gurney, John. *Brave Community: The Digger Movement in the English Revolution.* Manchester University Press, 2007.

Gutiérrez, Gustavo. *A Theology of Liberation: History, Politics, and Salvation.* Rev. ed. Orbis, 1988.

HadžiMuhamedović, Safet. *Waiting for Elijah: Time and Encounter in a Bosnian Landscape.* Berghahn, 2022.

Harney, Stefano, and Fred Moten. *The Undercommons: Fugitive Planning and Black Study.* Minor Compositions, 2013.

Hauerwas, Stanley. "The Reality of the Church: Even a Democratic State Is Not the Kingdom." In Stanley Hauerwas, *Against the Nations: War and Survival in a Liberal Society.* Winston, 1985.

Hauerwas, Stanley. "Seeing Peace: L'Arche as a Peace Movement." In Stanley Hauerwas and Romand Coles, *Christianity, Democracy, and the Radical Ordinary.* Cascade, 2008.

Hayden, Cori. "From Connection to Contagion." *Journal of the Royal Anthropological Institute* 27, no. S1 (2021): 95–107.

Hayes-Mota, Nicholas. "Public Theology in North America: Commonality amid Plurality." In *T&T Clark Handbook of Public Theology*, ed. Christoph Hübenthal and Christiane Alpers. Bloomsbury, 2022.

Henry, Michel. *I Am the Truth: Toward a Philosophy of Christianity.* Stanford University Press, 2003.

Henry, Michel. *Marx: A Philosophy for Human Reality.* Trans. Kathleen McLaughlin. Indiana University Press, 1983.

Heo, Angie. *Political Lives of Saints: Christian-Muslim Mediation in Egypt.* University of California Press, 2018.

"Herstory." Black Lives Matter, July 7, 2017. Accessed April 5, 2024. https://blacklivesmatter.com/herstory.

Heyer, Kristin E. "Migration and Structural Injustice." In *Christian Theology in the Age of Migration: Implications for World Christianity*, ed. Peter C. Phan. Lexington, 2020.

Hickman, Jared. *Black Prometheus: Race and Radicalism in the Age of Atlantic Slavery*. Oxford University Press, 2016.

Hidalgo-Capitán, Antonio Luis, and Ana Patricia Cubillo-Guevara. "Deconstruction and Genealogy of Latin American Good Living (Buen Vivir): The (Triune) Good Living and Its Diverse Intellectual Wellsprings." *International Development Policy/Revue Internationale de Politique de Développement* 9, no. 9 (2017): 23–50.

Hirschkind, Charles. *The Feeling of History: Islam, Romanticism, and Andalusia*. University of Chicago Press, 2020.

Hirschkind, Charles. "On the Virtues of Holding Your Tongue." *Critical Times* 3, no. 3 (2020): 471–77.

Honig, Bonnie. *Emergency Politics: Paradox, Law, Democracy*. Princeton University Press, 2011.

Hulsether, Lucia. *Capitalist Humanitarianism*. Duke University Press, 2023.

Hulsether, Lucia. "Tabitha's Trauma: Christian Nationalism, Centrist Jeremiad, and the Reconstruction of the American Family." In *Political Theology Reimagined*, ed. Alex Dubilet and Vincent Lloyd. Duke University Press, 2025.

Invernizzi-Accetti, Carlo. *What Is Christian Democracy? Politics, Religion and Ideology*. Cambridge University Press, 2019.

Iqbal, Basit Kareem. "Economy of Tribulation: Translating Humanitarianism for an Islamic Counterpublic." *The Muslim World* 112, no. 1 (2022): 33–56.

Iqbal, Basit Kareem. "Reprising Islamic Political Theology: Genre and the Time of Tribulation." *Political Theology* 23, no. 6 (2022): 525–42.

Isasi-Díaz, Ada María. "Afterwords: Strangers No Longer." In *Hispanic/Latino Theology: Challenge and Promise*, ed. Ada María Isasi-Díaz and Fernando F. Segovia. Fortress, 1996.

Isasi-Díaz, Ada María. *La Lucha Continues: Mujerista Theology*. Orbis, 2004.

Isasi-Díaz, Ada María. *Mujerista Theology*. Orbis, 1996.

Jäger, Anton, and Arthur Borriello. *The Populist Moment: The Left After the Great Recession*. Verso, 2023.

Jain, Kajri. *Gods in the Time of Democracy*. Duke University Press, 2021.

Jakobsen, Janet. *The Sex Obsession: Perversity and Possibility in American Politics*. New York University Press, 2020.

JanMohamed, Abdul. *The Death-Bound-Subject: Richard Wright's Archaeology of Death*. Duke University Press, 2005.

Jantzen, Matt R. *God, Race, and History: Liberating Providence*. Lexington, 2021.

Jennings, Willie James. *The Christian Imagination: Theology and the Origins of Race*. Yale University Press, 2010.

Joas, Hans. *Faith as an Option: Possible Futures for Christianity*. Trans. Alex Skinner. Stanford University Press, 2014.

Jobe, Sarah. *No Godforsaken Place: Prison Chaplaincy, Karl Barth, and Practicing Life in Prison*. T&T Clark, 2025.

Jobson, Ryan C. "The Case for Letting Anthropology Burn: Sociocultural Anthropology in 2019." *American Anthropologist* 122, no. 2 (2020): 259–71.

Jones, Donna V. *The Racial Discourses of Life Philosophy: Negritude, Vitalism, and Modernity*. Columbia University Press, 2010.

Jordan, Mark D. "St. Thomas and the Police." In Mark D. Jordan, *Rewritten Theology: Aquinas After His Readers*. Blackwell, 2006.

Jordan, Mark D. *Transforming Fire: Imagining Christian Teaching*. Eerdmans, 2021.

Kaba, Mariame. *We Do This 'Til We Free Us: Abolitionist Organizing and Transforming Justice*. Haymarket, 2021.

Kahn, Jonathon, and Vincent W. Lloyd, eds. *Race and Secularism in America*. Columbia University Press, 2016.

Kahn, Paul W. *Political Theology: Four New Chapters on the Concept of Sovereignty*. Columbia University Press, 2011.

Kahn, Victoria. "Political Theology and Liberal Culture: Strauss, Schmitt, Spinoza, and Arendt." In *Political Theology and Early Modernity*, ed. Graham Hammill and Julia Reinhard Lupton. University of Chicago Press, 2012.

Keeanga-Yamahtta Taylor, ed. *How We Get Free: Black Feminism and the Combahee River Collective*. Haymarket, 2017.

Keller, Catherine. *Cloud of the Impossible: Negative Theology and Planetary Entanglement*. Columbia University Press, 2014.

Keller, Catherine, and Maya Rivera. "The Coloniality of Apocalypse." The Immanent Frame, March 31, 2021. Accessed December 7, 2024. https://tif.ssrc.org/2021/03/31/the-coloniality-of-apocalypse.

Kilby, Karen. *God, Evil, and the Limits of Theology*. Bloomsbury, 2020.

Klein, Naomi. *Doppelganger: A Trip into the Mirror World*. Farrar, Straus and Giroux, 2023.

Kohn, Eduardo. *How Forests Think: Toward an Anthropology Beyond the Human*. University of California Press, 2013.

Kotsko, Adam. *The Prince of This World*. Stanford University Press, 2020.

Kwok Pui-lan, *Postcolonial Politics and Theology: Unraveling Empire for a Global World*. Westminster John Knox Press, 2021.

Kwok Pui-lan, ed. *Transpacific Political Theology: Perspectives, Paradigms, Proposals*. Baylor University Press, 2024.

Lamb, Michael. *A Commonwealth of Hope: Augustine's Political Thought*. Princeton University Press, 2022.

Lambelet, Kyle B. T. "The Lure of the Apocalypse: Ecology, Ethics, and the End of the World." *Studies in Christian Ethics* 34, no. 4 (2021): 482–97.

Lambelet, Kyle. *¡Presente! Nonviolent Politics and the Resurrection of the Dead*. Georgetown University Press, 2019.

Laniak, Timothy. *Shepherds After My Own Heart: Pastoral Traditions and Leadership in the Bible*. Intervarsity, 2006.

Largier, Niklaus. *Figures of Possibility: Aesthetic Experience, Mysticism, and the Play of the Senses*. Stanford University Press, 2022.

Largier, Niklaus. "The Plasticity of the Soul: Mystical Darkness, Touch, and Aesthetic Experience." *MLN* 125, no. 3 (2010): 536–51.

Larkin, Brian. *Signal and Noise: Media, Infrastructure, and Urban Culture in Nigeria*. Duke University Press, 2008.

Latour, Bruno. *Rejoicing: Or the Torments of Religious Speech*. Wiley, 2018.

Lefort, Claude. "The Permanence of the Theologico-Political?" In *Political Theologies: Public Religions in a Post-Secular World*, ed. Hent de Vries and Lawrence E. Sullivan. Fordham University Press, 2006.

Lemons, Derrick J. "An Introduction to Theologically Engaged Anthropology." *Ethnos* 86, no. 3 (2021): 401–7.

Lin, Weiqiang, Johan Lindquist, Biao Xiang, and Brenda S. A. Yeoh. "Migration Infrastructures and the Production of Migrant Mobilities." *Mobilities* 12, no. 2 (2017): 167–74.

Lloyd, Dana. *Land Is Kin: Sovereignty, Religious Freedom, and Indigenous Sacred Sites*. University Press of Kansas, 2023.

Lloyd, Vincent. *Black Dignity: The Struggle Against Domination*. Yale University Press, 2022.

Lloyd, Vincent. "Christian Responses to the Holocaust: Political Theology in Europe." In *T&T Clark Handbook of Political Theology*, ed. Rubén Rosario Rodríguez. T&T Clark, 2020.

Lloyd, Vincent. "Love, Judgment, and Antisemitism: The Case of Alice Walker." In *The King Is in the Field: Essays in Modern Jewish Political Thought*, ed. Julie E. Cooper and Samuel Hayim Brody. University of Pennsylvania Press, 2023.

Lloyd, Vincent, ed. *Race and Political Theology*. Stanford University Press, 2012.

Lloyd, Vincent. "Secularism's Two Ends." The Immanent Frame, November 10, 2017. Accessed November 7, 2024. https://tif.ssrc.org/2017/11/10/secularisms-two-ends/.

Lloyd, Vincent. "What Life Is Not: Aimé Césaire as Phenomenologist of Domination." *Symposium: Canadian Journal of Continental Philosophy* 26, nos. 1–2 (2022): 224–41.

Löwith, Karl. *The Meaning of History: The Theological Implications of the Philosophy of History*. University of Chicago Press, 1949.

Lucci, Diego. *John Locke's Christianity*. Cambridge University Press, 2021.

Luciani, Rafael. *Pope Francis and the Theology of the People*. Orbis, 2017.

Lynch, Thomas. *Apocalyptic Political Theology: Hegel, Taubes and Malabou*. Bloomsbury, 2019.

Lyons, Kristina M. *Vital Decomposition: Soil Practitioners and Life Politics*. Duke University Press, 2020.

MacKinnon, Donald. "Tragedy and Ethics." In Donald MacKinnon, *Explorations in Theology 5*. SCM, 1979.

Mahadev, Neena. *Karma and Grace: Religious Difference in Millennial Sri Lanka*. Columbia University Press, 2023.

Mahmood, Saba. *Religious Difference in a Secular Age: A Minority Report*. Princeton University Press, 2015.

Mahmood, Saba. "Secularism, Hermeneutics, and Empire: The Politics of Islamic Reformation." *Public Culture* 18, no. 2 (2006): 323–47.

Manoukian, Setrag. "Thinking with the Impersonal: An Ethnographic View from Iran." *Antropologia* 6, no. 1 (2019): 199–215.

Marasco, Robyn. "The Real Possibility of Physical Killing: A Critique of Carl Schmitt." *American Journal of Political Science* 67, no. 4 (2023): 1067–79.

Marchant, Oliver. *Post-Foundational Political Thought: Political Difference in Nancy, Lefort, Badiou and Laclau*. Edinburgh University Press, 2007.

Marrow, Stanley. "κόσμος in John." *Catholic Biblical Quarterly* 64, no. 1 (2002): 90–102.

Marshall, Ruth. *Political Spiritualities: The Pentecostal Revolution in Nigeria.* University of Chicago Press, 2009.

Marx, Karl. *Capital.* Vol. 1. Trans. Ben Fowkes. Penguin, 1990.

Mathewes, Charles. *A Theology of Public Life.* Cambridge University Press, 2007.

Mayblin, Maya. "The Lapsed and the Laity: Discipline and Lenience in the Study of Religion." *Journal of the Royal Anthropological Institute* 23, no. 3 (2017): 503–22.

Mazzarella, William. "The Anthropology of Populism: Beyond the Liberal Settlement." *Annual Review of Anthropology* 48 (2019): 45–60.

Mazzarella, William. *The Mana of Mass Society.* University of Chicago Press, 2017.

Mbembe, Achille. *Necropolitics.* Duke University Press, 2019.

McAllister, Carlota, and Valentina Napolitano. "Introduction: Incarnate Politics Beyond the Cross and the Sword." *Social Analysis* 64, no. 4 (2020): 1–20.

McAllister, Carlota, and Valentina Napolitano. "Political Theology/Theopolitics: The Thresholds and Vulnerabilities of Sovereignty." *Annual Review of Anthropology* 50 (2021): 109–27.

McGinn, Bernard. *The Calabrian Abbot: Joachim of Fiore in the History of Western Thought.* Macmillan, 1985.

McLeod, Allegra M. "Prison Abolition and Grounded Justice," *UCLA Law Review* 62 (2015): 1156–239.

McQueen, Alison. *Political Realism in Apocalyptic Times.* Cambridge University Press, 2018.

McTighe, Laura. "Insurgent Cartography." Society for Cultural Anthropology, July 31, 2019. https://culanth.org/fieldsights/insurgent-cartography.

Medina, Lara. "Nepantla." In *Hispanic American Religious Cultures*, ed. Miguel de la Torre. ABC-CLIO, 2009.

Medina, Néstor. *Mestizaje: (Re)Mapping Race, Culture, and Faith in Latino/a Catholicism.* Orbis, 2009.

Mehring, Reinhard. *Carl Schmitt: A Biography.* Trans. Daniel Steuer. Polity, 2014.

Merino, Roger. "An Alternative to 'Alternative Development'? Buen Vivir and Human Development in Andean Countries." *Oxford Development Studies* 44, no. 3 (2016): 271–86.

Meskimmon, Marsha. "From the Cosmos to the Polis: On Denizens, Art and Postmigration Worldmaking." *Journal of Aesthetics and Culture* 9, no. 2 (2017): 25–35.

Metz, Johann Baptist. *Remembering and Resisting: The New Political Theology*. Wipf and Stock, 2022.

Mignolo, Walter D. "Foreword: On Pluriversality and Multipolarity." In *Constructing the Pluriverse: The Geopolitics of Knowledge*, ed. Bernd Reiter. Duke University Press, 2018.

Mignolo, Walter D. "What Does It Mean to Decolonize?" In Walter D. Mignolo and Catherine E. Walsh, *On Decoloniality: Concepts, Analytics, Praxis*. Duke University Press, 2018.

Mittermaier, Amira. "Dreams from Elsewhere: Muslim Subjectivities Beyond the Trope of Self-Cultivation." *Journal of the Royal Anthropological Institute* 18, no. 2 (2012): 247–65.

Mittermaier, Amira. *Giving to God: Islamic Charity in Revolutionary Times*. University of California Press, 2019.

Moin, Azfar. *The Millennial Sovereign: Kingship and Sainthood in Islam*. Columbia University Press, 2014.

Moin, Azfar, and Alan Strathern, eds. *Sacred Kingship in World History: Between Immanence and Transcendence*. Columbia University Press, 2022.

Mol, Annemarie. *Eating in Theory*. Duke University Press, 2021.

Moltmann, Jürgen. *The Coming of God: Christian Eschatology*. Trans. Margaret Kohl. Fortress, 2004.

Moltmann, Jürgen. "Political Theology and Liberation Theology." *Union Seminary Quarterly Review* 45 (1991): 205–17.

Moosa, Ebrahim. "The Idea of Progress and Its Discontents in Islamic Thought." Contending Modernities, January 10, 2023. https://contendingmodernities.nd.edu/theorizing-modernities/moosa-inaugural-lecture/.

Mosse, David. *The Saint in the Banyan Tree: Christianity and Caste Society in India*. University of California Press, 2012.

Mouffe, Chantal, ed. *The Challenge of Carl Schmitt*. Verso, 1999.

Mouffe, Chantal. *The Return of the Political*. Verso, 1993.

Moumtaz, Nada. *God's Property: Islam, Charity, and the Modern State*. University of California Press, 2020.

Moyn, Samuel. *Christian Human Rights*. University of Pennsylvania Press, 2015.

Murakawa, Naomi. *The First Civil Right: How Liberals Built Prison America.* Princeton University Press, 2014.

Nadasdy, Paul. *Sovereignty's Entailments: First Nation State Formation in the Yukon.* University of Toronto Press, 2017.

Napolitano, Valentina. "Francis, a Criollo Pope." *Religion and Society* 10, no. 1 (2019): 63–80.

Napolitano, Valentina. "Immanent Singularity." Political Theology Network, May 5, 2022. Accessed December 7, 2024. https://politicaltheology.com/immanent-singularity/.

Napolitano, Valentina. *Migrant Hearts and the Atlantic Return: Transnationalism and the Roman Catholic Church.* Fordham University Press, 2016.

Napolitano, Valentina. "On a Political Economy of Political Theology: El Señor de los Milagros." In *The Anthropology of Catholicism: A Reader*, ed. Kristin Norget, Maya Mayblin, and Valentina Napolitano. University of California Press, 2017.

Navaro, Yael. "The Aftermath of Mass Violence: A Negative Methodology." *Annual Review of Anthropology* 49 (2020): 161–73.

Navaro, Yael, et al., eds. *Reverberations: Violence Across Time and Space.* University of Pennsylvania Press, 2021.

Nelson, Eric. *The Hebrew Republic: Jewish Sources and the Transformation of European Political Thought.* Harvard University Press, 2010.

Nelson, Robert H. *Economics as Religion: From Samuelson to Chicago and Beyond.* Penn State University Press, 2002.

Newheiser, David. "Why the World Needs Negative Political Theology." *Modern Theology* 36, no. 1 (2020): 5–12.

Ng, Emily. *A Time of Lost Gods: Mediumship, Madness, and the Ghost After Mao.* University of California Press, 2020.

Ngong, David. *Senghor's Eucharist: Negritude and African Political Theology.* Baylor University Press, 2023.

Niebuhr, H. Richard. "The Grace of Doing Nothing." *Christian Century* 49 (1932): 378–80.

Nongbri, Brent. *Before Religion: A History of a Modern Concept.* Yale University Press, 2013.

Langholm, Odd. *The Legacy of Scholasticism in Economic Thought: Antecedents of Choice and Power.* Cambridge University Press, 1998.

O'Donovan, Oliver. *The Desire of the Nations: Rediscovering the Roots of Political Theology.* Cambridge University Press, 1996.

Oliphant, Elayne. "Beyond Blasphemy or Devotion: Art, the Secular, and Catholicism in Paris." *Journal of the Royal Anthropological Institute* 21, no. 2 (2015): 352–73.

Oliphant, Elayne. *The Privilege of Being Banal: Art, Secularism, and Catholicism in Paris*. University of Chicago Press, 2021.

Oliphant, Elayne. "The Secular and the Global: Rethinking the Anthropology of Christianity in the Wake of 1492." *Religion* 51, no. 4 (2021) 577–92.

Orsi, Robert A. *Between Heaven and Earth: The Religious Worlds People Make and the Scholars Who Study Them*. Princeton University Press, 2013.

Pandolfo, Stefania. *Knot of the Soul: Madness, Psychoanalysis, Islam*. University of Chicago Press, 2018.

Patta, Raj Bharat. *Subaltern Public Theology: Dalits and the Indian Public Sphere*. Palgrave Macmillan, 2023.

Pérez, Elizabeth. *The Gut: A Black Atlantic Alimentary Tract*. Cambridge University Press, 2022.

Pitt-Rivers, Julian. "The Law of Hospitality." In *The Fate of Shechem, or the Politics of Sex*, ed. Cambridge University Press, 1977.

Pitt-Rivers, Julian. "The Place of Grace in Anthropology." *HAU: Journal of Ethnographic Theory* 1, no. 1 (2011): 423–50.

Pitts, Frederick Harry, and Ana Cecilia Dinerstein. "Corbynism's Conveyor Belt of Ideas: Postcapitalism and the Politics of Social Reproduction." *Capital and Class* 41, no. 3 (2017): 423–34.

Pleij, Herman. *Dreaming of Cockaigne: Medieval Fantasies of the Perfect Life*. Trans. Diane Webb. Columbia University Press, 2001.

Povinelli, Elizabeth A. *Geontologies: A Requiem to Late Liberalism*. Duke University Press, 2016.

Prevot, Andrew. *The Mysticism of Ordinary Life: Theology, Philosophy, and Feminism*. Oxford University Press, 2023.

Prevot, Andrew. *Thinking Prayer: Theology and Spirituality amid the Crises of Modernity*. University of Notre Dame Press, 2015.

Pulcini, Elena. *Tra Cura e Giustizia: Le Passioni Come Risorsa Sociale*. Bollati Boringhieri, 2020.

Purnell, Derecka. *Becoming Abolitionists: Police, Protests, and the Pursuit of Freedom*. Astra, 2021.

Quashie, Kevin. *The Sovereignty of Quiet: Beyond Resistance in Black Culture*. Rutgers University Press, 2012.

Quayson, Ato. *Tragedy and Postcolonial Literature*. Cambridge University Press, 2021.

Quick, Joe, and James T. Spartz. "On the Pursuit of Good Living in Highland Ecuador: Critical Indigenous Discourses of Sumak Kawsay." *Latin American Research Review* 53, no. 4 (2018): 757–69.

Rahemtulla, Shadaab. *Qur'an of the Oppressed: Liberation Theology and Gender Justice in Islam*. Oxford University Press, 2017.

Rancière, Jacques. "Are Some Things Unrepresentable?" In Jacques Rancière, *The Future of the Image*. Verso, 2019.

Rasmusson, Arne. *The Church as Polis: From Political Theology to Theological Politics as Exemplified by Jürgen Moltmann and Stanley Hauerwas*. University of Notre Dame Press, 1995.

Reeves, Marjorie. *Joachim of Fiore and the Prophetic Future*. SPCK, 1976.

Riedl, Matthias. "Longing for the Third Age: Revolutionary Joachism, Communism, and National Socialism." In *A Companion to Joachim of Fiore*, ed. Matthias Riedl. Brill, 2017.

Robbins, Joel. "Beyond the Suffering Subject: Toward an Anthropology of the Good." *Journal of the Royal Anthropological Institute* 19, no. 3 (2013): 447–62.

Robbins, Joel. *Theology and the Anthropology of Christian Life*. Oxford University Press, 2020.

Roberts, Alastair. "The Politics of Eschatological Imminence—1 Corinthians 7:29–31." Political Theology Network, January 19, 2015. Accessed December 7, 2024. https://politicaltheology.com/the-politics-of-eschatological-imminence-1-corinthians-729-31.

Roberts, J. Deotis. *A Black Political Theology*. Westminster John Knox Press, 1974.

Roberts, J. Deotis. *Liberation and Reconciliation: A Black Theology*. Orbis, 2005.

Roberts, Tyler. "From Secular Criticism to Critical Fidelity." *Political Theology* 18, no. 8 (2017): 693–708.

Rodríguez, Dylan. "Abolition as Praxis of Human Being." *Harvard Law Review* 132, no. 6 (2019): 1575–1612.

Rogozen-Soltar, Mikaela H. *Spain Unmoored: Migration, Conversion, and the Politics of Islam*. Indiana University Press, 2017.

Roitman, Janet. *Anti-Crisis*. Duke University Press, 2014.

Rojas-Perez, Isaias. *Mourning Remains: State Atrocity, Exhumations, and Governing the Disappeared in Peru's Postwar Andes*. Stanford University Press, 2017.

Römhild, Regina. "Global Heimat: (Post)Migrant Productions of Transnational Space." *Anthropological Journal of European Cultures* 27, no. 1 (2018): 27–39.
Rosario-Rodríguez, Rubén. *Racism and God-Talk: A Latino/a Perspective.* New York University Press, 2008.
Rose, Gillian. *The Broken Middle: Out of Our Ancient Society.* Blackwell, 1992.
Rowlands, Anna. "The Politics of Mourning: Reading Gillian Rose in COVID Times." ABC Religion, May 24, 2020. Accessed December 7, 2024. https://www.abc.net.au/religion/anna-rowlands-gillian-rose-the-politics-of-mourning/12281170.
Rudnyckyj, Daromir, and Filippo Osella. *Religion and the Morality of the Market.* Cambridge University Press, 2017.
Rufinus of Sorrento, *De Bono Pacis.* Hahn, 1997.
Sahlins, Marshall, et al. "The Sadness of Sweetness: The Native Anthropology of Western Cosmology." *Current Anthropology* 37, no. 3 (1996): 395–428.
Sánchez, Rafael. *Dancing Jacobins: A Venezuelan Genealogy of Latin American Populism.* Fordham University Press, 2016.
Santner, Eric L. *The Weight of All Flesh: On the Subject-Matter of Political Economy*, ed. Kevis Goodman. Oxford University Press, 2016.
Sarr, Felwine. *Afrotopia.* University of Minnesota Press, 2020.
Scannone, Juan Carlos. "Pope Francis and the Theology of the People." *Theological Studies* 77, no. 1 (2016): 118–35.
Schmitt, Carl. *The Concept of the Political.* Trans. George Schwab. University of Chicago Press, 2007.
Schmitt, Carl. *Political Theology: Four Chapters on the Concept of Sovereignty.* Trans. George Schwab. University of Chicago Press, 2005.
Schmitt, Carl. *Political Theology II: The Myth of the Closure of Any Political Theology.* Trans. Michael Hoetzl and Graham Ward. Polity, 2008.
Schmitt, Carl. *Theory of the Partisan: Intermediate Commentary on the Concept of the Political.* Trans. G. L. Ulmen. Telos, 2007.
Schwarzkopf, Stefan, ed. *The Routledge Handbook of Economic Theology.* Routledge, 2020.
Shange, Savannah. "Abolition in the Clutch: Shifting Through the Gears with Anthropology." *Feminist Anthropology* 3, no. 2 (2022): 187–97.
Shortall, Sarah. *Soldiers of God in a Secular World: Catholic Theology and Twentieth-Century French Politics.* Harvard University Press, 2021.

Shulman, George. *American Prophecy: Race and Redemption in American Political Culture*. University of Minnesota Press, 2008.

Simpson, Audra. *Mohawk Interruptus: Political Life Across the Borders of Settler States*. Duke University Press, 2014.

Singh, Bhrigupati. *Poverty and the Quest for Life: Spiritual and Material Striving in Rural India*. University of Chicago Press, 2015.

Skrimshire, Stefan. *Politics of Fear, Practices of Hope: Depoliticisation and Resistance in a Time of Terror*. Continuum, 2008.

Smit, Dirk. "The Paradigm of Public Theology—Origins and Development." In *Contextuality and Intercontextuality in Public Theology*, ed. Heinrich Bedford-Strohm, Florian Höhne, and Tobias Reitmeier. LIT Verlag, 2013.

Smith, Caleb. *Thoreau's Axe: Disciplines of Attention in a Secular Age*. Princeton University Press, 2023.

Smith, Christian. *The Emergence of Liberation Theology: Radical Religion and Social Movement Theory*. University of Chicago Press, 1991.

Snarr, Melissa. *All You That Labor: Religion and Ethics in the Living Wage Movement*. New York University Press, 2011.

Spivak, Gayatri Chakravorty. "Religion, Politics, Theology: A Conversation with Achille Mbembe." *boundary 2* 34, no. 2 (2007): 149–70.

Springs, Jason. *Restorative Justice and Lived Religion: Transforming Mass Incarceration in Chicago*. New York University Press, 2024.

Stahly-Butts, Marbre, and Amna A. Akbar. "Reforms for Radicals? An Abolitionist Framework." *UCLA Law Review* 68 (2022): 1553–83.

Stengers, Isabelle. "The Challenge of Ontological Politics." In *A World of Many Worlds*, ed. Marisol de la Cadena and Mario Blaser. Duke University Press, 2018.

Stimilli, Elettra. *Debt and Guilt: A Political Philosophy*. Bloomsbury Academic, 2019.

Stimilli, Elettra. "Jacob Taubes e il Senso Antistorico dell'Escatologia." In *Escatologia Occidentale*. Quodlibet, 2019.

Strathern, Marilyn. *Partial Connections*. Rowman & Littlefield, 1991.

Strathern, Marilyn. *Relations: An Anthropological Account*. Duke University Press, 2020.

Sullivan, Winnifred. *Church State Corporation: Construing Religion in US Law*. University of Chicago Press, 2020.

Tamisari, Franca. *Enacted Relations: Performing Knowledge in an Australian Indigenous Community*. Berghahn, 2024.
Taussig, Michael. *The Magic of the State*. Routledge, 2013.
Taussig, Michael. *Shamanism, Colonialism, and the Wild Man: A Study in Terror and Healing*. University of Chicago Press, 2008.
Taylor, Charles. *A Secular Age*. Belknap, 2007.
Taylor, Jeremy. *Holy Living and Holy Dying*. 2 vols. Ed. P. G. Stanwood. Clarendon, 1989.
Thiem, Yannik [Publishing as Annika Thiem]. "Schmittian Shadows and Contemporary Theological-Political Constellations." *Social Research* 80, no. 1 (2013): 1–32.
Tinker, George E. "Tink." *American Indian Liberation: A Theology of Sovereignty*. Orbis, 2008.
Todeschini, Giacomo. *Franciscan Wealth: From Voluntary Poverty to Market Society*. Franciscan Institute, 2004.
Tonda, Joseph. *The Modern Sovereign: The Body of Power in Central Africa (Congo and Gabon)*. Trans. Chris Turner. Seagull, 2021.
Tran, Jonathan. *Asian Americans and the Spirit of Racial Capitalism*. Oxford University Press, 2021.
Trouillot, Michel-Rolph. "Anthropology and the Savage Slot: The Poetics and Politics of Otherness." In *Recapturing Anthropology: Working in the Present*, ed. Richard G. Fox. School of American Research, 1991.
Trouillot, Michel-Rolph. "The Otherwise Modern." In *Critically Modern: Alternatives, Alterities, Anthropologies*, ed. Bruce M. Knauft. Indiana University Press, 2002.
Tshaka, Rothney. "Karl Barth and Public Theologies! Why Black Theology of Liberation Is Still Relevant in the Wake of a Public Theology Euphoria." *Revista Pistis & Praxis* 14, no. 1 (2022): 62–87.
Tshaka, R. S., and M. K. Makofane. "The Continued Relevance of Black Liberation Theology for Democratic South Africa Today." *Scriptura* 105 (2010): 532–46.
Tsing, Anna Lowenhaupt. *Friction: An Ethnography of Global Connection*. Princeton University Press, 2005.
Turner, Denys. *The Darkness of God: Negativity in Christian Mysticism*. Cambridge University Press, 1995.
Tutu, Desmond. *God Has a Dream: A Vision of Hope for Our Time*. Rider, 2005.

Tuveson, Ernest. *Millennium and Utopia: A Study in the Background of the Idea of Progress.* University of California Press, 1949.

van der Veer, Peter. *Imperial Encounters: Religion and Modernity in India and Britain.* Princeton University Press, 2001.

Vanhulst, Julien, and Adrian E. Beling. "Buen Vivir: Emergent Discourse Within or Beyond Sustainable Development?" *Ecological Economics* 101 (2014): 54–63.

Vatter, Miguel. *Living Law: Jewish Political Theology from Hermann Cohen to Hannah Arendt.* Oxford University Press, 2021.

Viefhues-Bailey, Ludger. *No Separation: Christians, Secular Democracy, and Sex.* Columbia University Press, 2023.

Villa-Vicencio, Charles. *A Theology of Reconstruction: Nation-Building and Human Rights.* Cambridge University Press, 1992.

Voegelin, Eric. *The New Science of Politics: An Introduction.* University of Chicago Press, 1952.

Waldron, Jeremy. *God, Locke, and Equality: Christian Foundations of John Locke's Political Thought.* Cambridge University Press, 2002.

Walsh, Catherine E. "The Decolonial For." In Walter D. Mignolo and Catherine E. Walsh, *On Decoloniality: Concepts, Analytics, Praxis.* Duke University Press, 2018.

Walsh, Catherine. "Development as Buen Vivir: Institutional Arrangements and (De)colonial Entanglements." *Development* 53, no. 1 (2010): 15–21.

Warnock, Raphael. *The Divided Mind of the Black Church: Theology, Piety, and Public Witness.* New York University Press, 2014.

Waterman, Anthony. *Political Economy and Christian Theology Since the Enlightenment: Essays in Intellectual History.* Palgrave Macmillan, 2004.

Wenger, Tisa. *We Have a Religion: The 1920s Pueblo Indian Dance Controversy and American Religious Freedom.* University of North Carolina Press, 2009.

West, Cornel. "Subversive Joy and Revolutionary Patience in Black Christianity." In *The Cornel West Reader*, ed. Cornel West. Basic Books, 1999.

Whelan, Matthew. *Blood in the Fields: Óscar Romero, Catholic Social Teaching, and Land Reform.* Catholic University of America Press, 2022.

White, Lynn. "The Historical Roots of Our Ecological Crisis." *Science* 155 (1967): 1203–7.

Wilder, Gary. *Freedom Time: Negritude, Decolonization, and the Future of the World.* Duke University Press, 2015.

Wimbush, Vincent L. *White Men's Magic: Scripturalization as Slavery.* Oxford University Press, 2012.

Winchell, Mareike. *After Servitude: Elusive Property and the Ethics of Kinship in Bolivia.* University of California Press, 2023.

Winchell, Mareike. "Afterword: Theos | Cosmos | Ontos: Rethinking Religion's Politics from Latin America." *American Religion* 5, no. 2 (2024): 201–24.

Winstanley, Gerrard. "A Declaration to the Powers of England (The True Levellers Standard Advanced)." In *The Complete Works of Gerrard Winstanley*, ed. Thomas N. Corns, Ann Hughes, and David Loewenstein. Oxford University Press, 2010.

Wolin, Richard. "Carl Schmitt, Political Existentialism, and the Total State." *Theory and Society* 19, no. 4 (1990): 389–416.

Wynter, Sylvia. "The Re-Enchantment of Humanism." Interview by David Scott. *Small Axe* 8 (2000): 176–82.

Wynter, Sylvia. "Unsettling the Coloniality of Being/Power/Truth/Freedom: Towards the Human, After Man, Its Overrepresentation—An Argument." *CR: The New Centennial Review* 3, no. 3 (2003): 257–337.

INDEX

abolition, 137–52
activation: definition of 161–63; and Obeah 162; as methodology 171; and Pope Francis 177; of political theology 206
Afropessimism, 104, 137. *See also* Blackness
Agamben, Giorgio, 25–26, 51, 93, 209; on sovereignty, 226
Albán, Adolfo, 92
Alinsky, Saul, 73
American Academy of Religion, 238n40
American religion (field of study), 218–19
anarcho-capitalism, 79
Andalucismo (intellectual movement), 189–90. *See also* Andalusia
Andalusia, 190, 228, 261n42
Anidjar, Gil, 223
Anthropodom, 164
anthropology, 157–59, 160, 188–89; of the otherwise, 204; and political theology, 178–79, 190, 201, 224; of religion, 162–63; and theology, 160–61. *See also* ethnography
anti-Blackness, 104, 140. *See also* Blackness, Afropessimism
Antichrist, 50, 51, 76, 77, 169
apartheid, 18, 30, 44
Apess, William, 210
apocalyptic: Alinsky eschews, 73; Césaire on, 130, 254n43; challenges nation-state, 90; event, 80; movements, 76; orientation to politics, 81, 261n1; and politics realism, 23; topic of political theology, 31

L'Arche, 77
Arendt, Hannah, 23, 59, 64, 242n30, 243n31
Aristotle, 56–57, 241n20
Asad, Talal, 3, 31, 115, 227, 233n1, 248n77
Augustine, 40, 52, 211, 246n53, 256n55; on political theology, 57–58, 71
Augustinian: conception of political life, 74; tradition, 76–77
authoritarianism, 1–2, 19, 35, 49, 102
authority: abolishing, 141–42; commons and, 60; versus domination, 141–42; God as, 142; prophecy challenges, 31; of state, 174, 195; theology challenges, 8
Avis, Paul, 23
Azaransky, Sarah, 234n9
Azusa Street Revival, 212

Badiou, Alain, 25, 251n20
Bakhtin, Mikhail, 50
Bakunin, Mikhail, 19, 49, 86–87
Balthrop-Lewis, Alda, 218
Banerjee, Milinda, 60, 222, 258–59n15
Barth, Karl, 212, 243n34
barzakh, 183–84
Bassichis, Morgan, 105
Bellah, Robert, 32
Benjamin, Walter, 54, 67, 75, 169, 203, 247n75
Berry, Wendell, 16
Black Atlantic, 10, 11, 13, 209, 221
Black Lives Matter (movement), 101, 104, 107, 227
Black theology. *See* liberation theology

300 • INDEX

Blackness, 43, 253n36. *See also* anti-Blackness
Bloch, Ernst, 75, 78
Blumenberg, Hans, 247–48n76
borderlands, 190, 204
Bouteldja, Houria, 223, 253n35
Branch Davidians, 77
broken middle, 47, 183
Bruegel the Elder, Pieter, 78
Buber, Martin, 169
Buddhism, 39, 230
buen vivir, 94–97, 213
Bulgakov, Sergei, 41–42

de la Cadena, Marisol, 92–94
Cannell, Fenella, 3
Cannon, Katie, 16
capitalism: capitalist economy, 91–92, 178; Christianity and, 178, 234n10; entangles its critics, 219; fair trade, 219; Francis (Pope) and, 198; life and, 187–88; Marx's critique of, 46; Pentecostalism and, 212; public theology and, 18; racial, 43, 91, 244n42, 269n9; as religious, 25; Sahlins on, 166; Santner on, 178; and the social, 14–15. *See also* anarcho-capitalism
carcerality, 43, 140, 255n50
care: circle of, 55, 67, 69, 99; domination as, 69; duty of, 70–71; ethics of, 164; kin, 196; labor, 158; mutual, 56, 62, 70, 95, 212; pastoral, 71, 182; politics organizing, 57, 65; requires life-in-common, 55; self-care, 137; sovereignty and, 71, 177
Carter, J. Kameron, 253–54n36
de las Casas, Bartolomé, 11, 199
de Certeau, Michel, 17, 157, 165, 185–86, 200
Césaire, Aimé, 36, 106; intellectual development of, 124–26; poetry of, 126–35; and political theology, 135–36; 253–54n36. *See also* negritude
Cherniss, Joshua, 119
Christ. *See* Jesus
Christian Democracy, 24, 64
City of God (Augustine), 209, 246n53
civil rights movement (US), 15, 24, 29–30, 147, 234n9, 243n31
Cleage, Albert, 30, 252–53n30
climate change, 102, 167, 237n34
Cockaigne (fictional utopia), 78–80

Cold War, 18, 93, 95, 199
Colón-Emeric, Edgardo, 217
Combahee River Collective, 107
common good, 57, 109
common life, 46–47; antipolitical perspectives, 63; and Black liberation theology, 83, 247n70; and Christian political theology, 21, 33, 53, 55–59, 64–66, 75, 79, 84, 98–99; between human and nonhuman, 95; just war theory and, 242n28; and public theology, 236n23. *See also buen vivir*, commons
commons, 64–65, 90–91, 175; definition of, 60–62; economy of, 199; as human life, 56, 84, 98; storytelling and 175, 205. *See also* life-in-common
communion. *See* Eucharist
communism: as apocalyptic, 23; Césaire and, 126; Christianity and, 13; Müntzer as protocommunist, 75; political theology and, 14; public theology and, 18
The Concept of the Political (Schmitt), 65, 244n36, 245n43
Cone, James, 14, 212; and Black liberation theology, 82–83, 212, 252–53n30; versus Roberts, 247n70; on spirituals, 43
Confessions (Augustine), 38
consent, 74, 244n42
Constantine (Emperor), 70–71
cosmology, 94–97, 238–39n42; African, 254n39; Christian, 51; secularization and, 164; Western, 166–67
cosmopolitics, 94, 99, 167
cosmos, 52, 53, 87
lo cotidiano, 16–17
Council for World Mission, 11
COVID-19, 102–3, 156–58, 167, 255n50, 257n68
Crick, Bernard, 63–64

Day, Keri, 212
Dean, Jodi, 111
Delany, Martin, 30
democracy, 10–11, 15, 49; agonistic, 69; and Christian political theology, 64; commons and, 61; democratic citizenship, 212; democratic renewal, 2; democratic struggle, 30; Diggers and, 61; European liberal, 25–26; foundations,

25; Gandhi's vision, 29–30; Hauerwas and, 77; multispecies, 90; neighboring, 85; prophecy and, 31. *See also* Christian Democracy; social democracy
denizenship, 161, 195–99
Derrida, Jacques, 25
Detroit, 181–82, 187
Diggers (English radicals), 61
Diop, Alioune, 13, 125
domination: abolishing, 141–43, 148; affect of, 143–44; Agamben on, 51; all-pervasive, 118, 120; Augustine on, 57–58, 71, 211; Césaire on, 127–36; colonial, 127–28, 130–36, 141–45; beyond domination, 9, 55, 68, 107, 120, 136, 143, 145–46; God and, 142; as idolatry, 119–20; Kaba on, 152; liberation theology and, 122; love and, 57–58, 71; naturalizing, 120; political theology and, 2, 5–6, 19, 34, 123; in the quotidian, 16; sovereignty and, 6, 70, 71; spirituality and, 211; systems of, 19, 108–9, 112, 117, 119–20, 148; theology implicated in, 19, 121; Wynter on, 68–69. *See also libido dominandi*
Doostdar, Alireza, 230–31
Dorrien, Gary, 234n13
Douglass, Frederick, 43
Dumler-Winkler, Emily, 211
Dussel, Enrique, 96

Eckhart, Meister, 205
Ecumenical Association of Third World Theologians, 11
Eldridge, Aaron, 267n131
Elia, Matthew, 211, 256n55, 269n5
enemy, 68–69, 82, 244n36, 245n43. *See also* friend-enemy relation
Engels, Friedrich, 75
Equiano, Olaudah, 209–10, 268n2
Esack, Farid, 30
eschatology, 10, 54, 56, 76–77; in Césaire, 131–33; Christian, 247–48n76; and Christian theology, 44; eschatological fulfillment, 85; eschatological immanence, 189, 191; eschatological longing, 80; and incarnation, 187; occidental, 189; and negritude, 132–33. *See also* millenarianism
eschaton, 50, 56, 74–75

ethnography: description of, 184–85; as a discipline, 196; ecclesial, 213; of Gacko, 175; of kenosis and incarnation, 176; and political theology, 159–61, 170. *See also* anthropology
Eucharist, 124, 135, 155, 177
Eusebius of Caesarea, 70
existential, the: and abolition, 145; and Christianity, 115, 251–52n21; and philosophy, 27; and political theology, 27, 98, 106, 114; and politics, 46–47, 84, 106, 109, 110, 117; and racism, 107; and religion, 114; Schmitt on, 65, 112–14, 119; and social movements, 104, 105, 108, 112. *See also* existentialism
existentialism, 13, 23

Fanon, Frantz, 67, 108, 244n41
Fassin, Didier, 248n82
Federici, Silvia, 17
Fernando, Mayanthi, 203–4
fetish, 127, 171–72
fieldwork, 163, 181
Foster, Elizabeth, 13, 125
Foucault, Michel: on carcerality, 255n50; on confession, 100; on Iranian Revolution, 231; on pastoral power, 71, 87
Francis (Pope), 16, 155–58, 193–94, 198; on *buen vivir*, 95–97; "Laudato Si'," 198; "Querida Amazonia," 95–97; on technocratic paradigm, 21, 88
freedom: Agamben on, 51; Bretherton defends, 10, 207; intrinsic, 207; liberal notion of, 204; political theology affirms, 33; state versus society realizing, 15; world of freedom, 147, 152
friend-enemy relation: and Black liberation theology, 82–83; versus *buen vivir*, 97; Cone on, 82–83, 247n70; constitution of citizenship, 195; in political theology, 55, 62, 75, 79, 80, 84–85; Schmitt on, 42, 65–69, 113; Wynter on, 67–68. *See also* Carl Schmitt
Furani, Khaled, 164, 180–81
Furey, Constance, 202

Gago, Verónica, 17
Gandhi, Mohandas, 11–12, 29–30, 98, 234n9

Gandolfo, Elizabeth O'Donnell, 212–13
Garvey, Marcus, 30
Gauchet, Marcel, 25
gift: anthropological concept, 201–2; Christian theological concept, 52
Gillespie, Michael, 23
Gilmore, Ruth Wilson, 107
Gilroy, Paul, 43, 268n2
globalatinization, 189
God: anthropology and, 164, 167; Augustine on, 57–58; Bakunin on, 49, 87; Christian, 51–53, 118, 172, 252n28; and climate change, 237n34; Cone on, 82; creativity, 231; and domination, 142–43; else-where, 168; enmity with, 84; Hauerwas on, 77; image of, 63; in Islam, 180–81, 191; and justice, 121; kingdom of, 53, 61, 77, 81; knowing, 200, 203; love of God, 58; as magical, 172; multispecies approach, 204, 258n15; people of God, 40; and political theology, 38, 142, 146; presence of, 166, 168; revelation, 40–41, 81; as sovereign, 39, 48, 70, 89, 124, 135; talk of, 38–40, 121; in theology, 84, 166–68; transcendence, 48, 118; vulnerable, 118. *See also* gods, Jesus, theology
gods, 196, 258n15; false, 119; mortal god, 89; obligating, 196, 204; and political theology, 203–4, 225–26. *See also* God, idolatry
Good Samaritan, 69
grace, 149, 154, 158, 190, 207, 261n42
Great Recession, 102–3
Gregory of Nyssa, 200
Gutiérrez, Gustavo, 14, 240n1

Habermas, Jürgen, 18, 23, 93
HadžiMuhamedović, Safet, 174–75
Harney, Stefano, 143
Hauerwas, Stanley, 2, 77
Heidegger, Martin, 112
Heimat, 195
Henderson, Ash-Lee, 147
Henry, Michel, 134, 255n45
Heo, Angie, 218
Hickman, Jared, 4, 221
Highlander Research and Education Center, 147
Hirschkind, Charles, 228

Hobbes, Thomas, 15, 31, 46, 74, 88–89, 91, 241n20
Holocaust, 250n2
homo sacer (concept), 25–26
Hulsether, Lucia, 219, 233n3
humanism: *buen vivir* and, 97; Christian, 209; Gilroy on, 43; reparative, 268n2; Wynter on, 68
Hume, David, 32
Hurston, Zora Neale, 16

ideology, 44–46; critique of, 7, 44, 121–22; idolatry and, 216; morality as, 72; secularism as, 7, 34, 123, 124, 207, 229
Idle No More (movement), 102, 104
idolatry: critique of, 121, 135, 216; and enmity, 56, 84; and fallen political life, 56, 65, 70; naturalized, 119–20; sovereign as, 118; in Sri Lanka, 230
immanent frame, 10, 21, 22, 89, 207, 229
impossible, the, 105, 143, 184
incarnation: de Certeau on, 185; dis-incarnation, 231; of Jesus Christ, 52; and kenosis, 176, 201; mystery of, 187–88
International Journal of Public Theology, 236n24
Iqbal, Basit, 185–86
Isaiah (prophet), 45
Isasi-Díaz, Ada María, 16
Islam: in Africa, 11; Anidjar on, 223; Black nationalism, 30; Bouteldja on, 223; charity, 168; Doostdar on, 230; Furani on, 180; Hirschkind on, 228; liberation theology, 30; Pandolfo on, 183–84; and psychiatry, 191; "reformation," 32; tribulation, 183, 185–86. *See also* Sufism, Umma

Jakobsen, Janet, 220
James, Henry, 73
Jantzen, Matthew, 211–12
Jennings, Willie James, 160, 268n2
Jesus: and Black theology, 82; Body of Christ, 135, 187; and Christian political theology, 38, 41, 42, 46, 52, 53, 61, 83, 99; in Christianity, 252n28; Gandhi draws on, 29; and King, 64; and liberation theology, 121; Santner on, 178; and Schmitt, 113. *See also* God

Joachim of Fiore, 75–78
Joachimite tradition, 76–78
Jobson, Ryan Cecil, 164
Jordan, Mark D., 222
just war theory, 242n28

Kaba, Mariame, 151–53
Kant, Immanuel, 78, 90, 180
katechon, 50, 169
kenosis, 176, 187, 201. *See also* incarnation
khalifah, 180
Kilby, Karen, 216–17
King Jr., Martin Luther, 64, 72, 138, 252–53n30
kinship, 129, 175, 177, 187, 192–93, 225
Kwok Pui-lan, 11

laïcité, 229
Largier, Niklaus, 221–22
Latour, Bruno, 186
Lee, Alexander, 105
Lefort, Claude, 25, 231–22
Left (political), 106–22, 129, 255n54; new, 106, 116, 117, 122; old, 106, 116, 117; political theology and, 15, 19, 20, 103, 133, 138, 233n1, 236n24
Lenin, Vladimir, 72
Lessing, Gotthold Ephraim, 78
liberalism: Christian, 18; generates problem space, 6; and the Left, 9, 106, 117–19; and public theology, 18. *See also* secularism
liberation theology, 10–11, 50, 121–23, 253n31; American Indian, 14, 210; Black, 10, 14, 30, 43, 83, 91, 212, 252–53n30; Latin American, 13–14, 96, 213; in South Africa, 18, 30. *See also* James Cone, Enrique Dussel
libido dominandi, 58. *See also* domination
life-in-common, 55–57, 60–61; and *buen vivir*, 97; and politics, 84–85; and sovereignty, 74
Locke, John, 23, 74, 89, 241n20
Lord of the Miracles (*El Señor de los Milagros*), 192
love, 57–58, 65; Césaire on, 132, 133; and domination, 71; Eckhart on, 205; of enemies, 69, 85
Löwith, Karl, 247–48n76
de Lubac, Henri, 75

MacIntyre, Alasdair, 2, 4, 93
Mahadev, Neena, 229
Mahmood, Saba, 3, 31, 115, 227–28, 248n82
Malcolm X, 30, 71–72
mana, 166, 178, 231–32
Marasco, Robyn, 118
Marty, Martin, 17
martyrdom, 127, 132, 212, 226
Marx, Karl, 46, 245n49
Marxism, 5, 13, 72, 75, 101; Christians and, 13, 23, 121; Dussel's, 96; hostile to ethics, 245n49; messianic eschatology, 247–48n76; turn away from, 25, 93, 101, 126; vision of state, 15; Voegelin on, 78
Mashpee Revolt, 210
Mathewes, Charles, 236n23
Maxfield-Steele, Allyn, 256n60
Mazzarella, William, 231
Mazzini, Giuseppe, 48–49
Mbembe, Achille, 26, 91, 209
McQueen, Alison, 23
mestizaje, 243n32
mestizaje-mulatez, 16, 63
#MeToo, 102, 104–5
Metz, Johann Baptist, 13–14, 259n19
mezcolanza, 63
Mignolo, Walter, 95
migration, 183, 188–94, 197, 201
millenarianism: peasant, 61; Christian, 76–78
miracles, 54, 66, 113, 120, 171, 230
Moin, Azfar, 222
Moltmann, Jürgen, 6, 13, 75, 78
More, Thomas, 80
Moten, Fred, 143
mothers, 127–28, 179, 223
Mouffe, Chantal, 111
Mujerista theology, 16
Müntzer, Thomas, 75, 77
Murray, John Courtney, 17
mysticism: critical theory and, 239n46; Jewish, 75; Largier on, 221–22; Latour on, 186; Prevot on, 216; Thoreau as, 218

nationalism, 116; Black, 30, 71–72; ethnoreligious, 2, 18, 233n3; methodological, 188
necropolitics, 91, 187

negativity: abolition and, 144, 147; affect of, 156; life and, 105, 130–31, 134; methodology, 202–3; negative theology, 8, 135, 200, 216; political theology and, 36, 37, 114, 118; power of, 156, 199–203
negritude (concept), 125–26, 130, 132, 254n41
Negritude (movement). *See* negritude (concept)
neoliberalism, 26, 103, 117
nepantla (Nahault concept), 63
Neuhaus, Richard John, 233n1
Ngong, David, 217
Nicaea, Council of, 83
Niebuhr, Reinhold, 17, 74, 119
nonsecular, 160–61, 167, 241n13, 258n12; anthropology, 202, 204
Notebook of a Return to a Native Land (Césaire), 124–35

Obeah, 162
O'Donovan, Oliver, 241n18
Oliphant, Elayne, 229

pacifism, 149
pandemic. *See* COVID-19
Pandolfo, Stefania, 183–84
Paul (apostle), 66
Pentecostal Christianity, 10, 11, 172, 212, 229–30
Peterson, Erik, 13, 118
Plato, 48
pluriverse, 92, 96, 196
Polish Christ (statue), 181–82, 187
political, the, 54, 56, 59, 62–67, 70–75, 85; *buen vivir* and, 96; Cone on, 82–83; enclosed by secular, 88–89; Hobbes on, 91; versus politics, 111–12; Schmitt on, 112–14, 118. *See also* politics
political theology: 1–8, 20–23, 25, 29, 33–34; as anthropology, 224–25; Black Atlantic, 11; Christian, 165, 210–11, 213; as Christian talk, 39; as confession, 99–100; and continental philosophy, 25–26; and cosmologies, 94–96; as creole, 10; ecological, 203–4, 258n15; from below, 61, 106; future of, 207; as insurgent, 49–50; and interfaith relations, 29–33; Islamic, 185; and Jesus Christ, 40–42; and kinship, 225; Latinx, 63; leftist, 118; and life and

death, 116; new, 121–22; and prophecy, 31; and religious studies, 27–29; as response to crisis, 100; and secularism, 227–29; and technocracy, 88–89; and ultimate concern, 106–7; vernacular, 120
Political Theology (journal), 2, 153, 236n24
Political Theology (Schmitt), 112
Political Theology Network, 238n40, 253n35, 256n60
politics: Augustine on, 58; democratic, 15, 30, 64, 212; descriptions of, 59–60, 62–65; of the guts, 177; Hobbes and, 88–89, 91; Left, 108–10, 112, 114–15, 117–20; and life-death relation, 46–47; and political theology, 33, 106; reenchantment of, 187–88; religion and, 23, 98; substance of, 170, 186; talk of, 38–40; as technical practice, 108–10; and theology, 83–84; of transfiguration, 44; and war, 242n28; as zero-sum game, 71. *See also* the political
power: Black Power, 83; confession and, 100; constituent power, 111; experiments with, 162; in the "field," 163; of the flesh, 173; in hermeneutics, 21; incarnated, 170; of liturgy, 177; and the negative, 118, 156, 199–203; pastoral, 70–71, 87; political theology and, 21, 30, 36, 55; politics and, 72, 83, 85, 108; relational, 62, 85, 242n29; soul, 62; sovereign power, 87, 119, 169, 197; will to power, 19, 73
Prevot, Andrew, 211, 216–17, 256n59
primitive accumulation, 169, 170, 174, 179
Princeton University, 218, 238n41
Proudhon, Pierre-Joseph, 79, 86
Prometheus, 221
prophecy, 31, 46
Proudhon, Joseph-Pierre, 79, 86–87
public theology, 17–19, 251–52n21

QAnon, 177

Rauschenbusch, Walter, 78
Rawls, John, 18, 23
reform: abolition and, 138, 143, 148–50; Left and, 117; liberalism and, 110; prison reform, 151; reformist political theology, 7, 12, 14–15, 17, 78; reformist versus nonreformist reforms, 148–50; revolution and, 117

religion: abolition, 139, 256n57; Afro-Atlantic, 162; American, 218–21; anthropology of, 162; category of, 32–33, 122–23, 163; critique of, 154, 163; flattened (secularized), 24, 25, 27–28; liberation theology on, 122–23; Marx on, 46; and political theology, 23, 94, 98; of reason, 78; and social movements, 24–25, 138; Voegelin on, 78. *See also* God, religious studies, secularism, secularization

religious studies (discipline), 27–29, 33, 164, 218–19

restorative justice, 256–57n66

Right (political), 2, 15, 19, 102, 104, 110, 117, 233n1

ritual, 87, 124, 155, 177–79, 193, 230; Césaire's poetry as, 253n36

Robbins, Joel, 167

Roberts, J. Deotis, 83, 252–53n30

Roberts, Tyler, 153–54

Rodríguez, Dylan, 144–46

Roma, 175

Romero, Óscar, 217

Rose, Gillian, 47, 183

Rothbard, Murray, 79

Rowlands, Anna, 183

Ruether, Rosemary Radford, 14

Rufinus of Sorrento, 49

Sahlins, Marshall, 166

Sánchez, Rafael, 232

Santner, Eric, 178

Schmitt, Carl: on Catholic Church, 229; *The Concept of the Political*, 65; on friend/enemy distinction, 42, 65–69; 111, 113, 116, 118, 244n36, 245n43; historical context, 6, 101; on *katechon*, 50; on liberalism, 118, 119; pathos of objectivity, 88; political existentialism, 112–14, 118, 119; and political theology, 1, 13, 25, 42, 86, 113–14; *Political Theology*, 112; *Political Theology II*, 247–48n76; on sovereignty, 48, 50, 72, 118, 119; on war, 113; Wolin on, 112–13

Second Vatican Council, 125, 182, 194

secular/religious binary, 168, 220. *See also* secularism

secularism (ideology), Asad on, 115, 227, 233n1; Bretherton rejects, 207; critique of, 7, 33, 34, 115, 123–24, 189, 229, 233n1; defined, 123; Löwith on, 247–48n76; Mahmood on, 115, 227–28, 248n82; and social movements, 138, 146, 154. *See also laïcité*, secularization

secularization (historical process): Blumenberg on, 247–48n76; concept produced by theology, 31, 248n77; Furani on, 164; globalatinization as, 265; Löwith on, 247–48n76; political theology and, 86, 124; refusal of secularization thesis, 21; Schmitt on 247–48n76; shaping scholarship, 22, 24, 164. *See also* secularism

Senghor, Léopold Sédar, 13, 217

September 11 attacks, 6, 18, 101, 189, 220

Shulman, George, 120

Simpson, Audra, 191, 226

Singh, Bhrigupati, 225–26

Skrimshire, Stefan, 268n1

slavery, 69, 91, 120, 211; and abolitionism, 139–44; Césaire on, 130, 134

Snarr, Melissa, 213–14

social democracy, 72

Social Gospel, 15, 64, 213

social movements: defined, 250n5; existential origins, 109; of long 2010s, 6, 101–3, 137–38, 140–41; modern political form, 209; and new Left, 116–17, 121–22; and political theology, 15, 104, 122, 146, 154; secularism of, 24, 138–39, 146; tragedy, 150, 153

Sölle, Dorothee, 13

Sorel, Georges, 79

South Africa, 18, 30, 44, 239n34

sovereignty: African, 171; Agamben's concept of, 25, 226; from below, 164, 174, 176; and care, 71; confederal conception of, 15; divine, 118; domination and, 6, 19, 55, 70; exception and, 50; founding moment, 74; God's, 39, 48; Hobbesian, 15, 89; as *katechon*, 50; of the king, 178; mestizo, 225; modern, 55, 89, 180–81; nonsovereignty, 94; and order, 48, 50, 70, 73; pluralizing, 171–72; and political theology, 5–6, 19, 33, 70–74; Schmitt on, 50, 70, 72, 118; self- 192–93, 196, 198; sovereign authority, 70–75; sovereign decision, 36, 195; spiritual, 193. *See also* political theology, statecraft

Spade, Dean, 105

Spinoza, Baruch, 31, 46
Springs, Jason, 256–57n66
Standing Rock (protests), 102, 104
statecraft: versus democracy, 15; versus liberation, 15; in political theology, 70, 72, 89, 207; politics as, 59–60, 85, 242n29; politics beyond statecraft, 33, 60; theology and, 83
Stengers, Isabelle, 173
Stimilli, Elettra, 26
Stirner, Max (Johann Kaspar Schmidt), 78–79
Strathern, Alan, 222
suffering: anthropological political theology and, 159, 163, 165; in Christian theology, 217; domination and, 127, 129; eschatology and, 56; Metz on, 259n19; reformism and, 148; sovereignty and, 73; suffering slot (Robbins's concept), 167; unthinkable suffering, 203
Sufism, 230–31
Sullivan, Winnifred, 219–20

Taubes, Jacob, 189
Taylor, Charles, 4, 6, 22, 23, 93, 248n77
Taylor, Jeremy (divine), 240n3
Taylor, Keeanga-Yamahtta, 107
technocracy: administration of life, 95; anarcho-syndicalism and, 79; Francis (Pope) on, 21, 88; More on, 80; political theology that opposes, 29, 34, 94, 96; sense of politics, 73, 88–89, 108–11
theology, defined by Metz, 259n19. *See also* God, political theology, religion
theopolitics, 169–70; in Sri Lanka, 229–30. *See also* political theology
Thoreau, Henry David, 218, 257n70
Tinker, George "Tink," 14, 210
Tonda, Joseph, 171–72, 181
tragedy: abolitionism and, 150–52; Alinsky on, 73; Francis (Pope) and, 155; liberalism and, 119–20, political theology and, 34, 245–6n52; politics as, 73–74; Rose on, 47
Tran, Jonathan, 69, 269n9

tribulation, 166, 183, 185, 186, 203
Trouillot, Michel-Rolph, 174, 197
Tutu, Desmond, 11, 44

Umma, 158, 185. *See also* Islam
United Nations, 72, 90
University of Chicago, 17, 218
unwitnessing, 45
Urbi et Orbi (papal address), 155–59, 177, 197
utopia: Alinsky eschews, 73; Bloch embraces, 75; in Islamic political theology, 185; modern utopian thought, 80; *Utopia* (More), 80

Viefhues-Bailey, Ludger, 220
Vietnam War, movement against, 122
Voegelin, Eric, 47, 78
vulnerability: body and, 166; broken middle, 183; denizenship, 197; fueling Left, 117; negativity and, 199–201; pandemic, 156; political theology and, 36; racism and, 107; Schmitt on, 118; theology and, 259n19

waqf (charitable property), 164
war: anthropological approaches to, 202; as emergency, 50; and friend-enemy relations, 69; and the political, 62; Schmitt on, 113; total war, 245n43. *See also* just war
Warnock, Raphael G., 252–53n30
Whelan, Matthew, 217
White, Lynn, 87–88
Wilder, Gary, 136
Winchell, Mareike, 224–25
Wolin, Richard, 112–13
Wolin, Sheldon, 23, 64
Wollstonecraft, Mary, 211
Womanist theology, 15, 16, 212
World War I, 112, 116
World War II, 149
Wouters, Jelle, 60
Wynter, Sylvia, 67–69, 91, 108

Žižek, Slavoj, 25, 93

GPSR Authorized Representative: Easy Access System Europe, Mustamäe tee 50, 10621 Tallinn, Estonia, gpsr.requests@easproject.com